Teradata 14 Database Administration

An Authorized Teradata Certified Professional Program Study Guide

Exam TE0-144

First Edition

ISBN 978-0-9894005-3-4
Printed by Cerulium Corporation

Stephen Wilmes
Eric Rivard

Copyright

Trademarks

The following are registered names and/or trademarks, and are used throughout the book: Teradata, Teradata BYNET, Teradata Administrator, Teradata SQL Assistant, Teradata Raising Intelligence, Teradata Decision Experts, Teradata Source Experts, Raising Intelligence, Smarter.Faster.Wins., Active Enterprise Intelligence, DECISIONCAST, WEBANALYST, MYCOMMERCE, SEECHAIN, SEERISK, CLARAVIEW, GRIDSCALE, and XKOTO are registered trademarks and/or products of Teradata Corporation. Microsoft Windows, Windows 2003 Server, and .NET are either registered trademarks or trademarks of Microsoft Corporation. Intel and Xeon are registered trademarks of the Intel Corporation. Ethernet is a trademark of Xerox Corporation. UNIX is a registered trademark of The Open Group. Linux is a registered trademark of Linus Torvalds. Unicode is a registered trademark of Unicode, Inc. Sun Java is a trademark or registered trademark of Oracle Corporation in the U.S. or other countries. In addition to these product names, all brand and product names in this manual are trademarks of their respective holders in the United States and/or other countries.

Special Acknowledgement

A special thank you to the following individuals that contributed to the Study Guide content: Barbara Christjohn, Susan Hahn, David Micheletto, and James Petruzzelli.

About the Author - Steve Wilmes

Steve Wilmes founded Cerulium Corporation in 2007. As Chief Executive Officer, his goal is to establish Cerulium as a premier data warehousing Technology Company. Cerulium's strategic growth is globally focused on six lines of business including education, consulting, BI solutions, productivity tools, application integration and assessment services. These lines of business have been highly successful by utilizing strategic data warehousing solutions provided by Teradata that spans across the consumer, and commercial markets.

Mr. Wilmes has over 20 years of experience in the computer industry and is known to be a detail-oriented, results-focused leader. He is an internationally recognized expert in several aspects of data warehousing including hardware, software, SQL, operating systems, implementation, data integration, database administration, and BI solutions.

Mr. Wilmes earned a bachelor's degree in business administration and economics from Augsburg College and he is also a Teradata Certified Master.

Mr. Wilmes resides just outside of Columbia, South Carolina, with his wife, Becky. He has been involved with numerous civic, educational, and business organizations throughout his career. Some of his more recent associations include working with the Richland County Sheriff's Department – Region 4 Community Member, and volunteer for local organizations where he shares his technical expertise.

About the Author - Eric Rivard

Eric Rivard is the COO and Vice President of Cerulium Corporation, and is responsible for consulting and product development operations. Mr. Rivard has substantial industry experience across the telecommunications, retail, and healthcare industries, and has consulted at many Fortune 500 companies. His in-depth knowledge of the Teradata platform has enabled him to design and develop customized Teradata applications. He has worked with some of the largest data warehouses in the world, providing unique software solutions and solving complex business problems.

Mr. Rivard dedicated the bulk of his career to the pursuit of data heterogeneity. Outside of this Teradata expertise, he worked extensively with a variety of database platforms, and developed software products that integrate across the different RDBMS systems. He is an experienced Microsoft .NET developer, which has enabled him to use Microsoft's best-in-class development tools as a foundation for Cerulium Corporation's data warehouse applications.

Mr. Rivard resides just outside of Atlanta, Georgia, with his wife, Susana, and their three children. Outside of his professional career, he is actively involved in many community activities. In addition, he serves on the Advisory Board for the Management Information Systems (MIS) program at his alma mater, the Terry College of Business at the University of Georgia, where he earned his Bachelor of Business Administration in MIS and International Business.

Contents

Chapter 1: The Teradata Certified Professional Program

Pursue Teradata Certification with Confidence™

The Teradata Certified Professional Program (TCPP), launched in 1999, develops and manages Teradata's premier, and only, certification testing program. Teradata authorized training and proctored exams, available globally to customers, partners, associates, and students, are instrumental in establishing an industry-standard measure of technical competence for IT professionals using Teradata technology. Recognized as a leader in Data Warehouse RDBMS technology and valued by major global companies using Teradata, more than 57,000 Teradata Certifications have been awarded.

The new Teradata 14 Certification Track consists of seven exams that combine for achievement of six certifications and provides a logical progression for specific job roles. Starting with the core Teradata 14 Certified Professional credential, individuals have an opportunity to demonstrate knowledge by achieving Certification as a Technical Specialist, Database Administrator, Solutions Developer, Enterprise Architect, and the most prestigious Teradata Certification – Teradata 14 Certified Master.

The purpose of this Certification Exam Study Guide is to assist you with your goal to become Teradata Certified. This Guide will provide focused content areas, high level explanations around the key areas of focus, and help you to determine areas of further study prior to sitting for the Teradata Certification examination.

Although the Exam Study Guide will assist you in exam preparation, you must be knowledgeable of the subject areas in order to pass the exam. This Guide is intended for individuals who have completed the recommended training and have the recommended amount of

Teradata experience. **We do not guarantee that you will pass the exam simply by reading the Exam Study Guide.** Only hard work, hands-on experience, and a positive attitude will help you to achieve exam success. We wish you the very best of luck!

> *"When hiring, I always look for Teradata Certified Professionals. Not only does it provide me a good understanding of a candidate's knowledge level, it also shows a commitment to continuous learning and self-improvement. That's a great trait to have in every employee and the Teradata Certified Professional Program makes it easy to recognize."*
>
> *Teradata Certified Master, Insurance Industry*

The flowchart and matrix below are designed to help you define a path to the knowledge, skills, and experience needed to achieve Teradata 14 Certifications.

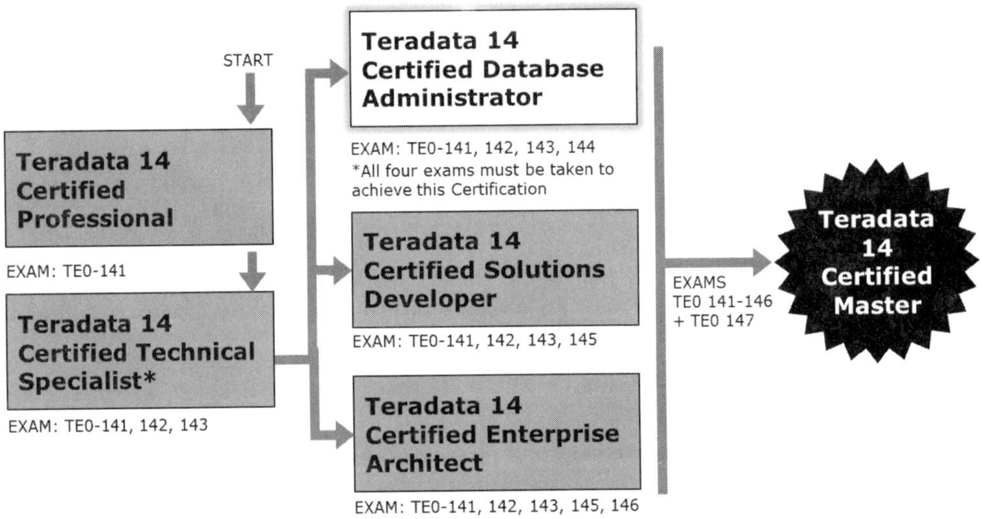

Your Teradata 14 Certification Upgrade Roadmap

Teradata 12 Certified candidates, in good standing, are eligible to take the *Teradata 14 Bridge from Teradata 12 Exam (TE0-14B).* The Bridge exam is a hybrid of all three (3) Teradata baseline Certification exams, and covers content changes to Teradata Basics, Teradata SQL and Teradata Physical Design & Implementation exams.

A passed exam result on the Bridge exam will yield the *Teradata 14 Certified Technical Specialist* designation. A candidate may then continue on the Teradata 14 track until achieving the desired Certification level.

<table>
<tr><th colspan="2">Teradata 14 Certifications</th></tr>
<tr><th colspan="2">Teradata 14 Certified Professional</th></tr>
<tr><td><u>Exams Required:</u>
• TE0-141 – Teradata 14 Basics

Must be passed before continuing on certification path</td><td><u>Recommended Teradata Experience:</u>
6-12 months

<u>Recommended Preparation Courses:</u>
• Introduction to the Teradata Database</td></tr>
<tr><th colspan="2">Teradata 14 Certified Technical Specialist</th></tr>
<tr><td><u>Exams Required:</u>
• TE0-141 – Teradata 14 Basics
• TE0-142 – Teradata 14 SQL
• TE0-143 – Teradata 14 Physical Design and Implementation

3 Exams to be passed in sequential order</td><td><u>Recommended Teradata Experience:</u>
1-2 years

<u>Recommended Preparation Courses:</u>
• Introduction to the Teradata Database
• Teradata SQL
• Advanced Teradata SQL
• Physical Database Design
• Physical Database Tuning</td></tr>
</table>

Teradata 14 Certified Database Administrator

Exams Required:

- TE0-141 – Teradata 14 Basics
- TE0-142 – Teradata 14 SQL
- TE0-143 – Teradata 14 Physical Design and Implementation
- TE0-144 – Teradata 14 Database Administration

4 Exams to be passed in sequential order

Recommended Teradata Experience:

2-3 years

Recommended Preparation Courses:

- Introduction to the Teradata Database
- Teradata SQL
- Advanced Teradata SQL
- Physical Database Design
- Physical Database Tuning
- Teradata Application Utilities
- Teradata Parallel Transporter
- Teradata Warehouse Management
- Teradata Warehouse Administration

Teradata 14 Certified Solutions Developer

Exams Required:

- TE0-141 – Teradata 14 Basics
- TE0-142 – Teradata 14 SQL
- TE0-143 – Teradata 14 Physical Design and Implementation
- TE0-145 – Teradata 14 Solutions Development

4 Exams to be passed in sequential order

Recommended Teradata Experience:

2-3 years

Recommended Preparation Courses:

- Introduction to the Teradata Database
- Teradata SQL
- Advanced Teradata SQL
- Physical Database Design
- Physical Database Tuning
- Teradata Application Utilities
- Teradata Parallel Transporter
- Teradata Application Design and Development

Teradata 14 Certified Enterprise Architect

Exams Required:

- TE0-141 – Teradata 14 Basics
- TE0-142 – Teradata 14 SQL
- TE0-143 – Teradata 14 Physical Design and Implementation
- TE0-145 – Teradata 14 Solutions Development
- TE0-146 – Teradata 14 Enterprise Architecture

5 Exams to be passed in sequential order

Recommended Teradata Experience:

2-3 years

Recommended Preparation Courses:

- Introduction to the Teradata Database
- Teradata SQL
- Advanced Teradata SQL
- Physical Database Design
- Physical Database Tuning
- Teradata Application Utilities
- Teradata Parallel Transporter
- Teradata Warehouse Management
- Teradata Warehouse Administration
- Teradata Application Design and Development

Teradata 14 Certified Master*

Exams Required:

- TE0-141 - TE0-146: Successful completion of all exams **PLUS:**
- TE0-147 – Teradata 14 Comprehensive Mastery Exam

7 Exams to be passed in sequential order

*Path for Teradata 12 Certified Masters

- TE0-147 – Teradata 14 Comprehensive Mastery Exam

Recommended Teradata Experience:

A minimum 5 years practical hands-on experience is highly recommended

Recommended Preparation Courses:

- Introduction to the Teradata Database
- Teradata SQL
- Advanced Teradata SQL
- Physical Database Design
- Physical Database Tuning
- Teradata Application Utilities
- Teradata Parallel Transporter
- Teradata Warehouse Management
- Teradata Warehouse Administration
- Teradata Application Design and Development

Note: Formal education recommendations may vary based on previous training and relevant job experience.

Certification... Knowledge Building to Mastery

Competition is fierce. Differentiate yourself while building critical IT technology knowledge and skills. Trust Teradata Certification to help you build the expertise employers are looking for in a demanding, data-driven global business environment. Teradata developed a new generation of certification exams that bring premium value to Teradata 14 Certification credentials.

Top 10 "What's new about the Teradata 14 Certification Track?"

1. Seven exams with all new content based upon the following database releases: Teradata Database 13.0, Teradata Database 13.1, Teradata Database 14.0 (including SLES 11)
2. The "*Teradata 14 Bridge from Teradata 12*" Exam allows Teradata 12 certified candidates to move, or "bridge", from the Teradata 12 Certification track to the Teradata 14 Certification track without starting the track from the beginning.
3. Eligibility-based exams to ensure compliance with Teradata Certification requirements (Bridge and Masters exams only)
4. Teradata 12 Certified Masters will take just one exam to update to Teradata 14 Certified Master status.
5. A Qualification exam is not required for those that have achieved a Teradata 12 Master Certification.
6. A new Candidate Agreement and revised security measures are in place to protect the value of your investment and integrity of all exams and certifications.
7. Newly designed electronic certificates, wallet cards, and logos.
8. An easy Certification verification process for individuals and employers.
9. More rigorous certification criteria including a combination of training, study, and practical, hands-on experience.

10. A team of dedicated, experienced, and knowledgeable individuals with a passion to help you achieve your Teradata Certification goals!

Path to Teradata 14 Mastery

A Teradata Certified Master enjoys a distinct advantage in the global marketplace. Employers seek Teradata Certified staff with verifiable knowledge and skills that support their business-critical Teradata systems. The TCPP process helps those individuals who want to deepen their knowledge and build their skills to the highest level.

The path to achieve Teradata 14 Certified Master status is summarized in the matrix below.

If You Are...	Exams Required for Teradata 14 Master Certification
Starting on the Teradata 14 Certification Track	• TE0-141 – TE0-147 All 7 Exams required
Teradata 12 Certified Master	TE0-147: Teradata 14 Comprehensive Mastery Exam

Exam Registration

All Teradata Certification exams are administered and proctored by authorized Prometric Testing Centers. Schedule exams at any authorized Prometric Testing Center by phone or online. In the US and Canada, you may call 1-877-887-6868. A listing of Prometric telephone numbers, by country, is available at: www.prometric.com/Teradata. Some countries do not offer online registration.

Where to Find More Information

Teradata Corporation's official certification exams and credentials are developed, copyrighted, and managed solely by the Teradata Certified Professional Program (TCPP) team. There are no other Teradata authorized exams, certifications, or legitimate credentials in the IT industry. To achieve your training and certification goals, pursue only authorized processes and approved courses of study as outlined on the official TCPP Website: www.Teradata.com/Certification. A mobile app with access to all study guides, practice questions, and many more Teradata Certification and related resources is also available for a variety of devices. Please refer to the web site for additional information.

Chapter 2 – Data Dictionary / Directory

Certification Objectives

- ✓ Given a scenario, identify the resource that should be used for the Data Dictionary.
- ✓ Given a scenario, identify the correct use of views to limit row or column accessibility.

Before You Begin

You should be familiar with the following terms and concepts.

Terms	Key Concepts
Dictionary Tables	The main tables associated with objects
Dictionary Views	User access to the dictionary tables
Timestamps	The format of Timestamp(0)

Supplied Data Dictionary Views

There are two types of views that can be installed in the Data Dictionary - Modern and Compatibility. Modern view names end with a V or VX, such as AllRightsV or AllrightsVX. Every modern view has a compatibility view. Compatibility view names end with an X or a non-X character, such as AllRights or AllrightsX. The compatibility views are deprecated and should not be used, since they will be discontinued in a future release.

AccessLogV	AccLogRulesV
AccountInfoV[X]	AllRightsV[X]
AllRoleRightsV	AllSpaceV[X]

AllTempTablesV[X]	All_RI_ChildrenV[X]
All_RI_ParentsV[X]	AMPUsageV[X]
ArchiveLoggingObjsV[X]	AssociationV[X]
AuthorizationsV[X]	BusinessCalendar
BusinessCalendarExceptions	BusinessCalendarPatterns
CharSetsV	CharTranslationsV
ChildrenV[X]	CollationsV
ColumnStatsV	ColumnsV[X]
ColumnUseCountV[X]	ConnectRulesV
ConstraintFunctionsV	ConstraintValuesV
CostProfiles_V	CostProfileTypes_V
CostProfileValues_V	Database_Default_JournalsV[X]
Databases2V[X]	DatabasesV[X]
DatabaseUseCountV[X]	DBCInfoV
DBQLRulesV	DeleteAccessLogV
DeleteOldInDoubtV	DeleteUseCountV[X]
DiskSpaceV[X]	ErrorTblsV[X]
Events_ConfigurationV[X]	Events_MediaV[X]
EventsV[X]	ExportWidthV
ExpStatsV	ExternalSPsV[X]
FunctionsV[X]	HostsInfoV
IndexConstraintsV[X]	IndexStatsV
IndexUseCountV[X]	IndicesV[X]
InDoubtLogV	InsertUseCountV[X]
JoinIndicesV	JournalsV[X]
LogOnOffV[X]	LogonRulesV
MultiColumnStatsV[X]	MultiExpStatsV
ObjectUseCountV[X]	PartitioningConstraintsV[X]
ProfileAsgdSecConstraintsV[X]	ProfileInfoV[X]
QryLockLogXMLV	QryLogEventHisV
QryLogEventsV	QryLogExceptionsV
QryLogExplainV	QryLogObjectsV
QryLogSQLV	QryLogStepsV
QryLogSummaryV	QryLogTDWMSumV

QryLogTDWMV	QryLogV
QryLogXMLV	QueryStatUseCountV[X]
RCC_ConfigurationV[X]	RCC_MediaV[X]
ReconfigDeleteOrderV	ReconfigInfoV
RedonfigRedistOrderV	ReconfigTableStatsV
RepCaptureRulesV	RepTablesV[X]
ResolvedDTSV[X]	RestrictedWordsV
RI_Child_TablesV[X]	RI_Distinct_ChildrenV[X]
RI_Distinct_ParentsV[X]	RI_Parent_TablesV[X]
RoleInfoV[X]	RoleMembersV[X]
SecConstraintsV[X]	SecurityDefaultsV
SecurityLogV[X]	SessionInfoV[X]
ShowColChecksV[X]	ShowTblChecksV[X]
Software_Event_LogV	StatsV
StatUseCountV[X]	Table_LevelConstraintsV[X]
Tables2V[X]	Tables3V[X]
TableSizeV[X]	TableStatsV
TablesV[X]	TableTextV[X]
TempTableStatsV	TriggersV[X]
UDTInfoV	UpdateUseCountV[X]
User_Default_JournalsV[X]	UserGrantedRightsV
UserRightsV	UserRoleRightsV
UsersV	UsrAsgdSecConstraintsV[X]

Figure 2.1

Using Restricted Views

As the name implies, "restricted views" limit what database elements users are allowed to see. In examining the above chart, additional system tables, such as DBC.AccessRights, DBC.DBase, DBC.Owners, DBC.RoleGrants, DBC.Roles, and others, are queried by the views. If a user's statement returns a "security violation" error, a reference to the "X" version of the view name may yield a valid result. If you are unable to access the views, then use the HELP commands to inquire about individual objects.

Selecting Information about Created Objects

DBC.ChildrenV[X] View

This view provides the names of all databases and users with the names of their parent.

DBC.ChildrenV[X]

Child	Parent

Figure 2.2

Example: Show all of the parents of a given database.

```
SELECT parent
FROM dbc.childrenV
WHERE child='csql_views'
ORDER BY parent;

Parent
------------------------------
csql00
DBC
tduser
```

Figure 2.3

Though the query shows all of the parents, it does not indicate the hierarchy of the relationships.

DBC.DatabasesV[X] View

This view provides information about the databases that the user can access.

DBC.DatabasesV[X]

DatabaseName	PermSpace	LastAlterTimeStamp
CreatorName	SpoolSpace	DBKind
OwnerName	TempSpace	AccessCount
AccountName	CommentString	LastAccessTimeStamp
ProtectionType	CreateTimeStamp	
JournalFlag	LastAlterName	

Figure 2.4

Example: Show the parentage for a particular database.

```
SELECT databasename, ownername
FROM dbc.databasesV
WHERE databasename
IN (SELECT parent
    FROM dbc.childrenV
    WHERE child = 'csql_views')
ORDER BY 1;

databasename  ownername
------------  ---------
csql00        tduser
DBC           DBC
tduser        DBC
```

Figure 2.5

In this query, you can see the hierarchy of ownership, DBC->tduser->csql00.

DBC.UsersV View

This view describes in detail all information about users that you control, including passwords. There is no [X] version.

DBC.Users[V]

UserName	StartupString	TimeZoneMinute
CreatorName	DefaultAccount	DefaultDateForm
PasswordLastModDate	DefaultDatabase	CreateTimeStamp
PasswordLastModTime	CommentString	LastAlterName
OwnerName	DefaultCollation	LastAlterTimeStamp
PermSpace	PasswordChgDate	DefaultCharType
SpoolSpace	LockedDate	RoleName
TempSpace	LockedTime	ProfileName
ProtectionType	LockedCount	AccessCount
JournalFlag	TimeZoneHour	LastAccessTimeStamp
ExportDefinitionName	ExportWidthRuleSet	

Figure 2.6

Example: Show information about current user's creation date and owner.

```
SELECT
 UserName
,DefaultAccount
,CreateTimeStamp
,OwnerName
FROM DBC.UsersV
WHERE UserName = USER ;

UserName   DefaultAccount   CreateTimeStamp       OwnerName
--------   --------------   -------------------   ---------
csql00     DBC              2010-07-15 10:18:20   tduser
```

Figure 2.7

DBC.TablesV[X] View

This view provides information about tables, views, stored procedures, join indexes, macros, user-defined types, user-defined methods, or user defined functions.

DBC.TablesV[X]

DatabaseName	ParentCount	LastAlterTimeStamp
TableName	ChildCount	RequestTxtOverFlow
Version	NamedTblCheckCount	AccessCount
TableKind	UnnamedTblCheckExist	LastAccessTimeStamp
ProtectionType	PrimaryKeyIndexId	UtilVersion
JournalFlag	RepStatus	QueueFlag
CreatorName	CreateTimeStamp	CommitOpt
RequestText	LastAlterName	TransLog
CommentString	CheckOpt	TemporalProperty
ResolvedCurrent_Date	ResolvedCurrent_TimeStamp	SystemDefinedJI
VTQualifier	TTQualifier	PIColumnCount
PartitioningLevels		

Figure 2.8

Example: Show all of the Fallback protected tables in a database.

```
SELECT tablename, protectiontype
FROM dbc.tablesV
WHERE databasename = 'csql_class'
AND protectiontype = 'f'
ORDER BY 1;

TableName                       ProtectionType
------------------------------  --------------
EmpJob                          F
enrollments                     F
EnrollStudent                   F
JobEmp                          F
```

Figure 2.9

DBC.ColumnsV[X] View

This view provides information about stored procedures, join indexes, the parameters of macros, user-defined types, user-defined methods, user-defined functions, and the columns of any table or view that the user can access.

DBC.ColumnsV[X]

DatabaseName	Nullable	CreatorName
TableName	CommentString	CreateTimeStamp
ColumnName	DecimalTotalDigits	LastAlterName
ColumnFormat	DecimalFractionalDigits	LastAlterTimeStamp
ColumnTitle	ColumnId	CharType
SPParameterType	UpperCaseFlag	IdColType
ColumnType	Compressible	AccessCount
ColumnUDTName	CompressValue	LastAccessTimeStamp
ColumnLength	ColumnConstraint	CompressValueList
DefaultValue	ConstraintCount	TimeDimension
VTCheckType	TTCheckType	ConstraintId
ArrayCol-ElementType	ArrayColScope	ArrayColNumber-OfDimensions
	PartitioningColumn	
ArrayColElement-UDTName	ColumnPartitionAC	ColumnPartitionNumber
ColumnPartitionFormat		

Figure 2.10

Example: Show the comments associated with a system table.

```
SELECT columnname, commentstring
FROM dbc.columnsV
WHERE databasename = 'dbc'
AND tablename = 'accountinfo'
ORDER BY 1;

   ColumnName  AccountName
CommentString  The AccountInfo.AccountName field specifies
               a valid account name for the user.
   ColumnName  UserName
CommentString  The AccountInfo.UserName field identifies a
               user or profile.
   ColumnName  UserOrProfile
CommentString  The AccountInfo.UserOrProfile field
               indicates whether the account name is for a
               user or a profile.
```

Figure 2.11

DBC.IndicesV[X] View

This view describes each of the indexes on each table.

DBC.Indices[V][X]

DatabaseName	IndexName	LastAlterName
TableName	ColumnName	LastAlterTimeStamp
IndexNumber	ColumnPosition	AccessCount
IndexType	CreatorName	LastAccessTimeStamp
UniqueFlag	CreateTimeStamp	UniqueOrPK
VTConstraintType	TTContrainstType	SystemDefinedJI

Figure 2.12

Example: Show all of the non-unique Primary Indexes in a database.

```
SELECT tablename, indextype, uniqueflag
FROM dbc.indicesV
WHERE databasename = 'csql_class'
AND indextype = 'p'
AND uniqueflag = 'n'
ORDER BY tablename;

TableName                       IndexType  UniqueFlag
------------------------------  ---------  ----------
b_words                         P          N
Emp_Job_table                   P          N
phcall                          P          N
phcall                          P          N
sales_stage                     P          N
Sales_table                     P          N
Student_Course_table            P          N
Temp_Employees                  P          N
```

Figure 2.13

DBC.IndexConstraintsV[X] View

This view provides information about index constraints on tables. Index constraints are implied constraints derived from a partitioning expression.

DBC.IndexConstraintsV[X]

DatabaseName	ConstraintType	CreatorName
TableName	ConstraintText	CreateTimeStamp
IndexName	ConstraintCollation	CharSetID
IndexNumber	CollationName	SessionMode
ResolvedCurrent_Date	ResolvedCurrent_ TimeStamp	

Figure 2.14

Example: Provides information about index constraints on tables.

```
SELECT DatabaseName
       ,TableName (TITLE 'Table/Join Index Name')
       ,ConstraintText
FROM DBC.IndexConstraintsV
WHERE ConstraintType = 'Q'
ORDER BY DatabaseName, TableName;

DatabaseName        Table/Join
                    Index Name    ConstraintText
------------------  -----------   --------------------------
retail              ITEMPPI       CHECK ((RANGE_N(l_shipdate
                                  BETWEEN DATE '1992-01-01'
                                  AND DATE '1998-12-01' EACH
                                  INTERVAL '1' MONTH ))
                                  BETWEEN 1 AND 00084)
```

Figure 2.15

DBC.ShowTblChecksV[X] View

This view provides information about table constraints.

DBC.ShowTblChecksV[X]

DatabaseName	CheckName	CreatorName
TableName	TblCheck	CreateTimeStamp
VTCheckType	TTCheckType	

Figure 2.16

Example: List all table checks for a given database.

```
SELECT tablename, checkname, tblcheck
FROM   dbc.showtblchecksV
WHERE databasename = 'csql_class'
ORDER BY 1;

TableName  CheckName     TblCheck
---------  ------------  -----------------------------
JOB_TABLE  job_no_range  CONSTRAINT job_no_range CHECK
                         ( job_no <  100000  )
```

Figure 2.17

DBC.TriggersV[X] View

This view provides information about event-driven, specialized procedures attached to a single table and stored in the database.

DBC.TriggersV[X]

DatabaseName	Event	CreateTimeStamp
SubjectTableDatabaseName	Kind	LastAlterName
TableName	OrderNumber	LastAlterTimeStamp
TriggerName	TriggerComment	AccessCount
EnabledFlag	RequestText	LastAccessTimeStamp
ActionTime	CreatorName	CreateTxtOverflow
VTEventType	TTEventType	

Figure 2.18

Example: Show all active triggers in the system.

```
SELECT
  databasename
, tablename
, triggername
, actiontime
FROM dbc.triggersV
WHERE enabledflag = 'y'
ORDER BY 1;

DataBaseName     TableName        TriggerName  ActionTime
--------------   ---------------  ----------   -----------
transportation   Frequent_Flyers  Awards       A
```

Figure 2.19

DBC.AllTempTablesV[X] View

The AllTempTables view provides information about all global temporary tables materialized in the system.

DBC.AllTempTablesV[X]

HostNo	UserName	B_TableName
SessionNo	B_DatabaseName	E_TableId

Figure 2.20

Example: List all materialized temporary tables.

```
SELECT databasename, tablename
FROM dbc.AllTempTablesV
WHERE databasename = 'manufacturing'
AND tablename = 'pclevel';


DatabaseName          TableName
------------------    --------------------
manufacturing         PCLevel
```

Figure 2.21

DBC.Databases2V[X] View

This view provides ID definition information about databases.

DBC.Databases2V[X]

DatabaseName	DatabaseId	UnResolvedRICount

Figure 2.22

Example: List the parents of a given database in databaseid order.

```
SELECT parent
FROM dbc.childrenV
JOIN dbc.databases2V
ON parent = databasename
AND child='csql_views'
ORDER BY databaseid;

Parent
------------------------------
DBC
tduser
csql00
```

Figure 2.23

Compare the results of this query to the one using dbc.databases. Since objects are assigned their IDs in numerical sequence, parents will have a lower databaseid than their children, unless GIVE statements have caused a higher databaseid to own lower databaseids.

Time Stamps in Data Dictionary

All of the timestamp columns appearing in Data Dictionary tables are defined as TIMESTAMP (0). The three main time stamp columns are CreateTimeStamp, LastAccessTimeStamp, LastAlterTimeStamp. The following figure shows the dictionary tables where these three time stamp columns appear.

Table Name	Create TimeStamp	LastAccess TimeStamp	LastAlter TimeStamp
AccessRights	Y	Y	N
AccLogRuleTbl	Y	Y	N
ArchiveLoggingObjsTbl	Y	N	N
ColumnCorrelation	Y	N	Y

Table Name	Create TimeStamp	LastAccess TimeStamp	LastAlter TimeStamp
ConstraintNames	Y	Y	N
Dbase	Y	Y	Y
ErrorTbls	Y	N	N
Indexes	Y	Y	Y
LogonRuleTbl	Y	Y	N
ObjectUsage	N	Y	N
Profiles	Y	N	Y
QueryStatsTbl	Y	N	N
ReferencedTbls	Y	Y	N
ReferencingTbls	Y	Y	N
RepGroup	Y	N	Y
RoleGrants	Y	N	N
Roles	Y	N	N
SecConstraints	Y	N	Y
StatsTbl	Y	N	Y
TableConstraints	Y	Y	N
TriggersTbl	Y	Y	Y
TVFields	Y	Y	Y
TVM	Y	Y	Y

Figure 2.24

Practice Questions

1. Which of the following dictionary views is deprecated and should not be used?
    a. DBC.CharSets
    b. DBC.AllSpaceVX
    c. DBC.AuthorizationsV
    d. DBC.ExternalSPsV

2. Which of the following is not a valid dictionary view?
    a. DBC.BusinessCalendar
    b. DBC.BusinessCalendarExceptions
    c. DBC.BusinessCalendarPatterns
    d. DBC.BusinessCalendarProfile

3. Which of the following views does not contain an 'AccessCount' column?
    a. DBC.ColumnsV
    b. DBC.TablesV
    c. DBC.DatabasesV
    d. DBC.ChildrenV

4. In which view will you find the 'UnResolvedRICount' column?
    a. DBC.DatabasesV
    b. DBC.Databases2V
    c. DBC.ShowTblChecksV
    d. DBC.TablesV

5. Which of the following views does not have an [X] version?
    a. DBC.TriggersV
    b. DBC.ChildrenV
    c. DBC.UsersV
    d. DBC.AllTempTablesV

Chapter Notes

Utilize this space for notes, key points to remember, diagrams, areas of further study, etc.

Chapter 3 Database Space

Certification Objectives

- ✓ Identify the types of data that need to be collected for future capacity planning.
- ✓ Identify what is monitored to diagnose immediate capacity shortfalls.

Before You Begin

You should be familiar with the following terms and concepts.

Terms	Key Concepts
Perm Space	How it is defined and allocated, and what consumes it
Spool Space	What is Spool Space and how does it work
Temp Space	Explain the methods of using Temporary Space

Permanent Space Terminology

CurrentPerm

CurrentPerm is the total number of bytes (including table headers) currently allocated to existing data tables, index tables (and subtables), stored procedures, triggers, and permanent journals residing in a particular database/user.

PeakPerm

PeakPerm is the largest number of bytes ever used to store data in a user or database since the last reset of this value to zero.

Note: This value is maintained on each AMP. To reset the PeakPerm value to zero, use the DBC.ClearPeakDisk macro. Please see Figure 3.2 for more information.

MaxPerm

MaxPerm is the maximum number of bytes available for storage of all (current and future) data tables, index tables and subtables, stored procedures, triggers, and permanent journals owned by a particular database/user.

For each database or user in the system, the number of permanent bytes allocated is divided by the number of AMPs in the configuration. The result is recorded on each AMP and may not be exceeded on any AMP. Uneven data distribution can cause a premature "Database Full" error.

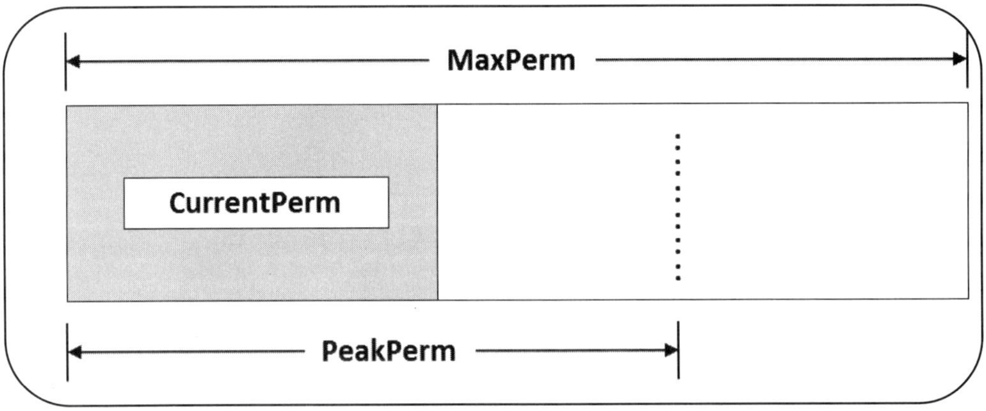

Figure 3.1

Spool Space Terminology

MaxSpool

MaxSpool is a value used to limit the number of bytes the system allocates to create spool files for a user. The value you specify may not exceed the value of the immediate parent (database or user) at the time you create the user. If you do not specify a value, MaxSpool defaults to the MaxSpool value of the parent.

Specify the spool limit for each user; taking into consideration the tables they access, to reduce the impact of "runaway" transactions, such as accidental Cartesian product joins.

PeakSpool

PeakSpool is the maximum number of bytes used by a transaction for a user since the value was last reset by the ClearPeakDisk Macro.

CurrentSpool

CurrentSpool is the number of bytes in use for resolving queries. This value is maintained on each AMP for each user.

Temp Space Terminology

MaxTemp

MaxTemp specifies the limit of space available for global temporary tables. The value may not exceed the limit of:

- The creator or modifier of the profile, when setting TEMPORARY in a profile

- The immediate owner of the user being created or modified, if a profile does not apply

If you do not specify a value and the user is associated with a profile, MaxTemp defaults to the value of the profile, if defined. If the profile TEMPORARY is set to NULL or NONE, or the user is not associated with a profile, MaxTemp defaults to the value of the user's parent.

PeakTemp

This is the maximum temporary space used since the last session. Temporary space is released when the session terminates.

CurrentTemp

This is the amount of space currently in use by Global Temporary tables.

DBC.ClearPeakDisk macro

Here is the syntax of the ClearPeakDisk macro that was mentioned earlier.

```
REPLACE MACRO DBC.ClearPeakDisk
AS  ( UPDATE DataBaseSpace
SET PeakPermSpace = 0, PeakSpoolSpace = 0,
PeakTempSpace = 0 ALL; );
```

Figure 3.2

Assigning Perm and Spool Limits

Perm space is the number of bytes to be reserved for permanent storage of the new user or database. The space is taken from unallocated space in the database or user space of the immediate owner.

Spool is the number of bytes allowed for spool files and volatile temporary tables for this user. The default is the largest value that is not greater than the owner spool space. It must not exceed the size of the owner spool space. Databases do not consume spool space.

If necessary, the defined PERM, SPOOL, or TEMPORARY space is changed to the highest multiple of the number of AMPs on the system less than or equal to the requested space.

Giving One User to Another

The GIVE command transfers *ownership* of a database or user and its space to another user. It also moves all children (i.e. databases and users) owned by the database or user that is being given. It has no effect on access rights.

Consider the following GIVE example:

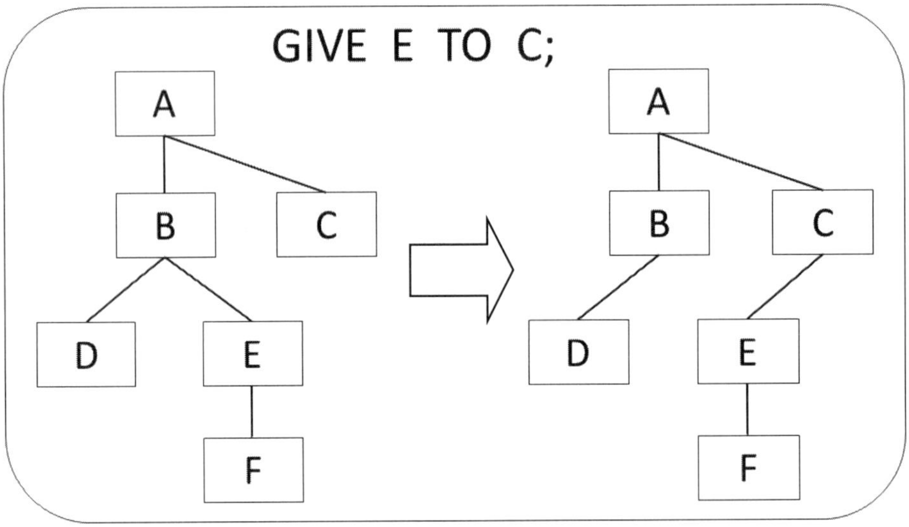

Figure 3.3

When database E was created, its Perm space came from database B. The Perm space for database F came from the space allocated to database E. So, if database F is dropped, its Perm space goes back to database E, and if database E is dropped, its Perm space goes back to database B.

However, the GIVE command is used to transfer the Perm space ownership from database to database (i.e. GIVE E TO C). So if you dropped databases F and E, then C gets all of the space that once belonged to B.

In addition, the GIVE can be used to remove a database/user from the middle of the hierarchy. Suppose that database B is to be removed. The previous GIVE statement (GIVE e TO c;) transferred E and F over to C. The following statement (GIVE d TO a;) will leave B at the bottom of the hierarchy where it can be dropped. The perm space allocated to B (minus the perm space allocated to D) will be credited back to A.

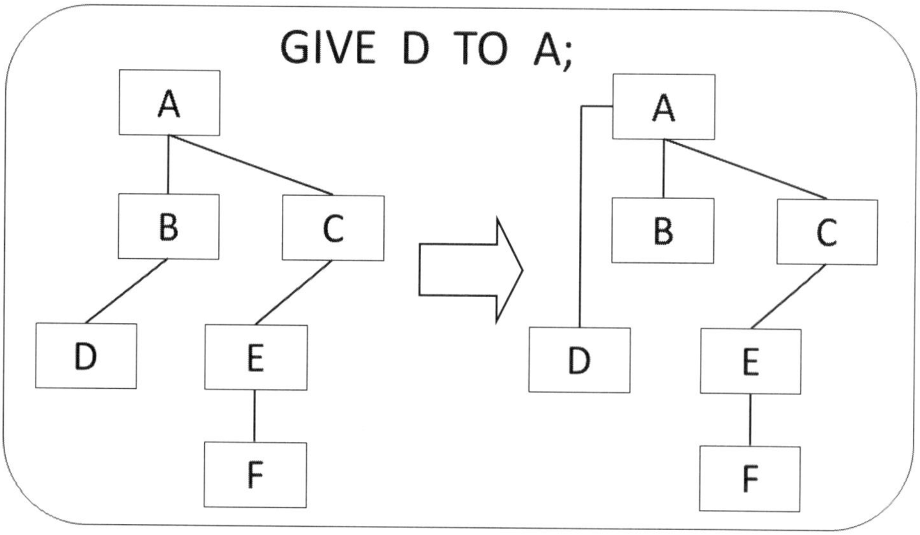

Figure 3.4

Views for Space Allocation Reporting

DBC.TableSizeV[X] View

DBC.TableSizeV[X]

Vproc	AccountName	CurrentPerm
DatabaseName	TableName	PeakPerm

Figure 3.5

DBC.AllSpaceV[X] View

DBC.AllSpaceV[X]

Vproc	MaxTemp	PeakSpool
DatabaseName	CurrentPerm	PeakPersistentSpool
AccountName	CurrentSpool	PeakTemp
TableName	CurrentPersistentSpool	MaxProfileSpool
MaxPerm	CurrentTemp	MaxProfileTemp
MaxSpool	PeakPerm	

Figure 3.6

DBC.DataBaseSpace Table

The DBC.DataBaseSpace table performs space accounting for each database and each table in a database. This is a non-fallback and non-hashed table.

DBC.DataBaseSpace

DatabaseId	PeakSpoolSpace	CurrentTempSpace
TableId	CurrentPermSpace	MaxProfileSpoolSpace
Vproc	CurrentSpoolSpace	MaxProfileTempSpace
MaxPermSpace	MaxTempSpace	PeakPersistentSpoolSpace
MaxSpoolSpace	PeakTempSpace	CurrentPersistentSpoolSpace
PeakPermSpace		

Figure 3.7

Different Views – Different Results

The DBC.AllSpaceV view provides object level space usage information. Objects include tables, join indexes, permanent journals, and stored procedures at either the database or user level. However, it is recommended that you either use DBC.DiskSpaceV or DBC.TableSizeV views to measure space usage because the DBC.AllSpaceV results can be misleading.

For example, the following query returns the total current permanent space each user or database.

```
sel databasename (char(30))
,sum(currentperm)
from DBC.AllSpaceV
group by 1 having sum(currentperm) > 0
order by 2 desc;


DatabaseName                    Sum(CurrentPerm)
------------------------------  ------------------
twm_md                               148,412,416
tpch                                  98,513,920
retail                                45,854,720
DBC                                   43,461,632
financial                             23,663,616
twm_source                            19,017,728
Sys_Calendar                           5,296,128
SysAdmin                               2,981,888
SYSLIB                                   643,072
SystemFe                                 299,008
CSQL_CLASS                               187,392
rex_20110212                             128,000
QCD_20110211                             109,568
manufacturing                            108,544
transportation                             8,192
csql00                                     6,144
```

Figure 3.8

The equivalent query referencing DBC.DiskSpaceV will return the same results.

Note: On certain Teradata Database Systems, this command can be more efficient.

```
sel databasename (char(30))
,sum(currentperm)
from DBC.DiskSpaceV
group by 1 having sum(currentperm) > 0
order by 2 desc;



DatabaseName                    Sum(CurrentPerm)
------------------------------  ------------------
twm_md                                  74,206,208
tpch                                    49,256,960
retail                                  22,927,360
DBC                                     21,730,816
financial                               11,831,808
twm_source                               9,508,864
Sys_Calendar                             2,648,064
SysAdmin                                 1,490,944
SYSLIB                                     321,536
SystemFe                                   149,504
CSQL_CLASS                                  93,696
rex_20110212                                64,000
QCD_20110211                                54,784
manufacturing                               54,272
transportation                               4,096
csql00                                       3,072
```

Figure 3.9

Practice Questions

1. Which of the following is not a column of DBC.TableSizeV?
    a. Vproc
    b. AccountName
    c. CurrentPerm
    d. MaxPerm
    e. PeakPerm

2. Which of the following is not a column of DBC.DataBaseSpace table?
    a. CurrentPermSpace
    b. MaxPermSpace
    c. MaxProfilePermSpace
    d. MaxProfileSpoolSpace
    e. MaxProfileTempSpace
    f. PeakPermSpace

3. Which view provides space usage at both the object and database level?
    a. DBC.TableSizeV
    b. DBC.DiskSpaceV
    c. DBC.AllSpaceV
    d. DBC.DatabasesV

4. Which of the following is not affected by a GIVE command?
    a. DBC.Owners
    b. DBC.AccessRights
    c. DBC.Parents
    d. MaxSpool

5. Which table is changed when someone does EXEC DBC.ClearPeakDisk; ?
    a. DBC.Dbase
    b. DBC.TVM
    c. DBC.Acctg
    d. DBC.DataBaseSpace

Chapter Notes

Utilize this space for notes, key points to remember, diagrams, areas of further study, etc.

Chapter 4 - Users and Databases

Certification Objectives

- ✓ Identify the methods of user authentication.
- ✓ Identify the account string expansion characters that should be used to capture the appropriate level of data.
- ✓ Identify the causes of a system prematurely running out of disk space.

Before You Begin

You should be familiar with the following terms and concepts.

Terms	Key Concepts
User	What are the characteristics of a User
Database	What are the characteristics of a Database
Account String	Explain how this can be used for user billing and priority scheduling

Creating Users & Databases

In the Teradata system, a User is a database that also represents a logon point into the system. It is through the CREATE USER and CREATE DATABASE commands that the hierarchical structure is built. In looking at the following database structure, all of the following are databases and, depending on the access rights you have been granted, you can access their contents. Some users may not be given any Perm space and only use Perm space given to other databases.

In the diagram below, all of these are databases, unless they have a password and you know what it is. That is why DBC, who is a user, is usually referred to as database DBC, since only a select few know its password.

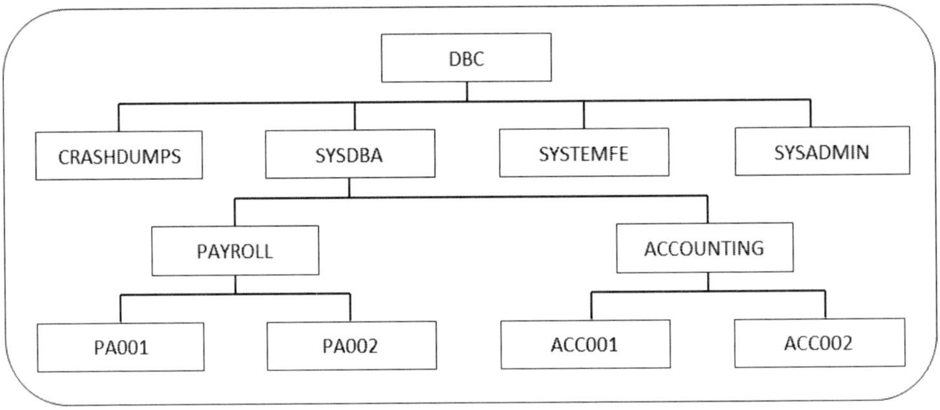

Figure 4.1

CREATE DATABASE Statement

Here is the syntax diagram of the CREATE DATABASE command. Compare it to the syntax of the CREATE USER command that follows.

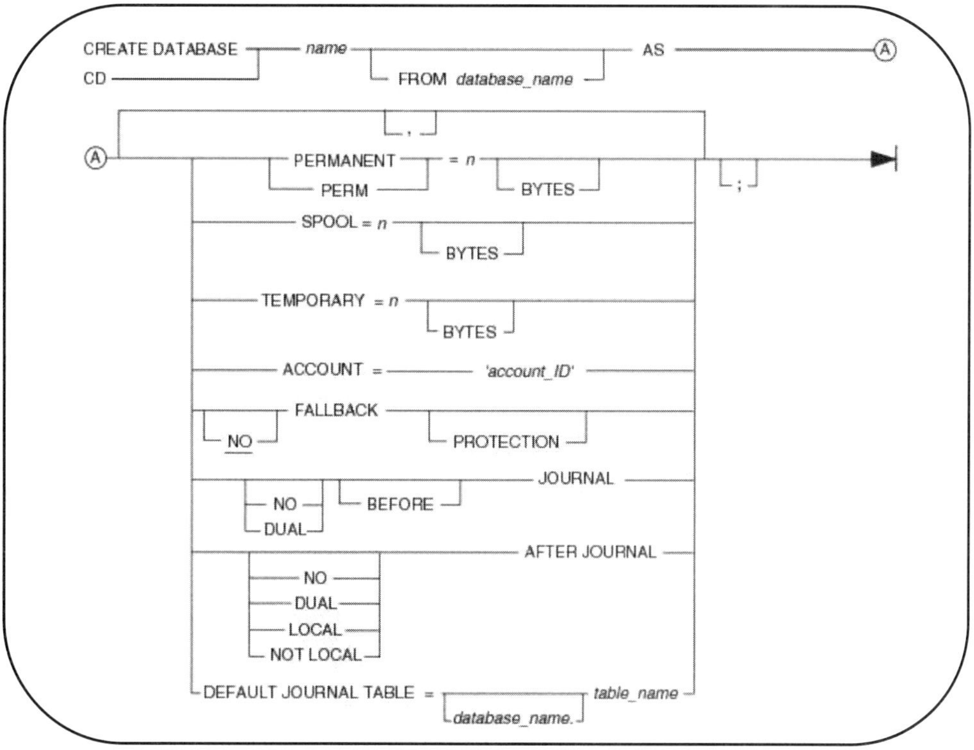

Figure 4.2

CREATE USER Statement

Here is the syntax diagram of the CREATE USER command. Notice the additional clauses that only apply to Users and not Databases.

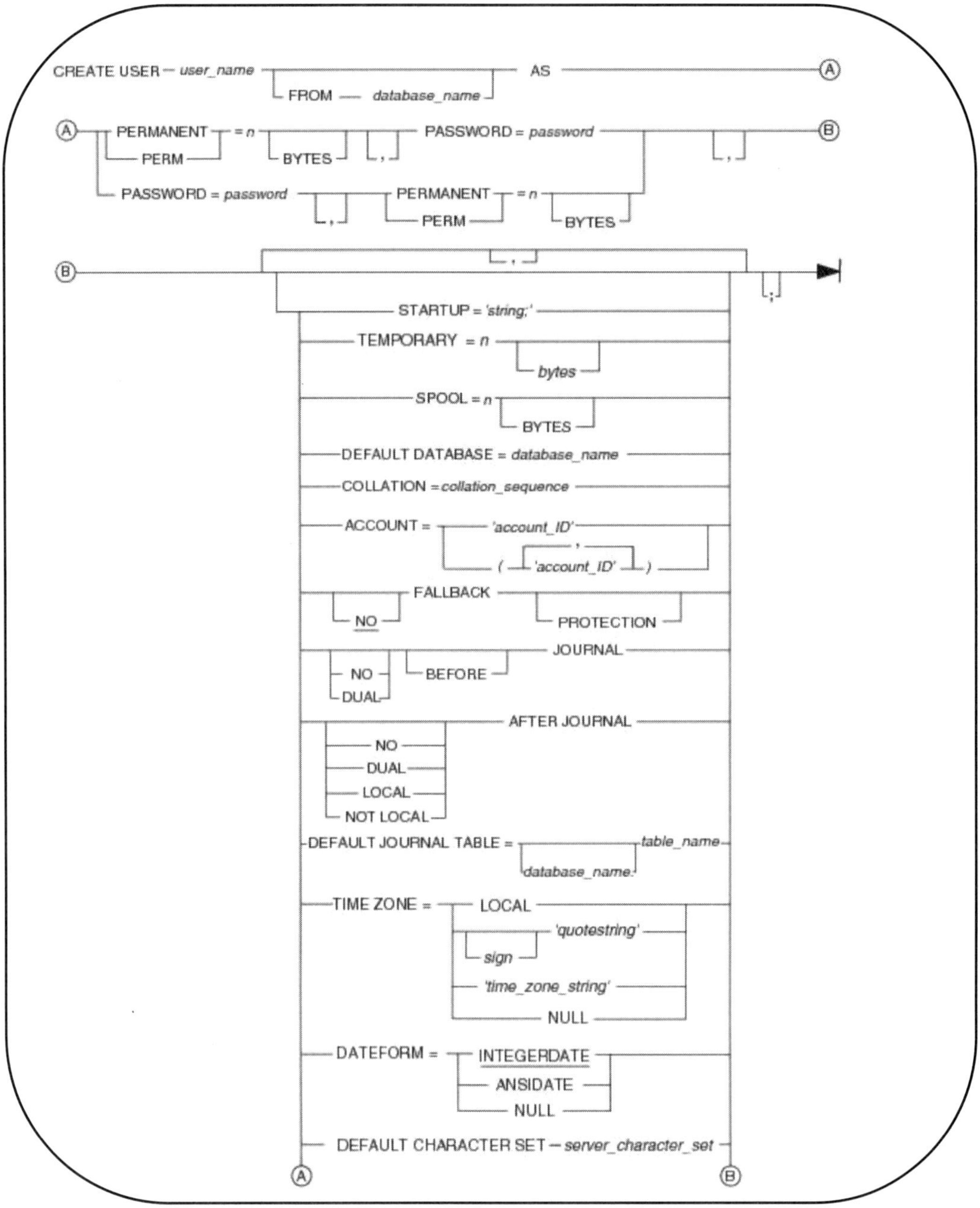
CREATE USER — user_name
FROM — database_name
AS
PERMANENT
PERM
= n
BYTES
PASSWORD = password
STARTUP = 'string;'
TEMPORARY = n
bytes
SPOOL = n
DEFAULT DATABASE = database_name
COLLATION = collation_sequence
ACCOUNT =
'account_ID'
NO
FALLBACK
PROTECTION
DUAL
BEFORE
JOURNAL
AFTER JOURNAL
LOCAL
NOT LOCAL
DEFAULT JOURNAL TABLE =
table_name
database_name.
TIME ZONE =
'quotestring'
sign
'time_zone_string'
NULL
DATEFORM =
INTEGERDATE
ANSIDATE
DEFAULT CHARACTER SET — server_character_set

Figure 4.3

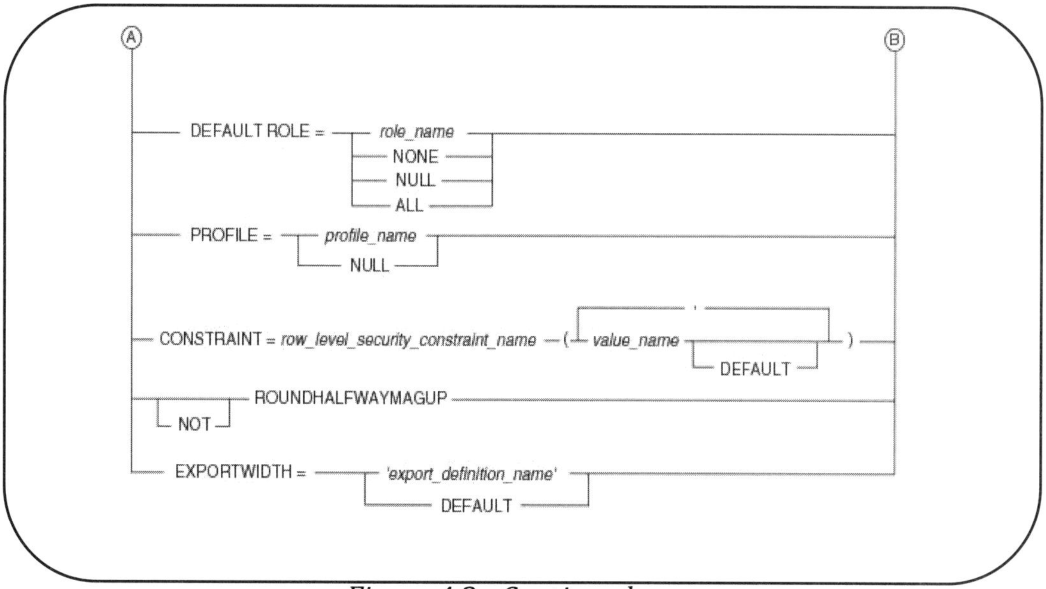

Figure 4.3 - Continued

CREATE USER and the Data Dictionary

An Explain of the following CREATE USER command shows the subsequent Data Dictionary tables being updated.

```
EXPLAIN
CREATE USER tester001 AS
PERM = 0 BYTES
PASSWORD = $gbh9XYZ#
TEMPORARY = 1000000
SPOOL = 1000000
DEFAULT DATABASE = csql_class
NO FALLBACK ;
```

Figure 4.4

AccessRights *Privileges for users and databases*	**Accounts** *Account logon information*
DatabaseSpace *Database/Table space accounting*	**Dbase** *Each database and user in the system*
Owners *Database ownership*	**Parents** *Database parentage*

Figure 4.5

MODIFY USER Statement

In the CREATE USER command (above), in addition to a username, a declaration of Perm space and a Password are required entries. In the MODIFY USER command, only the username is required, and all of the other definitions are optional.

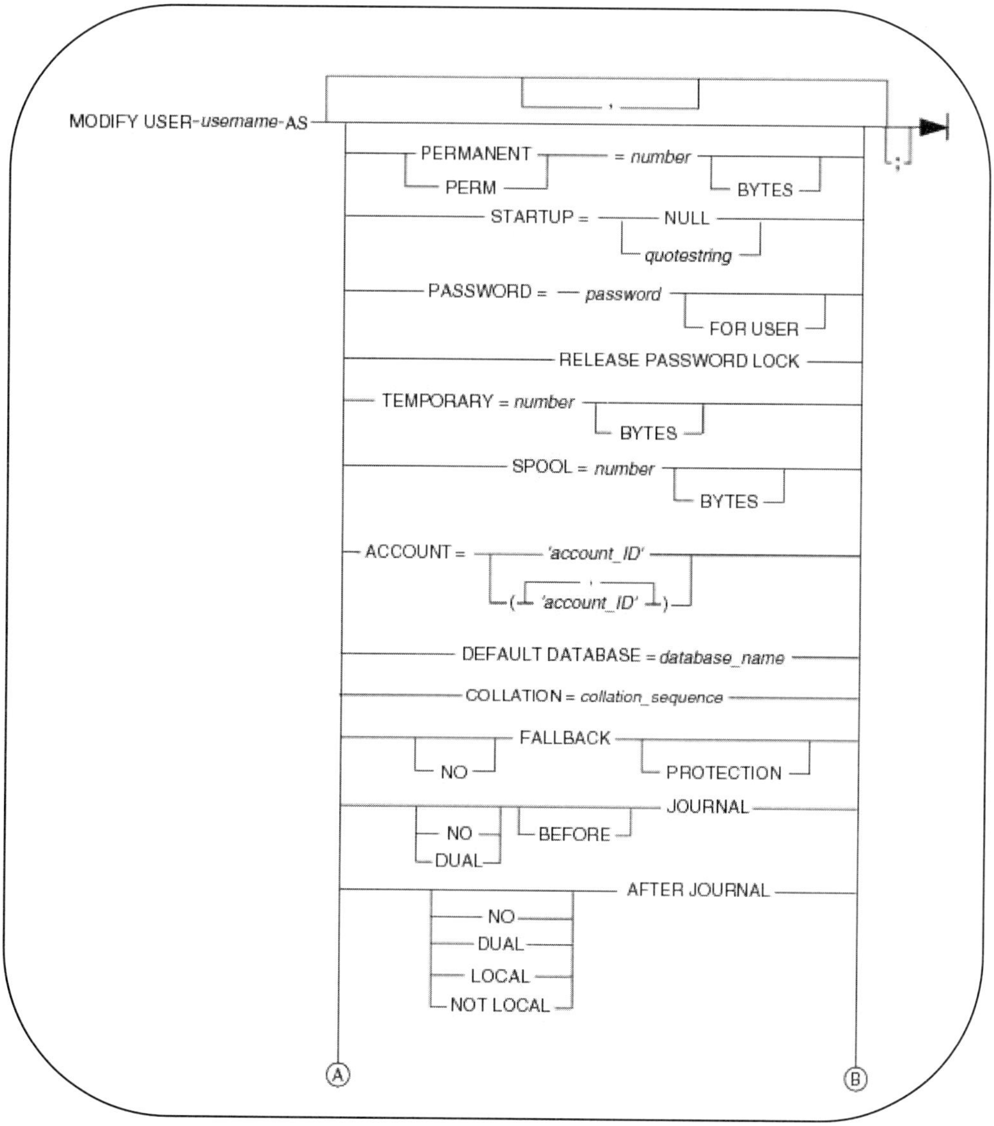
MODIFY USER-username-AS
,
;
PERMANENT
PERM
= number
BYTES
STARTUP =
NULL
quotestring
PASSWORD =
password
FOR USER
RELEASE PASSWORD LOCK
TEMPORARY = number
BYTES
SPOOL = number
BYTES
ACCOUNT =
'account_ID'
('account_ID')
DEFAULT DATABASE = database_name
COLLATION = collation_sequence
FALLBACK
NO
PROTECTION
JOURNAL
NO
DUAL
BEFORE
AFTER JOURNAL
NO
DUAL
LOCAL
NOT LOCAL
A
B

Figure 4.6

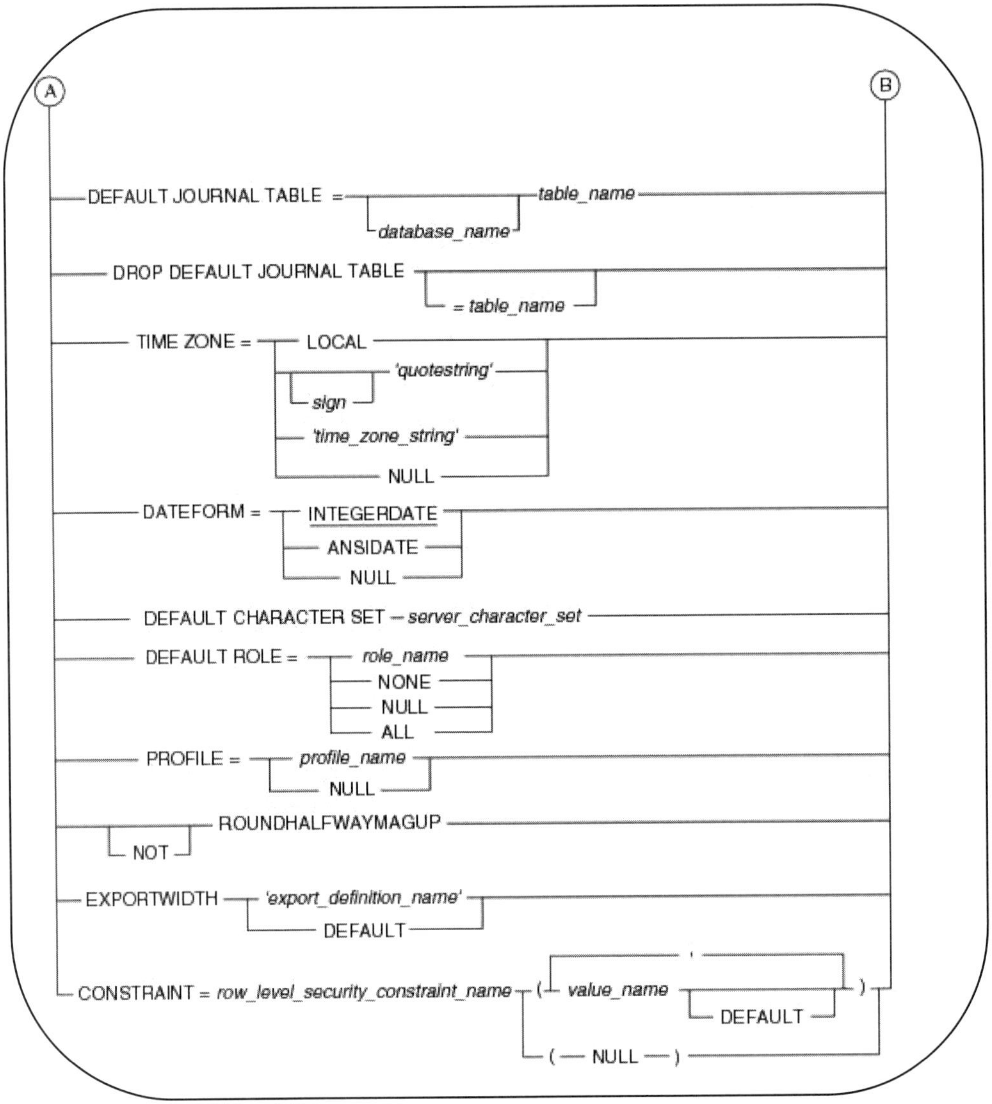

Figure 4.6 - Continued

Creating and Using Account IDs

Users may have more than one account. As an example, contractors might split their time between different projects, and have an Account ID for each one, as shown below.

```
CREATE USER contract001
PERM = 1000000000
PASSWORD = pa$$w0rd
ACCOUNT = ('Payroll', 'Accounting', 'Billing');
```

Figure 4.7

When contract001 logs on, the logon request takes the form:

```
.LOGON username, password [, accountid ]
```

So, the valid logons for contract001 are:

```
.LOGON contract001, pa$$w0rd, 'Payroll'
.LOGON contract001, pa$$w0rd, 'Accounting'
.LOGON contract001, pa$$w0rd, 'Billing'
.LOGON contract001, pa$$w0rd
```

Figure 4.8

If contract001 does not specify an account ID (as shown as the last entry), then the first one in the list (Payroll) becomes the default.

If contract001 wants to change accounts, the user can either logoff and logon using the different account ID, or simply execute the following.

```
.SET SESSION ACCOUNT = 'Accounting'
```

ACCOUNT PRIORITIES

There are a series of choices the system evaluates when a user does not specify an account ID when they log on. The following diagram shows the order of evaluation.

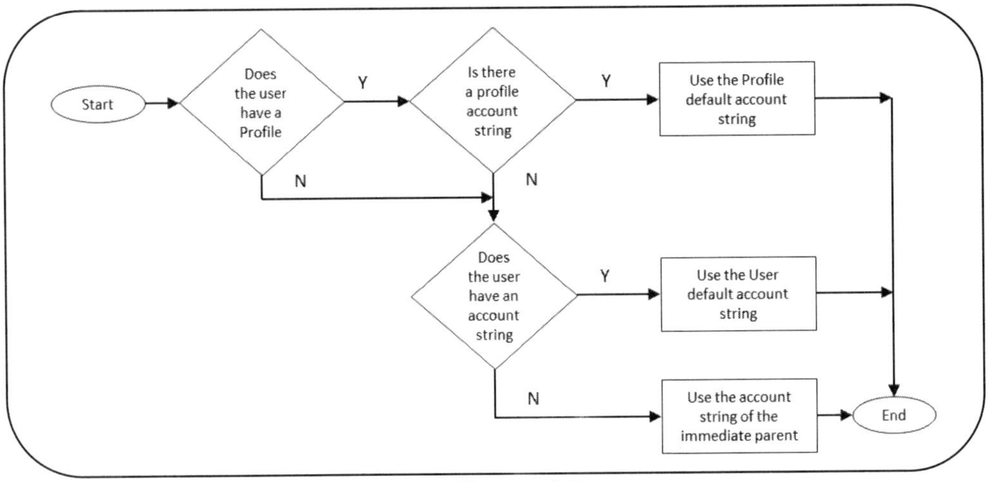

Figure 4.9

ACCOUNT STRING EXPANSION (ASE)

In addition to an account ID, an account string may contain a performance group name, and/or ASE designators. The maximum length of an account string is 30 bytes.

Performance group names are bracketed by dollar signs (*$groupname$*), and are discussed in Chapter 7. If appearing in an account string, a performance group name must appear first such as *$groupname$account_id&char.*

The following chart shows the ASE designators (&*char*)

VARIABLE	FORMAT	DESCRIPTION
&D	YYMMDD	Date substitution. The system replaces the date it received with the account string. **Note:** If &D is in position 26 or higher of the account definition, it will be truncated.
&H	HH (24 hour clock)	Hour substitution. The system replaces the hour of day with the account string. This is option is used for identifying users during peak periods who are consuming large amounts of resources. If you are using charge back accounting methods, use &H to identify and provide billing rates to usres for running queries during on/off-peak time periods. If the &H variable is used without the &D variable, the system will extrapolate and sum up the data collected for a specified hour on one day and apply these valuses to the same hour on other days. **Note:** If &H is in position 30 of the account definition, it will be truncated.
&I	LLLLSSSSSSSSSRRRRRRRRR	The system replaces the logon host ID, current session number, and sequential request number with the account string. **Note:** A stored procedure CALL command with more then one query will be reported under one request number.
&L	YYMMDDHHMMSS.hh	Logon date-time replacement. The system substitutes the logon timestamp with the account string. This value will not dynamically change in real time. It will only be modified when the user logs off and then logs on again.

VARIABLE	FORMAT	DESCRIPTION
		Note: If &L is in position 17 or higher of the account definition, it will be truncated.
&S	SSSSSSSSS	The system replaces the current session number with the account string.
&T	HHMMSS (24 hour clock)	Time substitution. The system replaces the time of day it received the SQL request with the account string. **Caution:** The &T option can be very resource intensive. If you see system performance impacted, delete rows from DBC.Acctg and refrain from using. **Note:** If &T is in position 26 or higher, it will be truncated.

Figure 4.10

The recommended ASE variable combination is &S&D&H. An account string is limited to 30 characters on systems where extended object naming is not enabled. Any characters exceeding position 30 will be truncated, as shown in the next diagram.

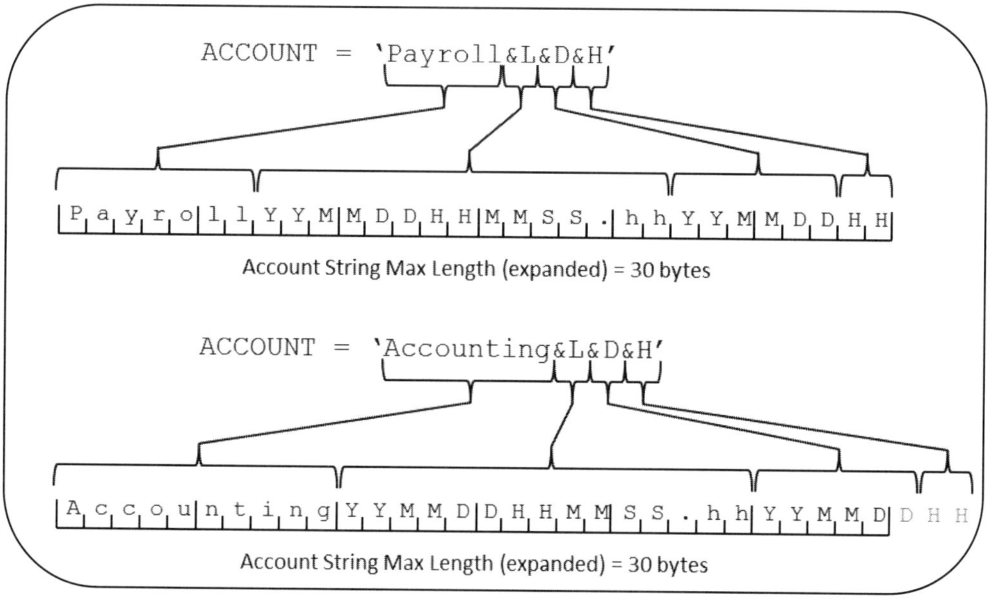

Figure 4.11

System Accounting Views

The Teradata Database provides the following views to support administration of accounts and accounting functions:

- DBC.AccountInfoV
- DBC.AMPUsageV

By auditing the information in these views, you can see which users heavily or rarely use the system. You can also make adjustments to the priority assigned to specific accounts.

You can also use the accounting features of Teradata Viewpoint to collect data and report on system usage.

DBC.ACCOUNTINFOV VIEW

The DBC.AccountInfoV view returns information about all valid accounts for all databases, users, and profiles.

Use DBC.AccountInfoV to find out:

- What accounts are valid for which user
- The assignment of:
  - Priority Scheduling codes
  - ASE codes

DBC.AccountInfoV[X]

UserName	AccountName	UserOrProfile

Figure 4.12

The following shows the account information for a single user.

```
SELECT * FROM dbc.accountinfoV
WHERE username = 'csql00'
ORDER BY 1;

Name      AccountName    UserOrProfile
------    -----------    -------------
csql00    DBC            User
```

Figure 4.13

DBC.AMPUSAGEV VIEW

The DBC.AMPUsageV view provides information about the usage of each AMP for each user and account. It also tracks the activities of any console utilities. By user, account, or console utility session, DBC.AMPUsageV stores information about:

- CPU time consumed
- Number of read/write (I/O) operations generated

AMPUsageV reports logical I/Os explicitly requested by the database software, even if the requested segment is in cache and no physical I/O is performed.

Use the information provided by DBC.AMPUsageV to do the following:

- Bill an account for system resource use.
- Determine what resources were used, by user and account string, after hours as well as during the day.
- Summarize and archive the information, then zero it out on a per-shift, per-day, or per-week basis.
- Determine if one or more tables has skewed row distribution across AMPs.
- Determine which session caused reduced performance.
- Derive capacity needs to plan for expansion.

DBC.AMPUsageV[X]

AccountName UserName CPUTime	DiskIO CPUTimeNorm Vproc	VprocType Model

Figure 4.14

The following is an example of summarizing information for a single user.

```
SELECT TRIM(accountname) AS AccountName
, TRIM(username) AS UserName
, SUM( CPUTIME) AS CpuTime
, SUM(DiskIO) AS DiskIO
, SUM(CpuTimeNorm) AS CpuTimeNorm
FROM DBC.AMPUsageV
WHERE UserName = 'csql00'
GROUP BY 1,2 ;


AccountName   UserName   CPUTIME     DiskIO      CpuTimeNorm
-----------   --------   -------   ---------     -----------
DBC           CSQL00       51.94   419181.00           90.90
```

Figure 4.15

Practice Questions

1. Which clause applies to CREATE USER but not CREATE DATABASE?
    a. PERMANENT =
    b. FROM =
    c. DEFAULT JOURNAL TABLE =
    d. ACCOUNT =
    e. PROFILE =

2. Which table is not affected by a CREATE USER statement?
    a. DBC.AccessRights
    b. DBC.Acctg
    c. DBC.Dbase
    d. DBC.DatabaseSpace
    e. DBC.Parents
    f. DBC.Owners

3. If a user is created with multiple accounts, what account will the system use as the default if the user fails to supply an account upon logging into the system?
    a. The default account in the DBSControl record
    b. The account of the immediate owner
    c. The last account in the list of accounts provided in the CREATE USER
    d. The first account in the list of accounts provided in the CREATE USER

4. Which ASE character supplies the longest string of values?
    a. &D
    b. &H
    c. &I
    d. &L
    e. &S
    f. &T

5. Which ASE variable combination is recommended?
    a. &D&S&L
    b. &L&I&T
    c. &S&D&H
    d. &T&S&H

Chapter Notes

Utilize this space for notes, key points to remember, diagrams, areas of further study, etc.

Chapter 5 - Access Rights

Certification Objectives

- ✓ Given a scenario, identify the effects of granting access rights.
- ✓ Given a scenario, identify the effects of revoking access rights.

Before You Begin

You should be familiar with the following terms and concepts.

Terms	Key Concepts
Access Rights	The right to access or manipulate another object within the Teradata Database
Implicit, Automatic, and Explicit Rights	How are access rights are acquired
GRANT and REVOKE	What Access Rights can be GRANTed or REVOKEd
GIVE command	Assigning a user/database to a different user/database

Privileges/Access Rights

Sometimes referred to as rights, access rights, or permissions, a privilege is the right to access or manipulate another object within the Teradata Database. Privileges control user activities such as creating, executing, viewing, deleting, or tracking objects. Privileges also include the ability to grant privileges to other users in the database.

There are two types of privileges -- Explicit and Implicit.

Privilege Type	Description
EXPLICIT PRIVILEGE	• A privilege that you explicitly grant with the GRANT statement. • A privilege that is automatically granted by the system as though a GRANT statement was issued. • An Inherited Privilege is an explicit privilege that is assigned by means of a role.
IMPLICIT PRIVILEGE	A privilege for a user who directly or indirectly owns an object.

Figure 5.1

The creator of an object is the user who submitted the CREATE statement. Every object has only one creator.

An owner of an object is any database or user above the object in the database hierarchy. The immediate owner of a new object is the database space in which the new object resides.

The default database is the database of the creating user, but can be a different database if you precede the object name with the database name and a period separator, such as databasename.objectname, in the CREATE statement.

The Teradata Database only recognizes rights as they appear in the DBC.AccessRights table. CREATEs insert rights into this table giving the "creator" automatic rights to this object. While explicitly granted rights insert the necessary rows to support the granted rights. You then remove those rows (subsequently the rights) by either dropping the object (removing creator rights), or revoking privileges (removing granted rights).

Note: In some cases, creator rights may be revoked by owners.

The following diagram and chart explain creators and owners.

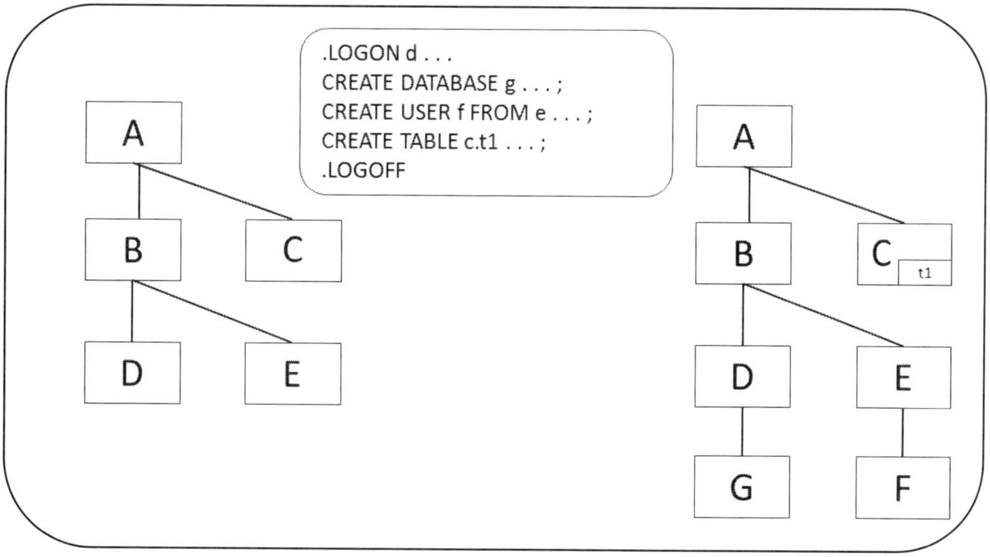

Figure 5.2

OBJECT	CREATOR	IMMEDIATE OWNER	ALL OWNERS
F	D	E	E B A
G	D	D	D B A
t1	D	C	C A

Figure 5.3

Access Rights Mechanisms

Privileges automatically granted to the creator of a database/user	Privileges automatically granted to the created database/user
CHECKPOINT CREATE AUTHORIZATION CREATE DATABASE	CHECKPOINT CREATE AUTHORIZATION - - -

Privileges automatically granted to the creator of a database/user	Privileges automatically granted to the created database/user
CREATE MACRO	CREATE MACRO
CREATE TABLE	CREATE TABLE
CREATE TRIGGER	CREATE TRIGGER
CREATE USER	- - -
CREATE VIEW	CREATE VIEW
DELETE	DELETE
DROP AUTHORIZATION	DROP AUTHORIZATION
DROP DATABASE	- - -
DROP FUNCTION	DROP FUNCTION
DROP MACRO	DROP MACRO
DROP PROCEDURE	DROP PROCEDURE
DROP TABLE	DROP TABLE
DROP TRIGGER	DROP TRIGGER
DROP USER	- - -
DROP VIEW	DROP VIEW
DUMP	DUMP
EXECUTE	EXECUTE
INSERT	INSERT
SELECT	SELECT
RESTORE	RESTORE
STATISTICS	STATISTICS
UPDATE	UPDATE

Figure 5.4

The following privileges are not automatically granted, and must be explicitly granted.

For Creators	For Created User/Database
ALTER EXTERNAL PROCEDURE	ALTER EXTERNAL PROCEDURE
ALTER FUNCTION	ALTER FUNCTION
ALTER PROCEDURE	ALTER PROCEDURE
- - -	CREATE DATABASE

For Creators	For Created User/Database
CREATE EXTERNAL PROCEDURE	CREATE EXTERNAL PROCEDURE
CREATE FUNCTION	CREATE FUNCTION
CREATE PROCEDURE	CREATE PROCEDURE
- - -	CREATE USER
- - -	DROP DATABASE
- - -	DROP USER
EXECUTE FUNCTION	EXECUTE FUNCTION
EXECUTE PROCEDURE	EXECUTE PROCEDURE
SHOW	SHOW

Figure 5.5

The following table lists additional privileges that must be granted explicitly.

ABORTSESSION	CONNECT THROUGH	CONSTRAINT ASSIGNMENT
CONSTRAINT DEFINITION	CREATE GLOP	CREATE PROFILE
CREATE ROLE	CTCONTROL	DROP PROFILE
DROP ROLE	INDEX	MONRESOURCE
MONSESSION	NONTEMPORAL	OVERRIDE DELETE
OVERRIDE DUMP	OVERRIDE INSERT	OVERRIDE RESTORE
OVERRIDE SELECT	OVERRIDE UPDATE	REFERENCES
REPLCONTROL	SETRESRATE	SETSESSRATE
UDTMETHOD	UDTTYPE	UDTUSAGE

Figure 5.6

When a user creates a table in their own space, they are the immediate owner and creator of the table and are automatically granted the following table-level privileges.

CREATE TRIGGER	DROP TABLE	REFERENCE
DELETE	INSERT	RESTORE

DROP TRIGGER	INDEX	UPDATE
DUMP	RETRIEVE/SELECT	STATISTICS

Figure 5.7

Implicit, Automatic, and Explicit Rights

EXPLICIT PRIVILEGES	IMPLICIT PRIVILEGES
The object creator who issues a CREATE statement receives automatically granted explicit privileges.	An owner from which that user or database was created receives implicit privileges. An owner on any object it owns can grant explicit privileges to other users, databases, roles, and PUBLIC along with the WITH GRANT OPTION.
When an object is created, then system automatically assigns explicit privileges which are given through the GRANT statement or received to a user, database, role, or PUBLIC by another user automatically with the appropriate privileges.	Given by ownership. No additional GRANT statements required.
CREATE USER or CREATE DATABASE statements will automatically give explicit privileges for both the owner and the object the owner created. These rights will be into the DBC.AccessRights table.	CREATE USER or CREATE DATABASE statements will provide the owner of the object created with automatic privileges.
The GRANT command will add new rows into the DBC.AccessRights or	Owners of objects do not insert rows in the AccessRights table. Only rights GRANTED will insert

EXPLICIT PRIVILEGES	IMPLICIT PRIVILEGES
DBC.RoleGrants table. The DROP/DELETE, REVOKE, DROP, command will remove the rows.	rows into the DBC.Accessrights table if they currently do not exist. Any user (i.e. owner or a user with explicitly granted rights) can revoke privileges. However, the owner can GRANT any privilege back if revoked by a user with explicit rights.
Databases or users are unable to create other databases, users, stored procedures, user-defined functions, roles, or profiles by default	Implicit privileges cannot be refused or revoked. They cannot be taken away unless ownership is transferred or the owned entity is deleted or dropped.

Figure 5.8

GRANT Command

The GRANT command assigns one or more explicit privileges on a database, user, table, hash index, join index, view, stored procedure, user-defined function, user-defined method, user-defined type, or macro to a role, group of roles, user, or group of users or databases.

The GRANT takes the following general form.

GRANT *privilege_list*
ON *object_name*
TO *user_name*
[WITH GRANT OPTION]

The previous tables listed the privileges. The four following privileges have syntax that allows you to specify one or more, comma-separated columns in a column list. See Figure 5.12 for an example.

INSERT [(*column_list*)] REFERENCES [(*column_list*)]	SELECT [(*column_list*)] UPDATE [(*column_list*)]

Figure 5.9

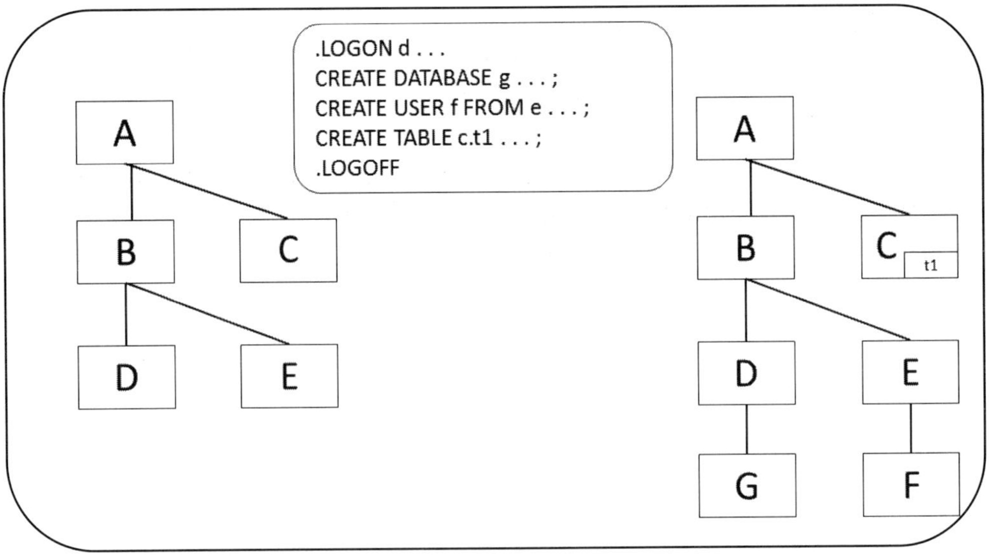

Figure 5.10

Referring back to the above diagram, if user *f* should have the right to create users, then the creator (*d*) or one of the owners (*e, b, a*) can execute the following statement.

```
GRANT CREATE USER, DROP USER ON f TO f;
```

Figure 5.11

If user *f* should be also able to read the data in c.t1, do inserts, and update certain columns (i.e. c3, c4, and c5) of that table, either the creator (*d*) or one of the owners (*c, a*) can execute the following command.

```
GRANT SELECT, INSERT, UPDATE (c3, c4, c5) ON c.t1 TO f;
```

Figure 5.12

REVOKE Command

REVOKE rescinds **explicit** privileges from one or more users, databases, or roles. The privileges might have been conferred either automatically or by a previous GRANT statement. **Implicit** privileges are governed by ownership and cannot be revoked. You can affect implicit privileges by using the GIVE statement to change ownership.

The REVOKE statements operate on explicit privileges recorded in the *DBC.AccessRights* table. This means that you cannot revoke implicit privileges because those privileges are not stored in *DBC.AccessRights.* Only those explicit privileges that have been granted automatically or explicitly can be revoked.

In most cases, implicit privileges only permit the user holding them to grant them to others, not to perform the SQL statements that correspond to those privileges. Generally, you must have explicit privileges to perform access protected SQL statements. The main exceptions to this rule are privileges on views, macros, and stored procedures.

The REVOKE statement takes the following general form.

REVOKE [GRANT OPTION FOR]
{ALL | *privilege_list* | ALL BUT *privilege_list*}
ON *object_name*
FROM *user_name*

In Figure 5.12, if user *f* should only be allowed to read rows in c.t1, then the following statement can be used.

```
REVOKE INSERT, UPDATE (c3, c4, c5) ON c.t1 FROM f;
```

Figure 5.13

Inheriting Access Rights

Two extensions to the GRANT are [ALL] *user_name* and PUBLIC. If you specify ALL *user_name*, then the object privileges are granted to the named database or user and to every database or user owned by that database or user now and in the future. If you specify PUBLIC, the privileges are inherited by all existing and future Teradata Database users and databases.

GRANT *privilege_list*
ON *object_name*
TO {ALL *user_name* | PUBLIC}
[WITH GRANT OPTION]

In the following diagram, *pa_001, pa_002, pa_003* inherit all of the rights on *pa_tvm* that *pa_user* has, and any new users added to *pa_user* will also receive the same rights. Also, *acc_001, acc_002, acc_003* will inherit all of the rights on *acc_tvm* that *acc_user* has, and any new users added *to acc_user* will also inherit the same rights.

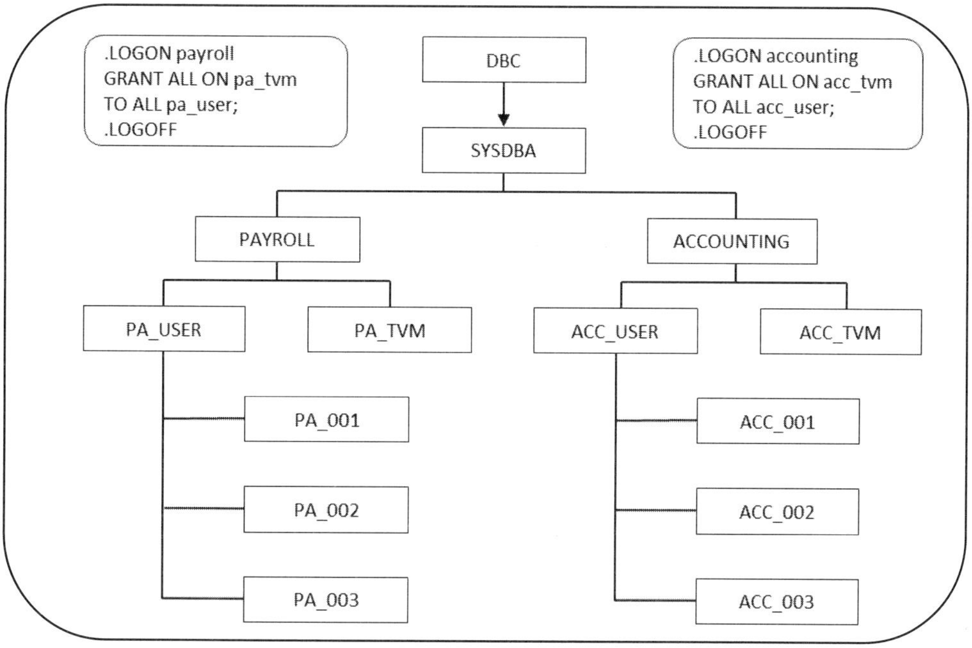

Figure 5.14

The GIVE Statement and Access Rights

In the previous diagram, suppose that user *pa_003* transfers to accounting. The user issuing a GIVE command would have to be an owner of both Payroll and Accounting (either SYSDBA, or DBC). The following diagram shows the result of the GIVE.

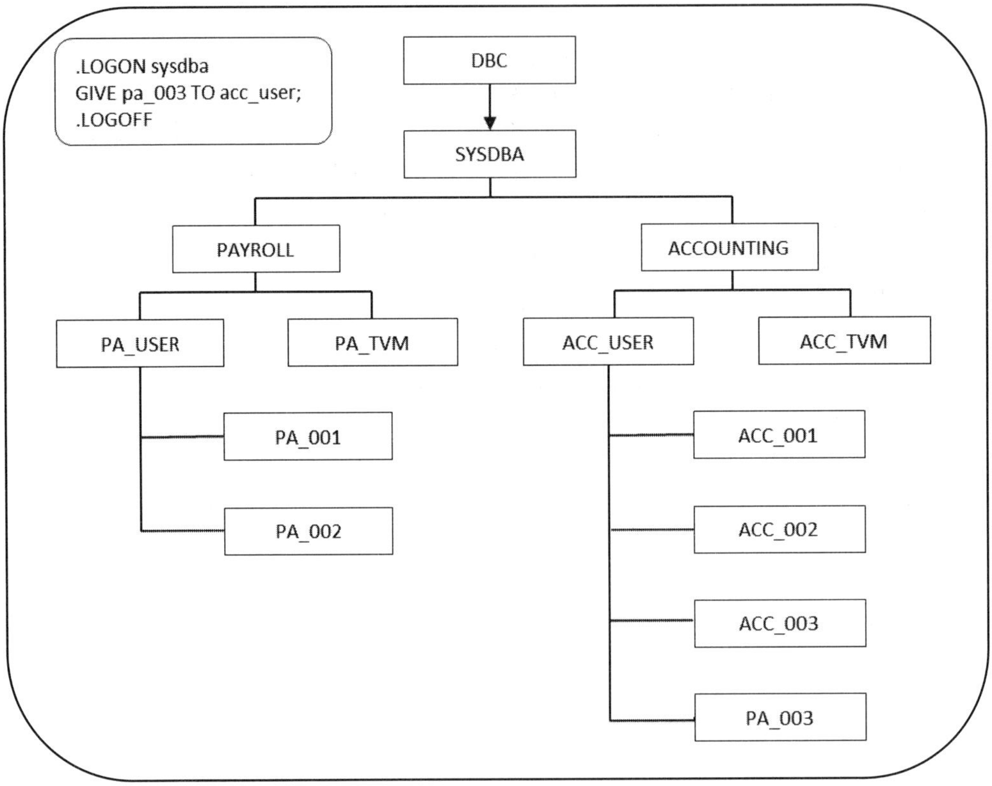

Figure 5.15

When you give a user to another immediate owner, explicit privileges are not altered. The GIVE statement **does not alter DBC.AccessRights**. The database or user that you GIVE does not receive any privileges from its new immediate owner, and does not lose any existing privileges.

The new owners gain only *implicit* privileges over the transferred object and the old owners lose them. The ALL option does not apply.

Therefore, *pa_003* still has all rights on *pa_tvm*, and does not inherit any privileges on *acc_tvm*.

The proper way to transfer *pa_003* to accounting is to do a DROP USER and a CREATE USER, as shown in the following diagram. Dropping *pa_003* removes all of that user's rights, and the newly created user inherits the granted rights on *acc_tvm*.

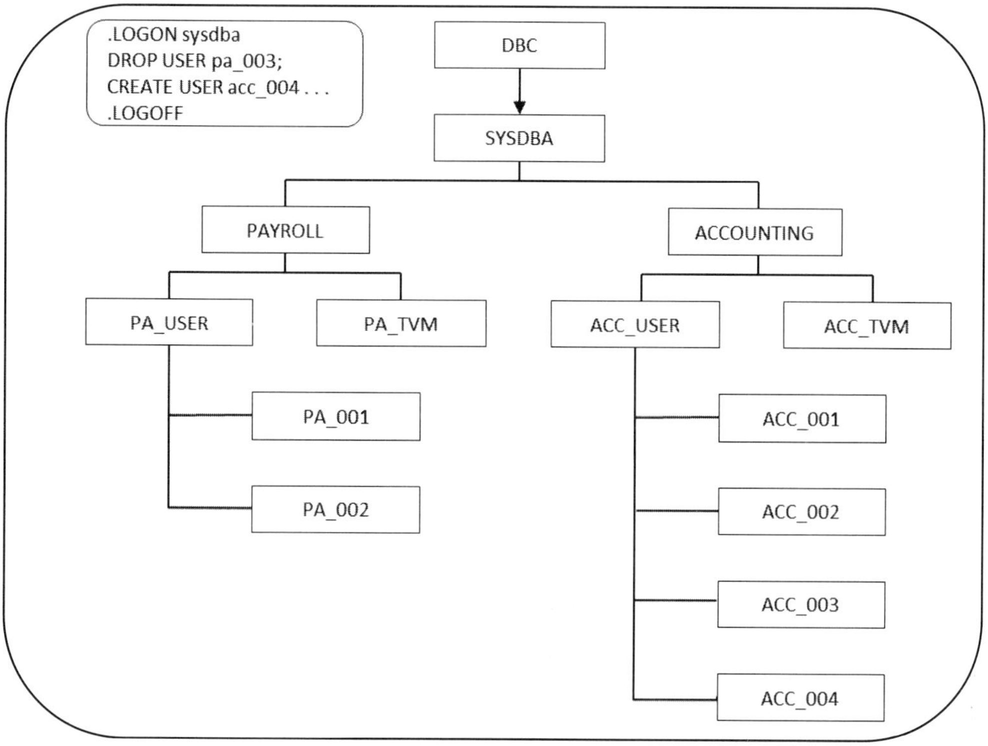

Figure 5.16

Access Rights and Views

In order to create a view, the creator must have the CREATE VIEW privilege. In addition, the creator must have the appropriate privileges (such as SELECT, INSERT, UPDATE, DELETE, . . .) on the objects being accessed by the view.

To allow someone else to retrieve data through a view, that user must be granted SELECT on the view.

To allow someone else to update (INSERT, UPDATE, DELETE) through a view, grant that user UPDATE on the view. Be certain to include the WITH CHECK OPTION if the view contains a WHERE clause that should be enforced.

System Views for Access Rights

The AllRightsV view provides information about all users who have been explicitly or automatically granted privileges, and the objects on which the privileges were granted including: databases, users, tables, views, stored procedures, macros, user-defined types, user-defined methods, and user-defined functions.

The AllRightsV view also returns PUBLIC rights.

DBC.AllRightsV[X]

UserName	AccessRight	AllnessFlag
Databasename	GrantAuthority	CreatorName
TableName	GrantorName	CreateTimeStamp
ColumnName		

Figure 5.17

The UserRightsV view provides information about objects on which the user has explicitly or automatically been granted privileges including the following: tables, views, join indexes, columns, stored procedures, macros, user-defined types, user-defined methods, or user-defined functions.

DBC.UserRightsV

DatabaseName	AccessRight	CreatorName
TableName	GrantAuthority	CreateTimeStamp
ColumnName	GrantorName	

Figure 5.18

The UserGrantedRights view provides information about objects on which the current user has explicitly granted privileges to other users.

DBC.UserGrantedRightsV

DatabaseName	Grantee	AllnessFlag
TableName	AccessRight	CreatorName
ColumnName	GrantAuthority	CreateTimeStamp

Figure 5.19

Practice Questions

1. When a user creates a table, which of the following privileges is not granted automatically?
    a. DROP TRIGGER
    b. STATISTICS
    c. REFERENCE
    d. DUMP
    e. CREATE PROCEDURE

2. Given the following BTEQ script, fill in the table below.

```
.logon dbc, . . .
create user b . . . ;
.logoff
.logon b, . . .
create database c from dbc . . . ;
create user d  from c . . . ;
.logoff
.logon d, . . .
create database e from b . . . ;
create database f from e . . . ;
.logoff
```

OBJECT	CREATOR	IMMEDIATE OWNER	ALL OWNERS
DBC			
B			
C			
D			
E			
F			

3. Which of the following is not a valid privilege?
    a. SETSESSIONRATE
    b. SETRESRATE
    c. MONSESSION
    d. CTCONTROL
    e. MONRESOURCE

4. Which privilege does not provide the ability to specify one or more columns in a comma separated list?
    a. INSERT
    b. UPDATE
    c. DELETE
    d. SELECT
    e. REFERENCES

5. Which view returns PUBLIC access rights?
    a. DBC.UserGrantedRightsV
    b. DBC.AllRightsV
    c. DBC.UserRightsV
    d. DBC.AllUserRightsV

Chapter Notes

Utilize this space for notes, key points to remember, diagrams, areas of further study, etc.

Chapter 6 - Security Management

Certification Objectives

- ✓ Explain the options for limiting access rights table growth.
- ✓ Given a scenario, determine how profiles should be used.
- ✓ Given a scenario, identify the correct use of views to limit row or column accessibility.
- ✓ Given a scenario, identify the process to locate a security violation, security breach, or password violation.
- ✓ Given a scenario, determine how roles should be used in relation to security management.
- ✓ Identify the methods of user authentication.
- ✓ Identify a situation where row level security is appropriate.
- ✓ Identify the new constraints for row level security (readclassification UDF).

Before You Begin

You should be familiar with the following terms and concepts.

Terms	Key Concepts
DBC.AccessRights	Why this is one of the largest system tables
Roles	How this simplifies access right management
Profiles	How this simplifies User management
Passwords	How to assign, modify, and control them
Limiting Access	Using views and row level security

What are Roles and Profiles?

Roles simplify the management of privileges for users. Roles help improve performance by reducing the number of rows added and deleted from DBC.AccessRights. Once a role is created, you can assign privileges to a specific role, and then grant the role to users. The users can then access all the objects on which their assigned role and nested roles have privileges.

Profiles simplify the management of user settings such as accounts, default database, spool space, temporary space, and password attributes for a group of users.

Advantages of Roles

Roles work best when based on job functions or responsibilities. Some users may belong to more than one role. By creating roles and granting them the necessary privileges, the DBA only has to grant or revoke roles to/from users as personnel and needs change. As the business changes, the DBA can grant or revoke privileges to the roles, and those changes will immediately affect all users of the modified role.

Roles do not consume space in their database. Their data rows are rows in DBC.AccessRights.

Access Rights without Roles

Suppose you have a database with 300 tables, and 50 users who need data from 23 to 100 of the tables, and at different times of the day or week or month. To manage a situation like this, you could create different databases that have been granted access to the various table sets with the allness flag, and then create users under the appropriate database where they would automatically inherit the necessary privileges. Since a user can only inherit privileges from one immediate parent, you would have to create different user definitions for those users with changing needs.

The following figure illustrates this issue.

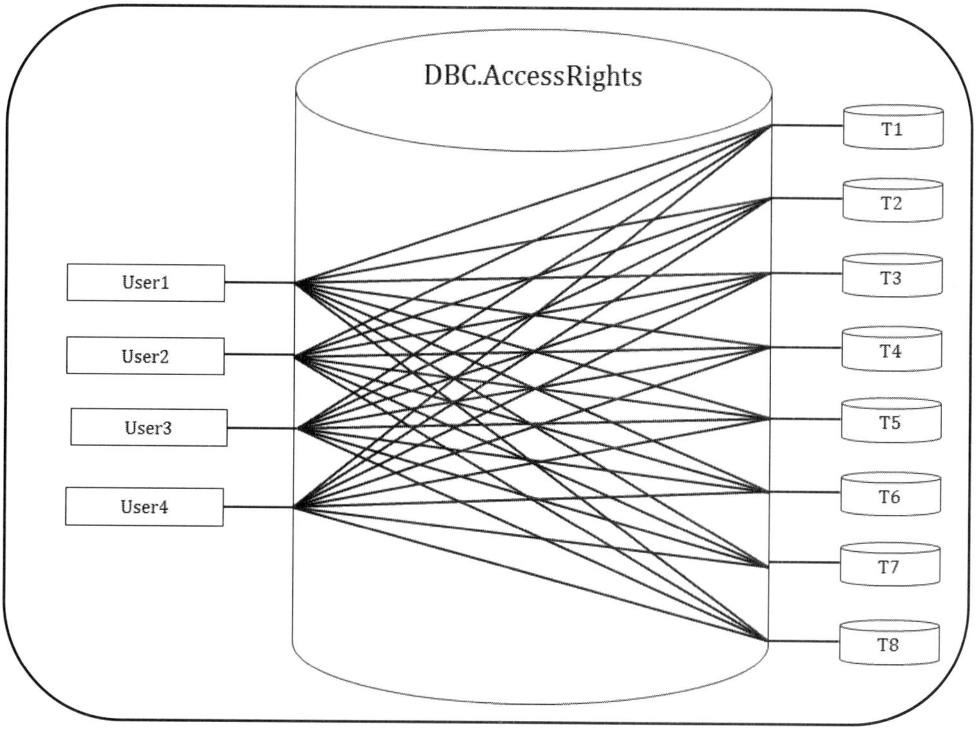

Figure 6.1

Access Rights using a Role

The problem stated above is easily solved by creating multiple Roles, and assigning them the privileges needed. Then, simply grant the necessary role(s) to the users.

The next figure shows how the use of roles reduces the number of entries in DBC.AccessRights.

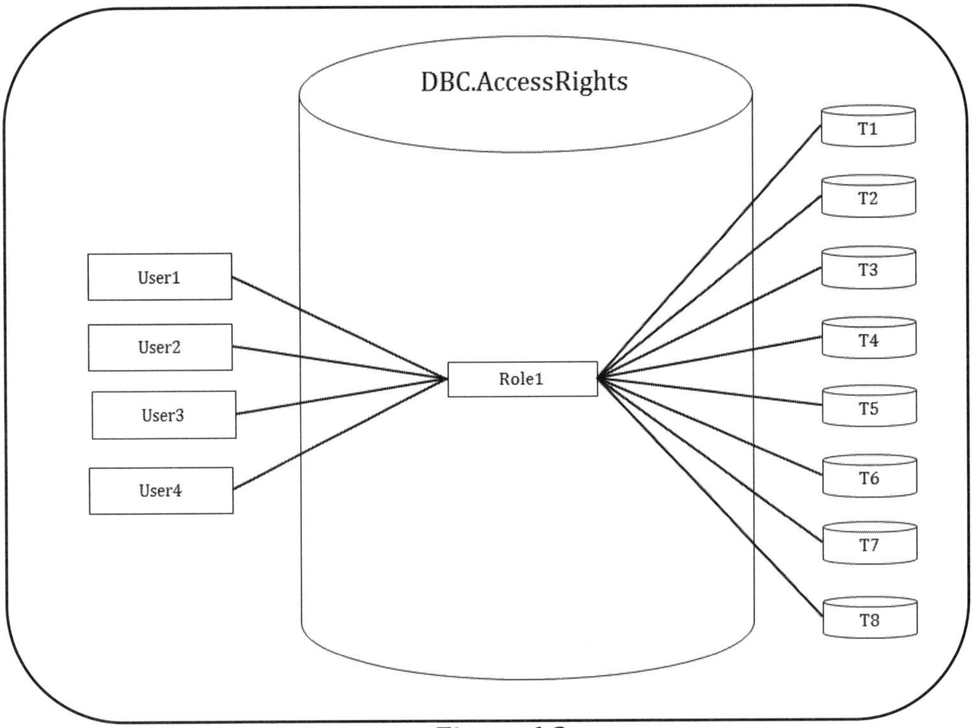

Figure 6.2

Note: Roles may be nested up to one level.

Users can switch between roles by issuing a SET ROLE command.

IF the user issues	THEN
SET ROLE NONE; SET ROLE NULL;	No privilege is needed to disable the current role for a session. Explicit privileges (either granted or inherited) remain in effect.
SET ROLE rolename;	The role must already be granted to the user.

SET ROLE ALL;	No privilege is needed and the user is not required to have any roles granted to them.
SET ROLE EXTERNAL;	The role must already be assigned to the user in the directory.

Figure 6.3

Implementing Roles

To start, roles are created with a CREATE ROLE command. You must have the CREATE ROLE privilege to execute it.

Then, through a series of GRANT statements, you assign specific database privileges to the roles.

Once a role has been created, it can be assigned as a default role through the MODIFY USER statement, or assigned using the GRANT command.

When a user logs on, the default role (if any) is current. The default role is assigned through the DEFAULT ROLE phrase of the CREATE USER or MODIFY USER command. This phrase has the following possible values.

DEFAULT ROLE = *role_name*
NONE
NULL
ALL

An active role is any role assigned to a user, either as the DEFAULT ROLE, or through a GRANT ROLE. The current role(s) for the session is the one activated by a SET ROLE statement.

Note: Nesting of roles is limited to one level.

Since the CREATE/MODIFY USER, the DROP *role_name*, the SET ROLE, and GRANT/REVOKE statements are DDL statements, their execution has an immediate effect on DBC.AccessRights.

The following is the syntax diagram for the SQL statements which support creating and using roles.

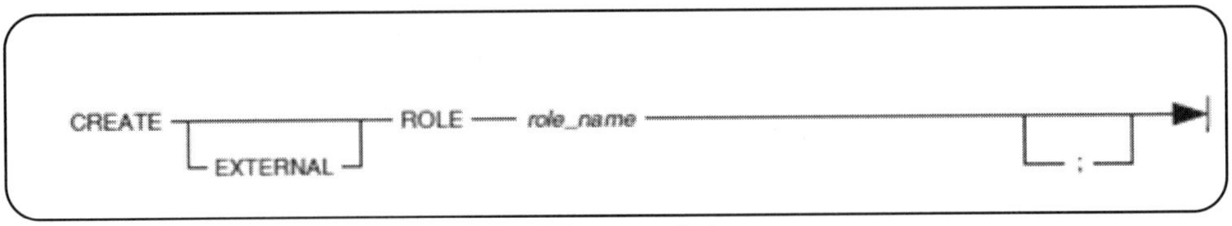

Figure 6.4

The next diagram provides support for granting roles to objects.

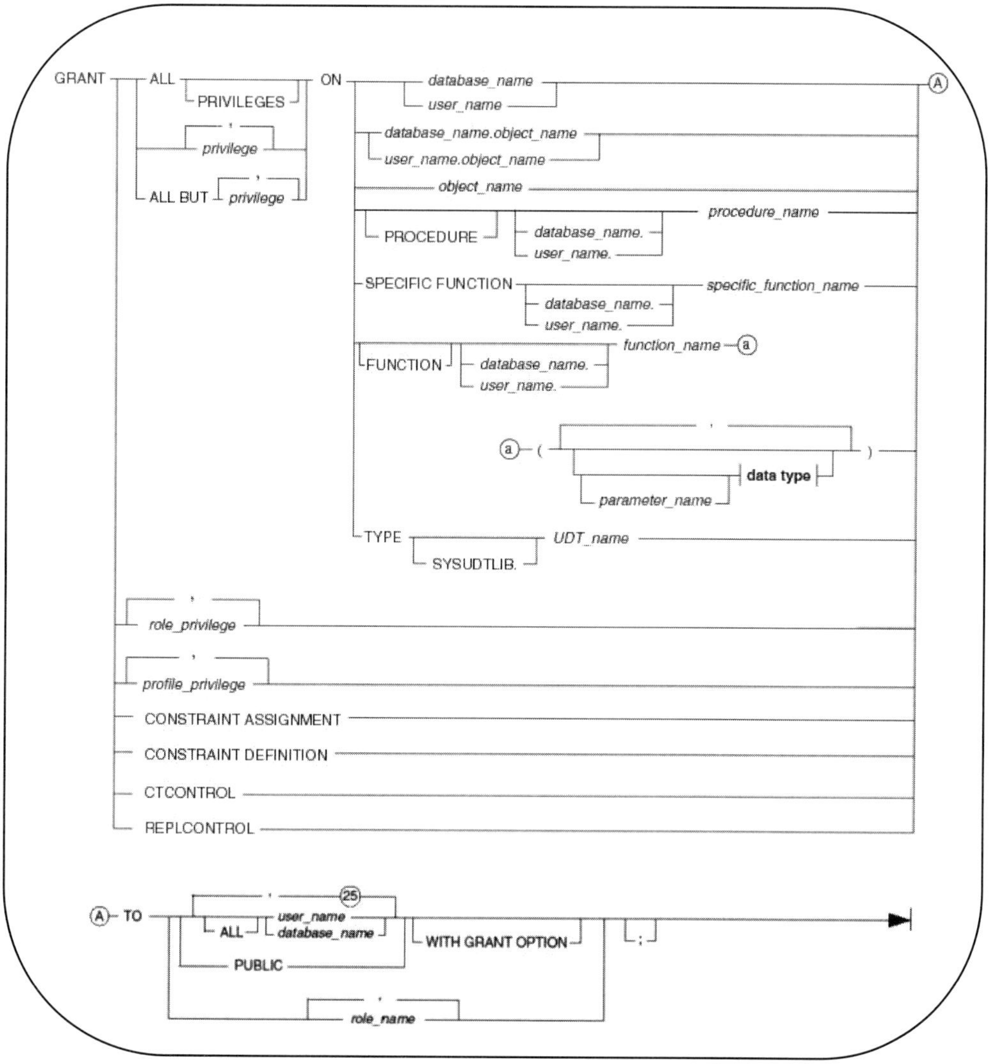

Figure 6.5

This diagram (excerpt) demonstrates how you CREATE users with roles.

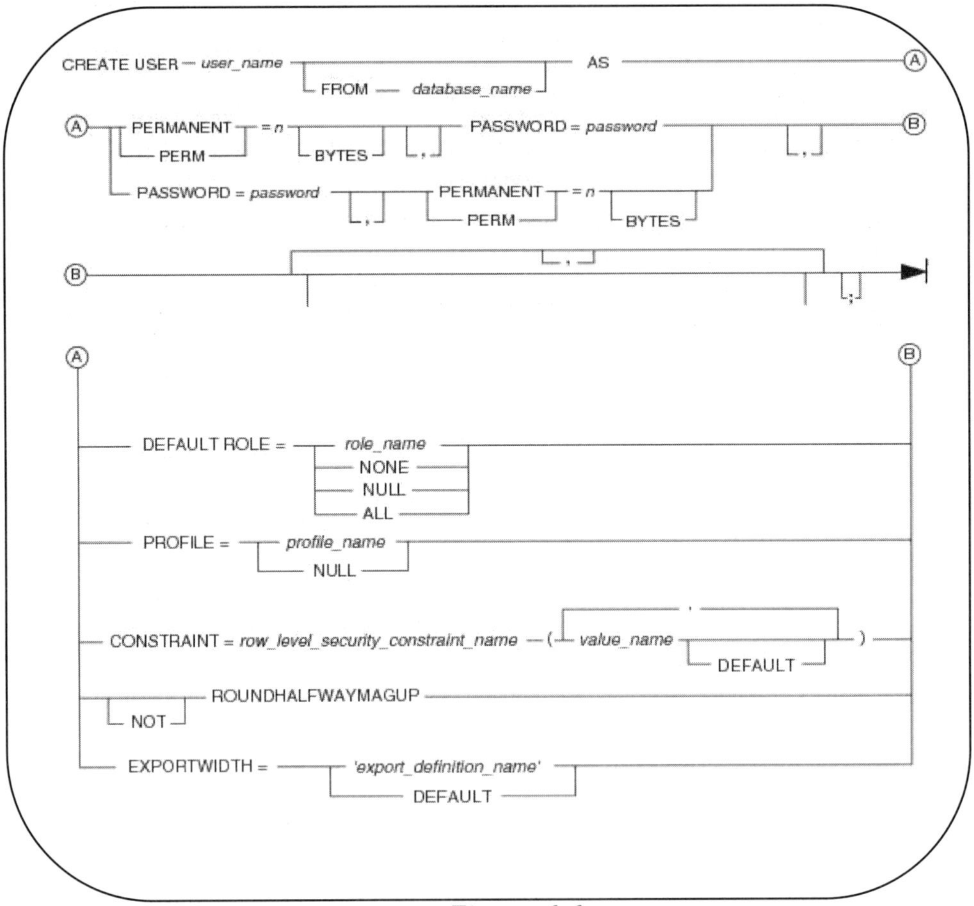

Figure 6.6

The last diagram illustrates how you GRANT roles to users.

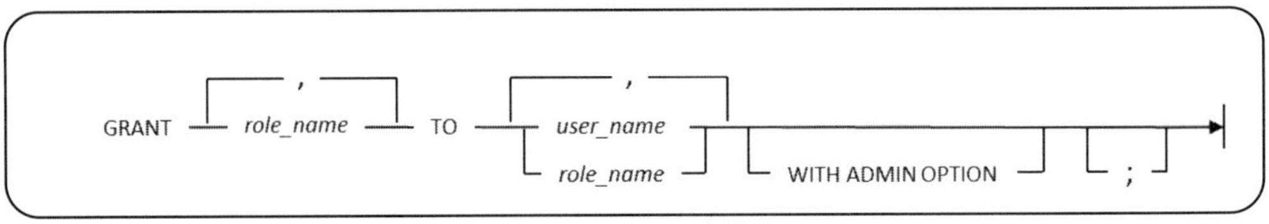

Figure 6.7

Dropping a Role

The privileges assigned to a role can be adjusted at any time through GRANT and REVOKE. The default role for a user can be changed through MODIFY USER. The roles available to a user can be changed using the GRANT *role_name* and REVOKE *role_name* commands. When a role is no longer needed, use the DROP ROLE statement.

The following syntax diagrams show SQL statements that can be used to modify, set, revoke, and drop roles.

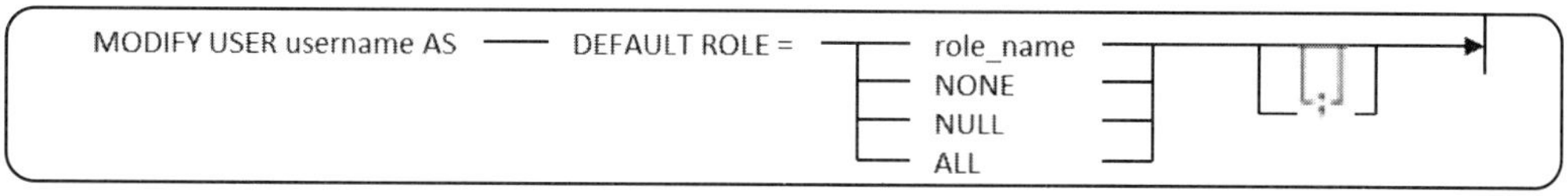

Figure 6.8

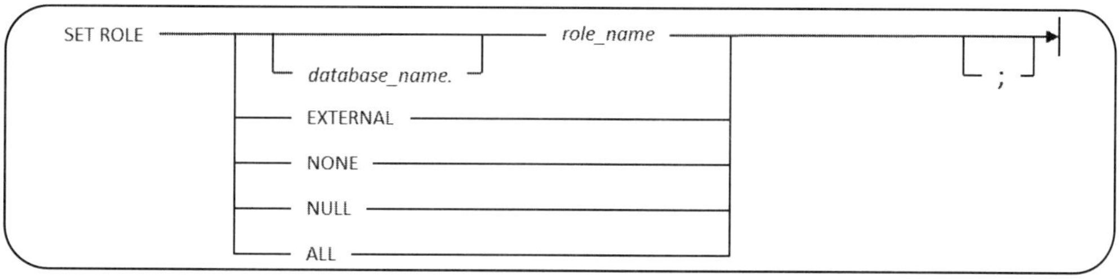

Figure 6.9

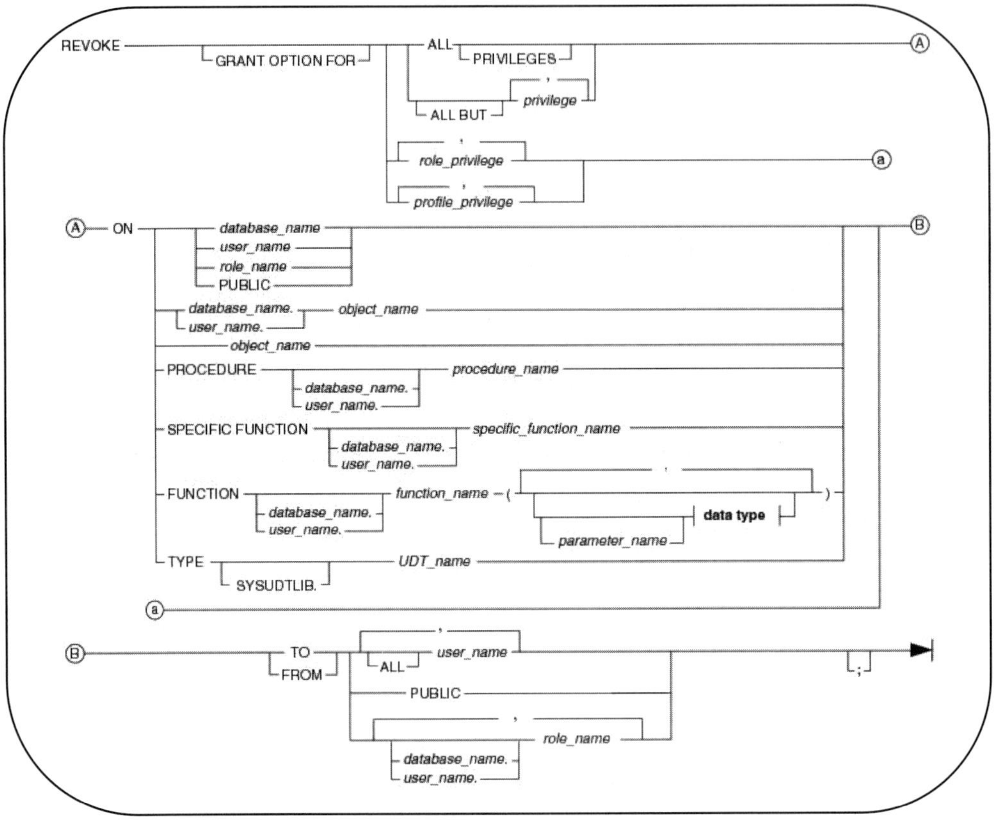

Figure 6.10

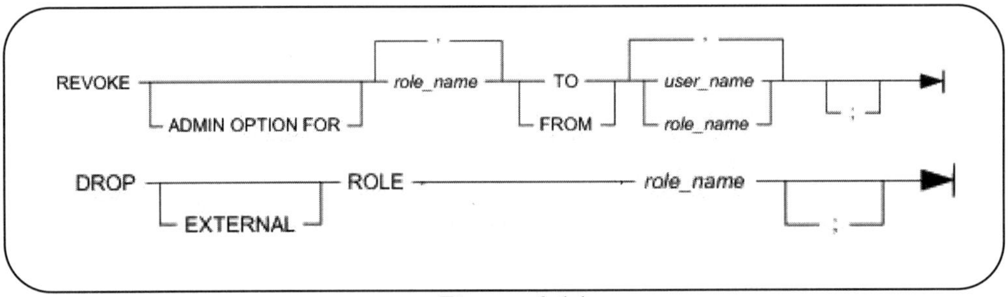

Figure 6.11

Role Views

The RoleInfoV view returns the names of role creators corresponding to each role.

DBC.RoleInfoV[X]

RoleName	CommentString	ExtRole
CreatorName	CreateTimeStamp	

Figure 6.12

The RoleMembersV view lists each role and all of its members.

DBC.RoleMembersV[X]

RoleName	Grantor	DefaultRole
Grantee	WhenGranted	WithAdmin
GranteeKind		

Figure 6.13

The RoleMemberVX view does not have the Grantee and GranteeKind.

The AllRoleRightsV view lists all rights granted to each role.

DBC.AllRoleRightsV

RoleName	ColumnName	GrantorName
DatabaseName	AccessRight	CreateTimeStamp
TableName		

Figure 6.14

The UserRoleRightsV view lists all rights granted to each role for the user.

DBC.UserRoleRightsV

RoleName	ColumnName	GrantorName
DatabaseName	AccessRight	CreateTimeStamp
TableName		

Figure 6.15

Steps to Implementing Roles

Here are the various things you need to do to implement and use roles.

1. Get the CREATE ROLE privilege.
2. Use the CREATE ROLE statement to create role names.
3. Grant necessary database privileges to the roles.
4. Establish default roles for users where necessary.
5. Grant additional roles to users as needed and instruct them on the use of the SET ROLE command.
6. Use MODIFY USER to change default profiles.
7. Use REVOKE to change database privileges given to roles.
8. Use REVOKE to remove a user from a role.
9. When a role is no longer needed, use DROP ROLE.

Advantages of Profiles

Profiles simplify the management of user settings such as accounts, default database, spool space, temporary space, and password attributes for a group of users. Assign specific settings to a profile, and then assign a profile to a user in the CREATE USER or MODIFY USER statement. This way, instead of managing settings for users on an individual basis, you can modify the settings for a profile to immediately apply the changes to all users that use the profile. You can also assign a user to a different profile any time using the MODIFY USER statement.

Implementing Profiles

All users (except DBC) must be explicitly granted the CREATE PROFILE privileges in order to create, drop, grant, and implement a profile.

When you create a profile, you automatically receive creator privileges (implicit privileges granted through ownership do not apply). This gives you the DROP PROFILE privilege on the profile.

Creator privileges do not enable you to assign a default profile to a user. These parameters are specified in the PROFILE clause of CREATE/MODIFY USER, for which you need the CREATE USER or DROP USER privilege, respectively.

To create a profile assigned to a user, follow this procedure:

1. Log on as user DBC or as the administrative user.
2. Grant the CREATE PROFILE privilege using WITH GRANT OPTION to your database administration user.
3. Log off as user DBC. Then log on again as your database administration user (DBADMIN).
4. Create a profile that defines the following:

- A profile name
- One or more of the following:
- PASSWORD attributes
- SPOOL space
- TEMPORARY space
- ACCOUNT (one or more IDs, with or without Priority Group and ASE codes)
- DEFAULT DATABASE

5. To assign the profile to a user, use the AS PROFILE modifier in the CREATE USER or MODIFY USER statement.

With profiles, you can manage the following attributes:

- Password settings, including:
    - Days before expiration
    - Number of minimum and maximum characters
    - Number of allowable logon attempts
    - Duration of user lockout (indefinite or elapsed time)
    - Number of times allowed for password reuse
    - Requiring mixed case, use of alpha, numeric, and/or special characters
    - Allowing or disallowing username, or any word listed in DBC.PasswordRestrictions, within the password string
- Account strings, including ASE codes and Performance Groups
- Default database assignments
- Spool and temporary space limits

In a profile, the SPOOL and TEMPORARY limits may not exceed the current space limits of the user submitting the CREATE/MODIFY PROFILE statement.

All members inherit changed profile parameters. The impact is immediate, or in response to a SET SESSION statement, or upon next logon, depending on the parameter:

- SPOOL and TEMPORARY space allocations are imposed immediately. This affects the current session of any member who is logged on at the time the profile is modified.
- Password attributes take effect upon next logon.
- Account IDs and a default database are considered at next logon unless the member submits a SET SESSION DATABASE or SET SESSION ACCOUNT statement. If that happens, the specified databasename or account ID must agree with the profile definition.

Profile definitions apply to every assigned user, overriding specifications at the system or user level. However, any profile definition can be NULL or NONE.

If you do not specify any profile definitions, the default value for the user session is determined as listed in the following table.

<table>
<tr><th>IF the following is null</th><th>THEN the default value is taken from</th></tr>
<tr><td>a password attribute</td><td>The system-wide specification for the corresponding attribute in the DBC.SysSecDefaults table.</td></tr>
<tr><td>all other attributes</td><td>The definitions in the CREATE USER or last MODIFY USER statement.

If none are specified, a value is determined as follows:

<table><tr><th>Parameter</th><th>Default Value</th></tr><tr><td>AccountID</td><td>The default account ID of the user.</td></tr></table></td></tr>
</table>

<table>
<tr><th>IF the following is null</th><th colspan="2">THEN the default value is taken from</th></tr>
<tr><td></td><td></td><td>If an account is not specified, it will inherit the account of its owner.</td></tr>
<tr><td></td><td>Performance group</td><td>Level M.</td></tr>
<tr><td></td><td>DEFAULT DATABASE</td><td>The setting defined for the user.</td></tr>
<tr><td></td><td>SPOOL</td><td>The SPOOL value will be inherited by immediate owner that is creating the user.</td></tr>
<tr><td></td><td>TEMPORARY</td><td>The setting defined for the user.</td></tr>
</table>

Figure 6.16

CREATE/MODIFY/DROP PROFILE Statements

The following is a syntax diagram for the CREATE PROFILE statement. Notice the similarities to the CREATE USER statement.

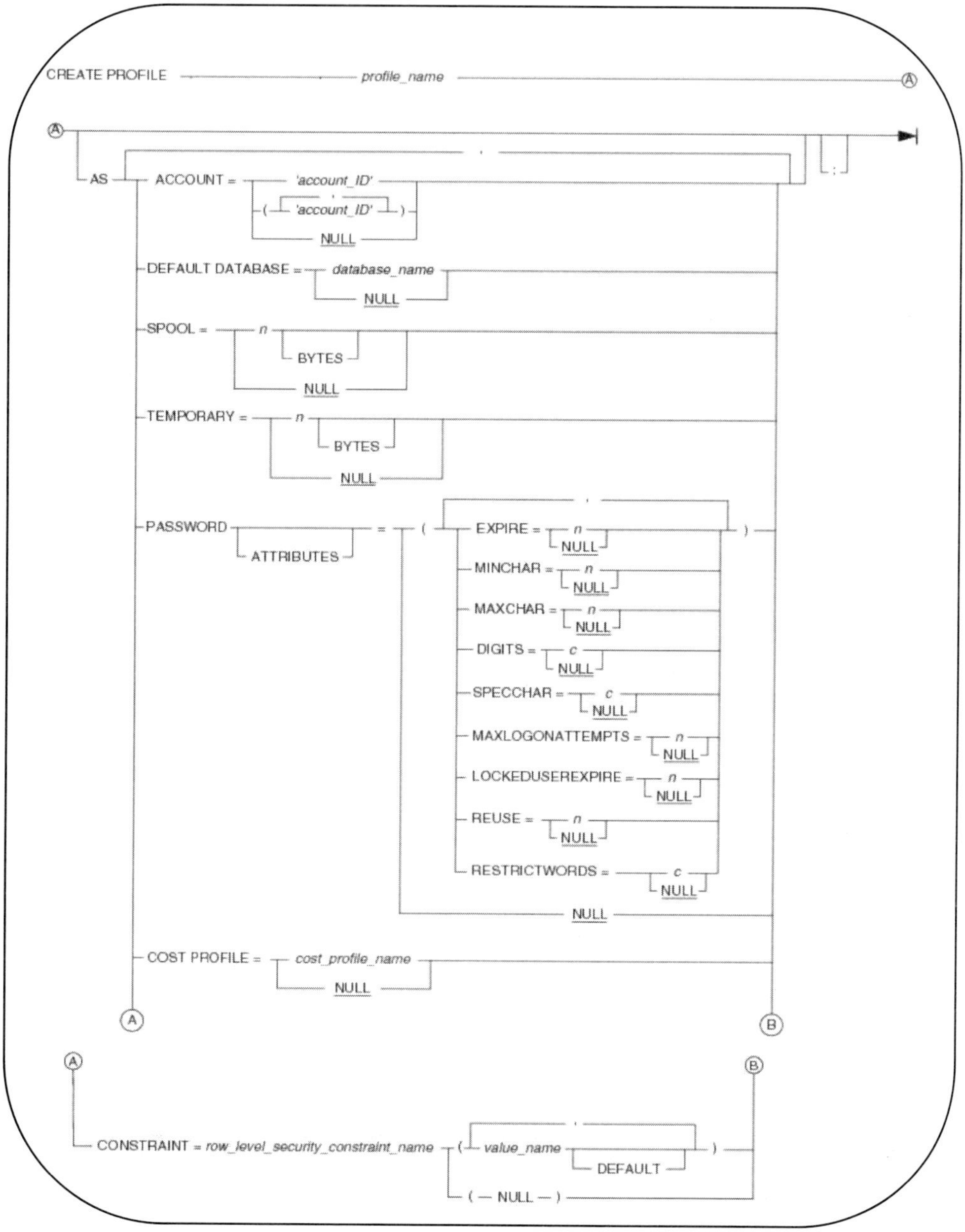
CREATE PROFILE
profile_name
AS
ACCOUNT =
'account_ID'
'account_ID'
NULL
DEFAULT DATABASE =
database_name
NULL
SPOOL =
n
BYTES
NULL
TEMPORARY =
n
BYTES
NULL
PASSWORD
ATTRIBUTES
EXPIRE =
n
NULL
MINCHAR =
MAXCHAR =
DIGITS =
c
SPECCHAR =
MAXLOGONATTEMPTS =
LOCKEDUSEREXPIRE =
REUSE =
RESTRICTWORDS =
NULL
COST PROFILE =
cost_profile_name
NULL
CONSTRAINT = row_level_security_constraint_name
value_name
DEFAULT
(— NULL —)

Figure 6.17

The following is a syntax diagram for the MODIFY PROFILE statement.

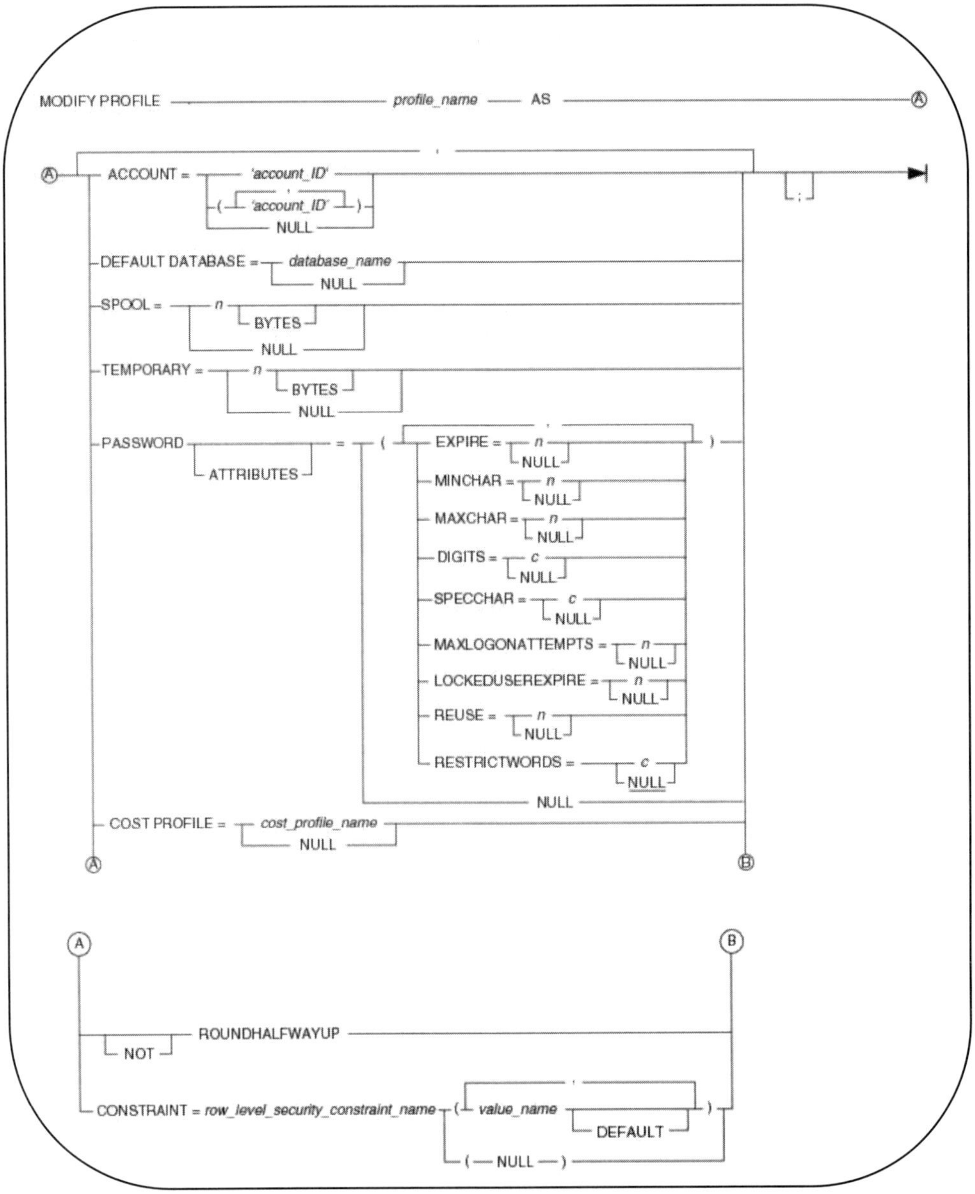

Figure 6.18

Password Attributes (CREATE/MODIFY PROFILE)

The following chart lists the password attributes and their meaning.

EXPIRE = *n*	The number of days to elapse before the password expires. A value of 0 for *n* indicates the password never expires.
MINCHAR = *n*	The minimum number of characters for a password string. The valid range for *n* is 1 to 30.
MAXCHAR = *n*	The maximum number of characters for a password string. The valid range for *n* is 1 to 30.
DIGITS = *c*	Parameter that specifies at least one digit must appear in a password string.
SPECCHAR = *c*	Parameter for user names to define if mixed case characters, or special characters are allowed, not required, or not allowed in a password string.
MAXLOGONATTEMPTS = *n*	The number of incorrect logon attempts allowed before locking the user from further attempts. A value of 0 for *n* indicates never to lock the user.
LOCKEDUSEREXPIRE = *n*	The number of minutes required before unlocking a user that has been locked.
REUSE = *n*	The number of days required before you reuse a password.

	A value of 0 for *n* allows the password to be reused immediately.
RESTRICTEDWORDS = *c*	Whether certain words are restricted from use within a password string.

Figure 6.19

Teradata Password Control

You control global security defaults for the password attributes by setting the fields of the DBC.SysSecDefaults table. Typically, you use the DBC.SecurityDefaults view to accomplish this. However, you must have the appropriate privileges to update the DBC.SecurityDefaults and the DBC.SysSecDefaults table directly.

Changes to DBC.SysSecDefaults table settings do not take effect until after the system restarts. Note also that profile password settings take precedence over global settings.

The value in each SysSecDefaults column applies to all users, or, if your site implements profiles, to all users of any profile with that attribute set to NULL or NONE. If you set MaxLogonAttempts and LockedUserExpire at the system level, user DBC could potentially be locked out; yet only DBC can submit MODIFY USER DBC to change the DBC password.

DROP PROFILE Statement

If you created the profile, then you have the right to issue this statement.

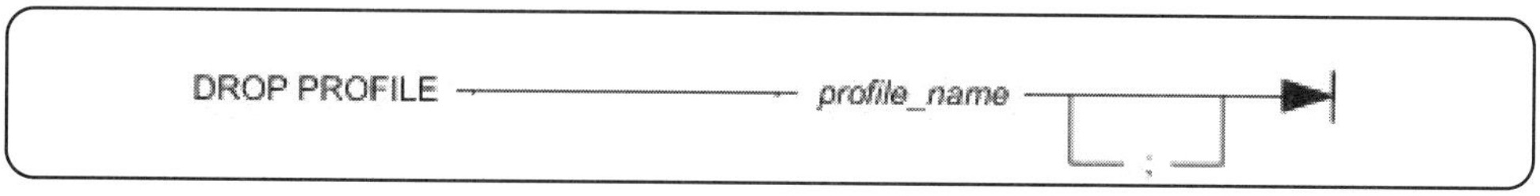

Figure 6.20

ProfileInfoV[X] View

The following are the columns of the ProfileInfo view.

DBC.ProfileV[X]

ProfileName	PasswordMaxChar	PasswordReuse
DefaultAccount	PasswordDigits	CommentString
DefaultDB	PasswordSpecChar	CreatorName
SpoolSpace	PasswordRestrictWords	CreateTimeStamp
TempSpace	MaxLogonAttempts	LastAlterName
ExpirePassword	LockedUserExpire	LastAlterTimeStamp
PasswordMinChar		

Figure 6.21

User Authentication

One method to control access to the Teradata Database is by utilizing LDAP. LDAP (Lightweight Directory Access Protocol) provides a means of managing and centralizing user accounts in a network environment. LDAP offers a scalable and secure approach to network management. By utilizing this method, you can use an LDAP to:

- Authenticate users

- Manage passwords
- Provide a Single Sign-On strategy
- Activate and deactivate accounts.

The directory username must match a Teradata Database username, and the matching Teradata Database username must have LOGON WITH NULL PASSWORD privileges.

After users have been authenticated, then they are logged onto the Teradata Database. From there, they are authorized to access only those objects allowed by their database privileges.

For mainframe users, you can use external authentication software, such as Kerberos. Keep in mind that all users authenticated by Kerberos must have LOGON WITH NULL PASSWORD privilege defined in each Teradata system to which they can log on.

Never GRANT LOGON WITH NULL PASSWORD to individual Teradata users unless you are using external authentication.

For every using client and each database system that can be accessed by the client and all Unity Director servers the clients can use to log on, you must verify that the corresponding external authentication mechanism is enabled.

Also, for users who log on to Teradata through Unity Director, the external authentication controls and WITH NULL PASSWORD privileges should be the same on all systems.

Teradata Wallet

To avoid having to code their password in a .logon or .logdata statement, users can store usernames and passwords on a PC workstation or application server installed with the Teradata Tools and Utilities 14.0 - Teradata Wallet software.

This software will enable you to securely store and protect passwords along with additional logon data and then retrieve the needed data when connecting to the database. Each wallet is configured for each specific user, and therefore, is not accessible by other users. When connecting to the Teradata system, the wallet software only accesses logon data belonging to that user.

Teradata Wallet can be utilized by either the .logon and .logdata statements for ODBC, CLI applications, and custom scripts.

Note: Teradata Wallet accepts replacement strings for ODBC, and CLI applications.

Users implementing custom scripts can incorporate password retrieval syntax that will add an extra layer of security by eliminating the need to include a password in the scripts.

In addition, Teradata Wallet can automatically and accurately retrieve username and password information when accessing multiple Teradata Database systems instead of having to store the information elsewhere.

Once Teradata Wallet has been installed on your client system, do the following:

1. Logon to your client system.
2. At a command prompt, execute Teradata Wallet to create a password alias name:

   ```
   tdwallet add <password_alias>
   ```

3. The software will prompt you to enter the password value for the alias name.

4. Then, reference your wallet in your script logon command.

```
.logon tdpid/username, $tdwallet (password_alias)
      [,"account "]
```

Identifying Security and Password Violations

Maintaining security is vital in protecting a company's data assets. This includes access rights, passwords, and abuse of special privileges.

Teradata provides many mechanisms to establish the proper level of Quality Of Protection (QOP), and the means to monitor it.

The following figure lists the system views associated with access logging.

DBC.AccessLogV DBC.AccLogRulesV	DBC.DeleteAccessLogV DBC.LogOnOffV[X]	DBC.LogonRulesV DBC.SecurityLogV[X]

Figure 6.22

The next figure lists the system views associated with users and privileges.

DBC.AllRightsV[X] DBC.AllRoleRightsV DBC.RoleInfoV[X] DBC.RoleMembersV	DBC.UsersV DBC.UserGrantedRightsV DBC.UserRightsV DBC.UserRoleRightsV

Figure 6.23

This last figure lists the system views associated with password control.

DBC.ProfileInfoV[X]	DBC.RestrictedWordsV	DBC.SecurityDefaultsV

Figure 6.24

The following query shows any failed logon attempts for the last ten days.

```
SELECT
 LogDate
,LogTime
,UserName (FORMAT 'X(20)')
,Event
FROM DBC.LogOnOffV
WHERE Event NOT LIKE ('%Logo%')
AND LogDate GT DATE - 10
ORDER BY LogDate, LogTime ;

LogDate       LogTime  UserName               Event
--------  -----------  --------------------  ------------
13/08/21  19:16:49.22  CSQL00                Bad Password
13/08/21  19:17:18.51  Non-existent User     Bad User
```

Figure 6.25

Limiting Column and Row Access Using Views

As a best practice, only the load utilities should have direct access to the base tables. All other access should be through views.

Views are very flexible. They can be single table or complex views. They can be updatable or read only. They can return all of the rows of the table(s) or just some. They can return all of the columns of the table(s) or just some.

The following figure shows the rows in the Employee_table.

```
SELECT employee_no, dept_no, mgr_employee_no AS mgr_no,
last_name(CHAR(10)) AS last_name, first_name (CHAR(10)) AS
first_name, salary FROM employee_table ORDER BY dept_no;

Employee_No  Dept_No       mgr_no  last_name   first_name      Salary
-----------  -------  -----------  ----------  ----------  ----------
    2000000        ?      1121334  Travolta    John          32800.50
    1000234       10      1121334  Gere        Richard       64300.00
    1232578      100      1256349  Student     Mandee        48850.00
    1333454      200      1121334  Roberts     Julia         48800.00
    1324657      200      1000234  Willis      Bruce         42788.88
    2312225      300      1333454  Mcfly       Loraine       40200.00
    1256349      400      1333454  Ford        Harrison      54590.00
    1121334      400            ?  Strickland  Stan          54590.00
    2341218      400      1256349  Clooney     George        35000.00
```

Figure 6.26

Here's an example of limiting the rows and columns of the table that a group of users can see.

```
CREATE VIEW dept_400_employees AS
SELECT employee_no, TRIM(first_name) || ' ' || TRIM(last_name)
AS employee
FROM employee_table
WHERE dept_no = 400;
```

Figure 6.27

Using the following query returns the following rows.

```
SELECT * FROM dept_400_employees;

Employee_No  employee
-----------  ---------------------------------
    1256349  Harrison Ford
    2341218  George Clooney
    1121334  Stan Strickland
```

Figure 6.28

As shown in Figure 6.28, views can be used to limit the rows available to users. However, creating separate views for each group of employees that users might need, and assigning access rights to those views would be cumbersome.

Another approach would be to create a table to identify which employee rows specific users can access, as shown in the next figure.

```
CREATE TABLE dept_filter
(userid CHAR(30) NOT NULL
,dept_no SMALLINT NOT NULL)
PRIMARY INDEX (userid);
```

Figure 6.29

Then insert the appropriate rows. Since the table has a NUPI, multiple rows can be inserted for those users requiring access to more than one department's employees.

```
INSERT INTO dept_filter VALUES ('gere', 200);
INSERT INTO dept_filter VALUES ('willis', 300);
INSERT INTO dept_filter VALUES ('willis', 400);
INSERT INTO dept_filter VALUES ('roberts', 400);
```

Figure 6.30

Then create a view, similar to the following and grant access to all users. If anyone whose userid doesn't appear in the filter table accesses the view, they simply get a "No rows found" message rather than a security error message.

```
CREATE VIEW employee AS
SELECT * FROM employee_table
WHERE dept_no IN
(SELECT dept_no FROM dept_filter
WHERE userid = USER)
WITH CHECK OPTION;
```

Figure 6.31

Since this is an updatable view, including the WITH CHECK OPTION restricts the rows which can be updated by an INSERT or UPDATE statement.

Using views and granting privileges at the column level instead of the table level provides a very robust level of security.

Row Level Security

Though controlling access to database objects is normally done by access rights, granting access rights is discretionary. This is referred to as Discretionary Access Control (DAC). The owner of an object has the right to grant access to that object to any other user. Though views are used to limit what data is made available, users cannot insert non-null values into columns they can't see, and they can't update columns or delete rows they cannot see.

Typically, views can be used to implement row level security for SELECT operations. However, any other operations which access the base table directly bypass the row level security check.

Now, with TD14, you can also use row level security in addition to object level privileges. Row Level Security (RLS) is referred to as Mandatory Access Control (MAC). However, implementing row level security can be complicated and should only be used when the more conventional DAC methods, mentioned above, are not sufficient.

With just DAC, users cannot be denied access to tables they own. Under MAC, users can be prohibited from accessing data in a table they own if they do not have the proper clearance.

Unlike view-based security, row level security is implemented at the base table level and can control SELECT, INSERT, UPDATE, and DELETEs.

In designing row level security, you create CONSTRAINT objects which identify the levels of security (hierarchical or compartments) and what SQL operations can be done at those levels. You assign appropriate CONSTRAINT(s) to users, and add CONSTRAINT columns to the tables to be protected. You must also create C language scalar UDFs to enforce the restrictions.

The following are some of the restrictions on Row Level Security (RLS) tables.

- Only permanent tables can have CONSTRAINT objects, and any table which has a CONSTRAINT object assigned to it cannot have any CHECK, UNIQUE, Primary Key, or Foreign Key constraints.

- CONSTRAINT object columns cannot be part of a Primary Index of a table, join index, or hash index, and cannot be part of a partitioning expression.

- A join index or hash index can only reference one RLS table.

- Multi-value compression and algorithmic compression are not allowed on CONSTRAINT object columns.

- Views and joins may reference both RLS and non-RLS tables. If a view or a join references more than one RLS table, all of the RLS tables must have the same set of CONSTRAINT objects.

- RLS tables cannot be referenced by a trigger.

Practice Questions

1. Which statement about RLS tables is false?
    a. A join index can only reference one RLS table.
    b. MLC and ALC are not allowed on CONSTRAINT object columns.
    c. RLS tables may be referenced by triggers
    d. A hash index can only reference a single RLS table.

2. Row Level Security is referred to as which of the following?
    a. Manual Authorization Control
    b. Manual Access Control
    c. Mandatory Authorization Control
    d. Mandatory Access Control

3. What is the maximum number of characters allowed in a password string?
    a. 8
    b. 15
    c. 30
    d. 45
    e. 60

4. Which of the following is not a valid role view?
    a. DBC.UserRoleRightsV
    b. DBC.AllRoleRightsVX
    c. DBC.RoleInfoVX
    d. DBC.RoleMembersVX

5. How many levels deep can roles be nested?
    a. 1
    b. 2
    c. 4
    d. 8

Chapter Notes

Utilize this space for notes, key points to remember, diagrams, areas of further study, etc.

Chapter 7 - Priority Scheduler and Workload Management

Certification Objectives

- ✓ Given a scenario, identify the steps to solve session management problems.
- ✓ Given a scenario using a web-based, mainframe, or BI application, identify the function that reduces authentication time.
- ✓ Given a shared userid scenario, identify the feature that uniquely identifies the user.
- ✓ Identify the usage and benefits of a trusted session.
- ✓ Given a scenario, identify alternative workload management methods and parameters that the Priority Scheduler can use for a system running SLES 11.
- ✓ Given a scenario, identify the Workload Designer features that should be used for a system running SLES 11.
- ✓ Identify the capability of the Workload Designer tool for analyzing and managing workloads for systems running SLES 11.
- ✓ Identify characteristics of AMP Worker Tasks (AWTs).

Before You Begin

You should be familiar with the following terms and concepts.

Terms	Key Concepts
Workload	What constitutes a workload and what you can control
Priority Scheduling	How users are assigned to a Performance Group

Reducing Authentication Time

To expedite accessing a Teradata system, Teradata allows single sign-on. This means that users who have logged onto the Windows domain can logon onto a Teradata system without having to submit a Teradata username and password.

To do this, an external authorization agent (LDAP, Kerberos) validates the user's domain name and password when they log onto their Windows system. When the user wants to connect to a Teradata system, the agent passes the user's domain name to Teradata. The user's domain name must match a Teradata username. Since the external agent has validated the user, a Teradata password is not needed. Teradata then authorizes the access privileges to the matching username.

Session Pooling

Using the START POOL command, the operator specifies how many sessions, using the same logon string, are to be started. The logon string supplied in the START POOL command will be authenticated against the corresponding username. If the logon is valid, the TDP creates the requested number of sessions, as shown in the following diagram. Many session pools can exist at the same time, as long as they each have a unique logon string, or different accounting information.

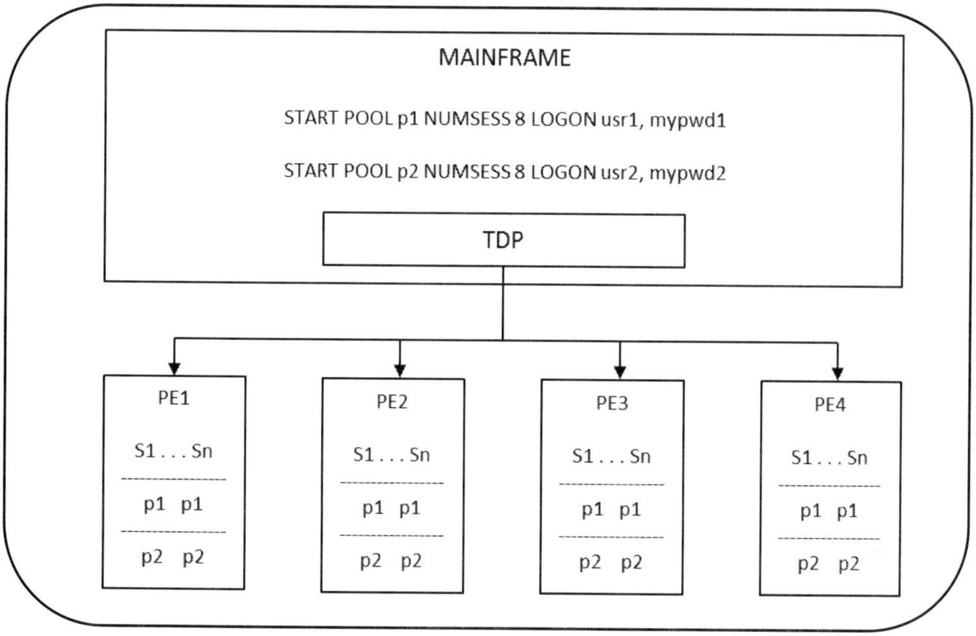

Figure 7.1

When the pool is first started, none of the sessions are in use. In the following diagram, when an application sends a logon request, the TDP checks to see if the logon string matches any established pools. If it does, such as for *usr1* and *usr2*, the TDP connects the application to the first available session established for that pool. If the user's logon string doesn't match any active pool, as shown for *usr3*, the user is connected to the first available general session.

Once a session is assigned, it cannot be given to any other application/user until the current user logs off.

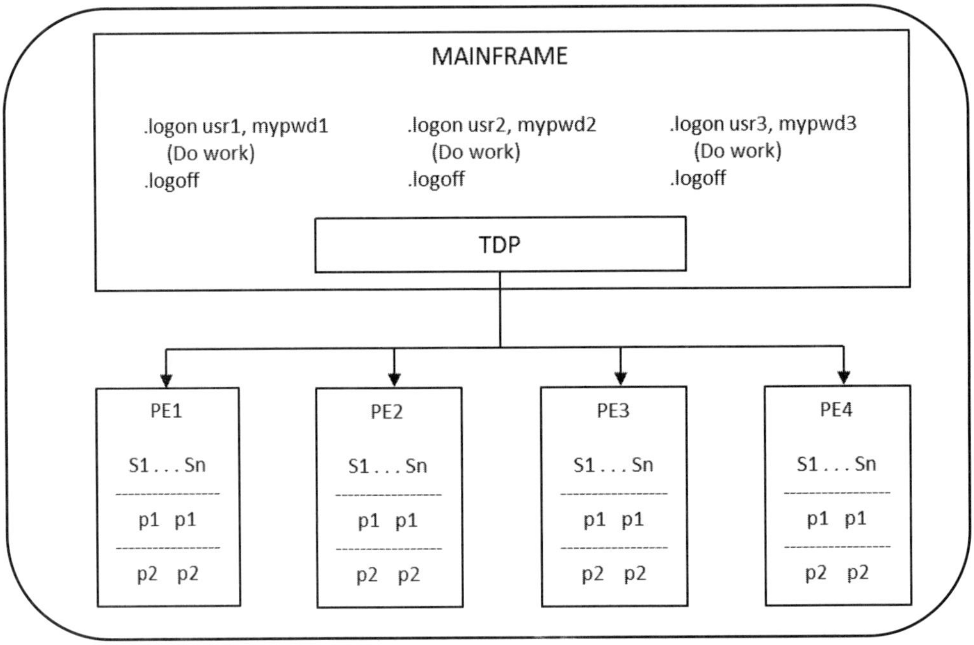

Figure 7.2

When the operator issues a STOP POOL command, the sessions established for that pool are returned for general use.

Identifying users

When the TDP establishes a session, it populates various columns in DBC.EventLog, DBC.SessionTbl, and the LogonSource column in various views such as DBC.LogOnOffV and DBC.SessionInfoV.

The following table lists the various columns that may get populated with specific EBCDIC values. Using these columns, along with the other columns in the two system tables will allow you to identify individual users.

ClientConnectionType	ClientGroupSecProd	ClientJobId
ClientOsName	ClientProgramName	ClientTDPReleaseId
ClientTdHostName	ClientCoordName	ClientCLIv2ReleaseId
ClientJobName	ClientTransactionId	ClientSessionDesc
ClientEnvName	ClientTerminalId	ClientWorkload
ClientUserIdSecProd	ClientUserOperId	

Figure 7.3

Trusted Sessions

Trusted sessions provide applications (i.e. proxy users) a middle-tier to logon and access the Teradata Database through a permanent user (trusted user). Trusted users are established through the following command.

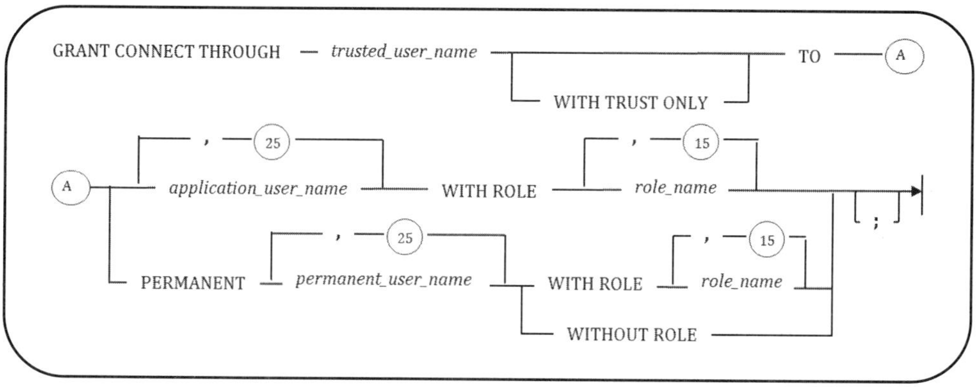

Figure 7.4

The person issuing this command must have the following privileges.

- CTCONTROL
- WITH ADMIN OPTION on each of the roles specified
- DROP USER on each of the PERMANENT users specified as proxy users

The *trusted_user_name* shouldn't be an end-user. It should identify a middle tier CRM application or Teradata Viewpoint.

The *application_user_name* is the name of an application user who should have proxy logon privilege. The intent is to create a list of application user names that should have access to the system if creating permanent users for every end-user of the application wouldn't be feasible. Application user names can be anything which represents the client connecting to the middle tier, such as an ATM identifier or a client name.

Though there is a limit of 25 *application_user_names* in a GRANT statement, there is no limit on how many *application_user_names* can be granted logon privileges to a *trusted_user_name*.

The *role_names* in a WITH ROLE must be internal roles managed by Teradata, rather than external roles which are directory-managed, and are roles that are to be assigned to the proxy user. Only a permanent proxy user can be defined without a role.

Levels of Workload Management

Using Teradata Viewpoint Workload Designer, you can establish rules with the portlet to provide different kinds of workload control.

- **Filters** to reject query requests before they are executed to a specific database object for some or all types of SQL requests. Queries can be prohibited to run if they are estimated to access too many rows, take too long, and/or perform joins that take too many resources.
- **Throttles** can be applied to specific objects where you can impose session and query concurrency limits. In other words, you can restrict the number of query requests against a database object (i.e. table). You can also apply throttles to Priority Scheduler Performance Groups (PGs). Throttles can

also be applied on FastLoad, MultiLoad, FastExport, and Archive/Restore when it comes to enforcing concurrency limits. In other words, you can restrict the type and/or number of utilities that run simultaneously.
- **Workload Definitions** that specify how the Teradata Database should regulate or manage queries by specifying parameters for up to 36 separate workloads. The default is 5.

Priority Scheduler Facility

Priority Scheduler Facility (PSF) is used to control resource consumption, specifically CPU. It does not directly control resources such as I/O, AWTs, Memory, etc. PSF cannot alter the PG's automatically or regulate access to AWTs. With Priority Scheduler, you can:

- Balance resource usage across different applications and utilities.
- Authorize users for access to prioritized levels of service based on the PG, carried in the user account string.
- Dynamically alter the PG of a user or user group (with profiles).
- Regulate access to AMP Worker Tasks (AWTs).
- Dynamically modify parameters that define your scheduling strategy, plus:
    - Record these parameters as profiles.
    - Automatically change the profiles at scheduled times.
- Set CPU usage limits at a variety of levels.

PSF is a weight-based system. It uses weights to determine the relative priority of a query. It is the relative priority that determines how much and how frequently CPU will be offered to a query. The main components of the PSF are:

- Resource Partitions

- Performance Groups
- Performance Periods
- Allocation Groups

Of those, Allocation Groups determine the ultimate relative priority of a query. The parameters available for defining your scheduling strategy include:

- A prioritized weighting system
- Methods for dynamically adjusting your strategy based on resource use or calendar schedule.

These capabilities allow you to control your workload flow.

SLES 10 Priority Scheduler Architecture

Priority Scheduler consists of Resource Partitions, Resource Groups, and Allocation Groups, as shown in the following diagram.

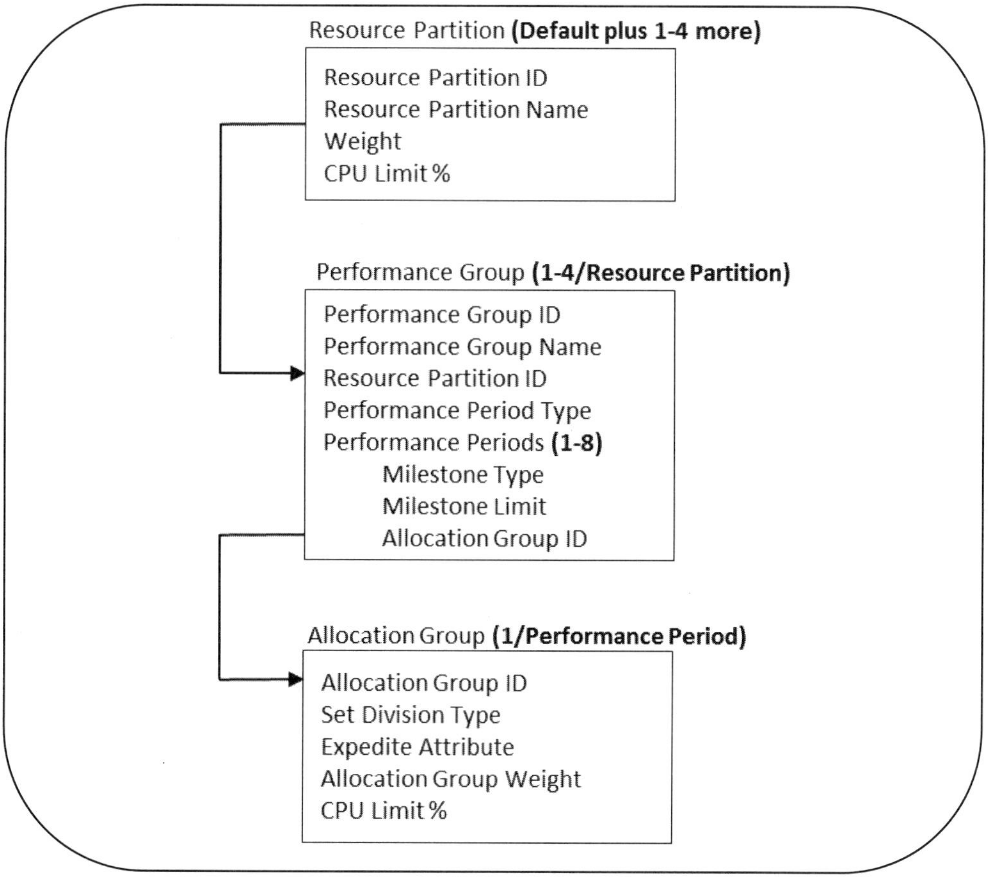

Figure 7.5

Resource Partition 0 (RP0) is the Default, and if required, you can create an additional 4 RPs. The default number of PGs (L, M, H and R) is 4 with the option to create an additional 36 PGs (max 40). Each PG can have up to 8 Performance Periods. Each performance period can map to only 1 AG, and *multiple RPs or PGs can map to the same AG.* In addition, an AG can map to multiple PG or PP, but only one RP. Lastly, there is a maximum of 200 AGs.

Resource Partitions and Performance Groups

WHAT IS A WEIGHT?

Every Teradata Database logon session is assigned to a Performance Group. Performance Groups control the prioritization of jobs started by sessions under their control. When a Performance Group is defined, it is assigned to a Resource Partition.

Weights are assigned at the Resource Partition level and to Allocation Groups within a Resource Partition. Weights are used at these levels to determine the relative proportion of resources to allocate to the user. Basically, weights are:

- A numeric value used at the Resource Partition Level to compute a relative weight (compared to other Resource Partitions) to determine the proportion of resources the processes of the entire Resource Partition are to receive.

- A numeric value used at the Allocation Group Level to compute a relative weight (within the Resource Partition) to determine the proportion of resources the processes of the Allocation Group is to receive.

Allocation Groups are also associated with Performance Groups. Like Resource Partitions, Allocation Groups have weights that determine the proportion of resources allocated relative to the other Allocation Groups that are active within the same Resource Partition.

EXAMPLE OF PRIORITY WEIGHTS

Let's assume there are four defined Resource Partitions, with individual weight assignments of R1 = 10, R2 = 20, R3 = 40, and R4 = 80. These weights mean nothing to Priority Scheduler unless more than one Resource Partition is active. If there are multiple active

Resource Partitions, the weights are used to determine how much of the system's resources a given partition will receive compared to the other active partitions. The formula is very straight forward: Divide the weight of the active partition being measured by the sum of the weights of all of the active partitions. As an example, if R1 and R2 are active, their combined weights add up to 30. This means the R1 will receive 10/30 (.33, or 33%) of the system's resources, and R2 will receive 20/30 (.66 or 66%) of the system's resources. If partitions R2, R3, and R4 are active, the sum of their weights is 140. That means that the system's resource will be distributed across the three active partitions as R2 = 14% (20/140), R3 = 28% (40/140), and R4 = 57% (80/140). If only one Resource Partition is active, it gets 100% of the system's resources.

This same process is used to determine the percentage of resources Allocation Groups within a Resource Group can use. Let's assume the three Allocation Groups under R4, have assigned weights of U1 = 30, U2 = 60, and U3 = 90. If all of them are active, the amount of resources available to R4 will be distributed as U1 = 16% (30/180), U2 = 33% (60/180), and U3 = 50% (90/180).

When a user logs on, a PG can be specified in the Account String during logon time, but it is not required. PGs do not link RPs and AGs. Queries will be assigned to a PG, either through specifying it in the account string, the default PG or the Milestone. The AG of the query step will be assigned to is based on the Performance Period(s) defined.

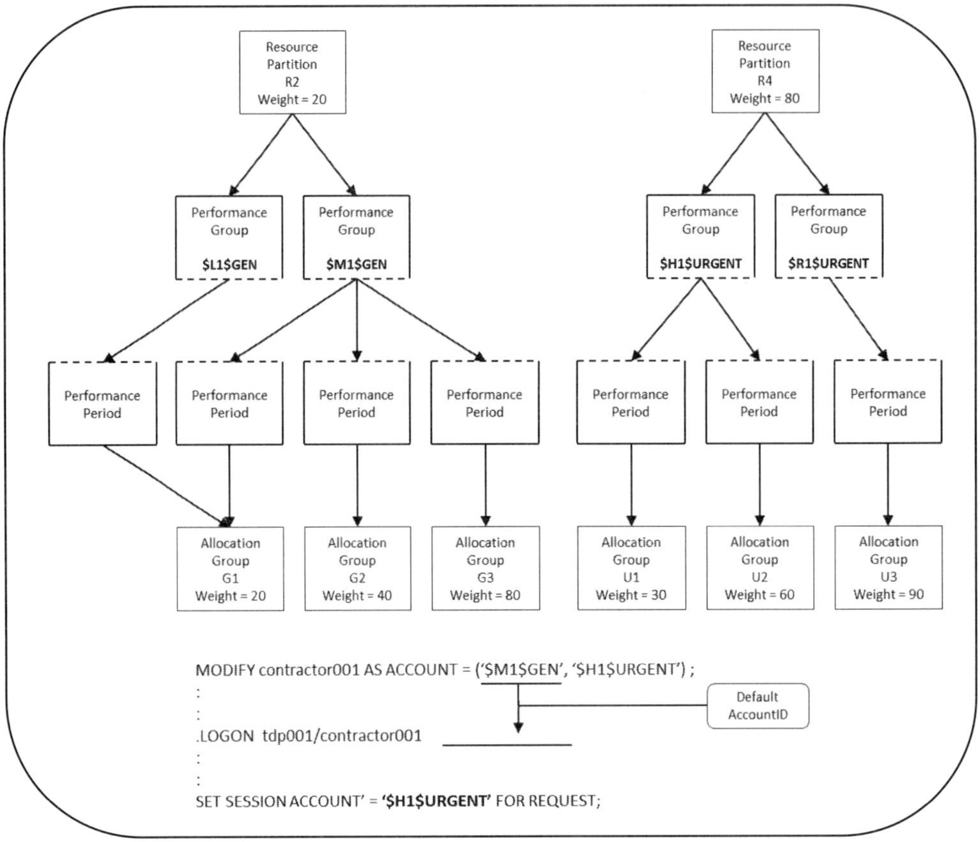

Figure 7.6

Referring to the example illustrated in Figure 7.6, only Resource Partitions R2 and R4 are active at the moment, and the Allocation Groups shown are active. When *contractor001* logged on, the default AccountID put the user in Performance group $M1$GEN. Presently, R2 can use 20% of the system's resources, and R4 can use 80%. Since all three Allocation Groups are active, G1 can use 14% of R2's 20%, G2 can use 28%, and G3 can use 57%. To determine the relative weight of a Performance Group (what percentage of the total system's resources a Performance Group can use), the system simply has to multiply the Resource Partition's active weight against the Allocation Group' active weight. The rules defined for the individual Performance Groups will determine which Allocation Group will service *contractor001*'s requests. Based upon parameters, like time-of-day, contractor001's requests may dynamically switch Allocation Groups. Assuming that all three Allocation Groups remain active, here are the relative Performance Group weights for $M1$GEN depending upon which Allocation Group is used.

G1 = 20/(20+80) * 20/(20+40+80) = .2 * .14 = 2%
G2 = 20/(20+80) * 40/(20+40+80) = .2 * .28 = 5%
G3 = 20/(20+80) * 80/(20+40+80) = .2 * .57 = 11%

When *contractor001* switches AccountIDs, the next request will be processed by U1 or U2. At the present time, if all three Allocation Groups under R4 are active, the relative Performance Group weight for $H1$URGENT can vary across the two Allocation groups.

U1 = 80/(20+80) * 30/(30+60+90) = .8 * .16 = 12%
U2 = 80/(20+80) * 60/(30+60+90) = .8 * .33 = 26%

PERFORMANCE PERIODS

As shown earlier, each Performance Period defines a Milestone and an Allocation Group. A Milestone is made up of a Milestone Type and a Milestone Limit. The following chart explains their content.

Component	Definition
Milestone Type	Thresholds defined for each Performance Period / Performance Group. You can express the following parameters: • Time-of-day (T) • Session resource usage (S or R) • Query resource usage (Q)
Milestone Limit	Thresholds to change Performance Periods / Performance Group. You can express the following parameters: • A valid time-of-day (i.e. 0800 for 8:00 A.M.). • A number of seconds of CPU usage.
Allocation Group	Used to control sessions in the Performance Period.

Figure 7.7

All Performance Periods with in a Performance Group must use the Milestone Type.

When the threshold for the Performance Period is exceeded, the session is transferred to the next Performance Period, and the processes belonging to that session are placed under the control of a different Allocation Group. Typically, the change is to a lower-priority Allocation Group. Consequently access to resources will be progressively reduced for longer-running sessions. This is expressed in seconds to hundredths of a second, representing an amount of session CPU resource consumption per node.

Note: The compare and adjust concept monitors resource consumption and will modify queries that exceed threshold and that have been established by the workload parameters.

Time-of-day Performance Periods monitor the clock time, and optionally, the day of the week. This is expressed in military time, representing time periods during a 24-hour day. For example, 0800 is 8:00 A.M. These types of Performance Periods are used to dynamically switch the Allocation Group of a session based on changes in business priority of different work at different times of day. For example, a session can be switched to a higher-priority Allocation Group after business hours or on weekends, when competition for database resources is not high.

CPU USAGE LIMITS WITH PRIORITY SCHEDULER

Priority Scheduler uses Milestones and CPU limits to manage CPU usage.

Milestones (either Query or Session) monitor CPU consumption for each query step and moves the query to another AG once the threshold is met. Milestones are time-based; you can limit a Resource Partition to a specified percentage of CPU resource usage.

CPU limits restrict CPU consumption on the system. This limit has no effect on the scheduling strategy defined by other Priority Scheduler parameters. The relative weights of Allocation Groups and Resource Partitions are observed. The normal distribution of resources prevails within the specified amount of CPU usage.

Note: You can also limit the percentage of total CPU usage by sessions controlled by an Allocation Group. The Milestone Limit of CPU usage is defined in seconds or fractions of seconds.

Schmon Utility

The schmon utility, schmon, is a command line interface that enables you to show and modify Priority Scheduler parameters.

Schmon runs on the following platforms and interfaces:

Platform	Interface
Windows	Command line ("Teradata Command Prompt") Database Window
Linux	Command line Database Window

Figure 7.8

Note: If Workload Definitions have been activated using Teradata Viewpoint Workload Designer portlet, schmon cannot be used to modify the Priority Scheduler parameters.

SLES 11 Priority Scheduler

The Priority Scheduler no longer uses the SLES 10 Resource Groups, Resource Partitions, and Allocation Groups discussed above. Teradata Active System Management (TASM) now manages Priority Scheduler and Teradata Viewpoint monitors and configures these settings with workload management portlets. In addition, the Teradata Viewpoint provides a portlet to assist in converting SLES 10 definitions to SLES 11.

Priority Scheduler deals with virtual partitions, which are also referred to as environments.

Initially, all of the system's resources are assigned to the fixed partition named **Always.**

Within a virtual partition, you can create three resource groupings or tiers, one for Tactical workloads, another for SLG workloads, and one for Timeshare workloads, as shown in the next figure.

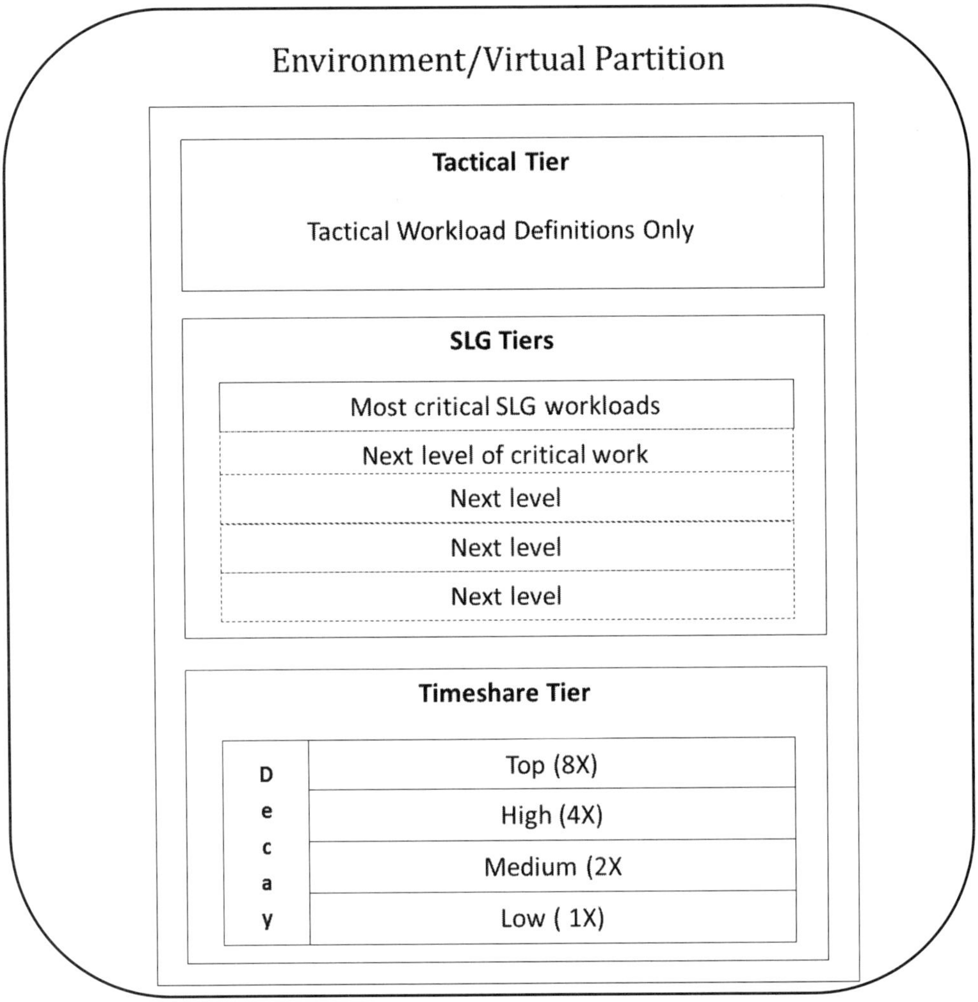

Figure 7.9

Tactical workloads get all of the resources they need. The SLG tier workloads then have access to the remaining resources after all tactical demands are fulfilled. Timeshare workloads have access to the remaining resources after Tactical and SLG resource requirements are met.

The timeshare tier has a Decay option to prevent problematic queries from monopolizing system resources. The decay automatically lowers the workload's resource access rate.

Multiple environments can be defined. As an example, you might want one for the weekend, another for month end, another for midnight, and so on. The following figure shows there is no limit to the number of environments that can be defined for a system.

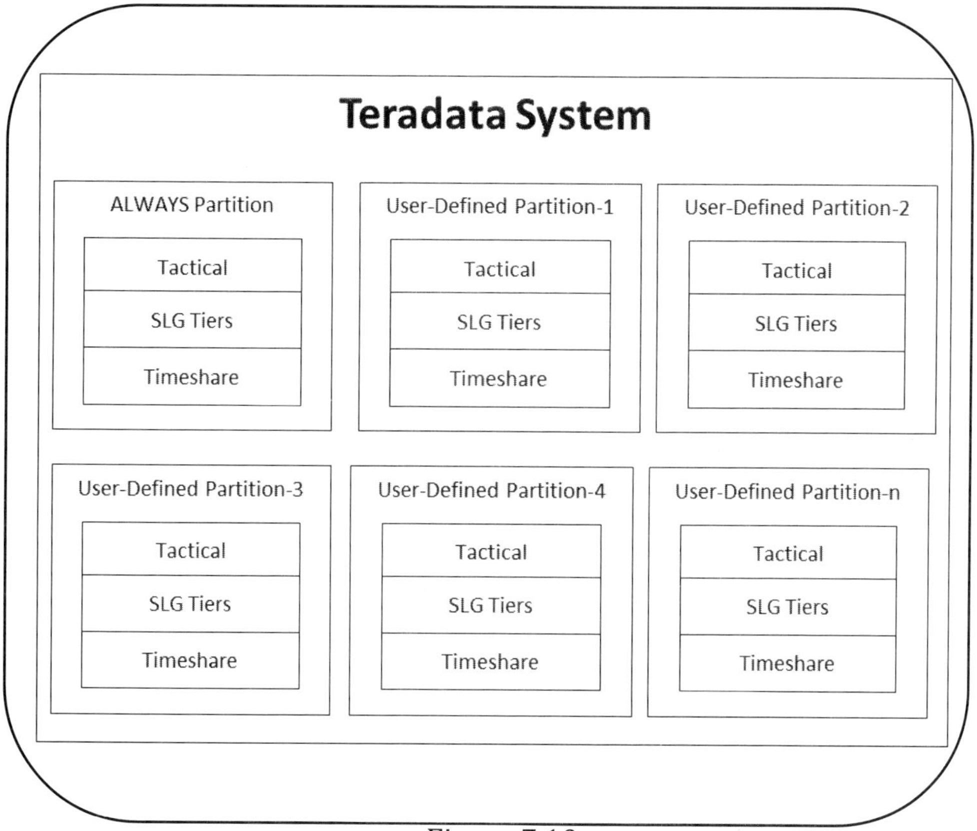

Figure 7.10

An environment does not consume any resources until one of its workloads is activated.

AMP Worker Task (AWT)

Amp worker tasks (AWTs) are processes that will help an AMP to finish any database work. AWTs are considered powerful resources to an AMP. AWTs are always ready for any action, which gives it the advantage of being able to quickly respond to almost all database execution needs. Here is how AWTs are utilized:

1. The PE will dispatch the first step of the query
2. This step will be given a AWT to process the work
3. The database will execute and finish the work
4. When this step is completed, two things occur:
    a. The AWT assigned to the step will be returned to the pool of available AWTs
    b. The step is sent back to the AMP
5. Then the AMP will dispatch the step and wait for the next step from the Optimizer

The AWT Monitor utility, *awtmon*, collects and shows easy-to-read summary information of the AMP Worker Task(s) (AWT) in the Teradata Database system. This information, which can be captured for a single node or for all nodes, can be used for debugging purposes, such as isolating hot-AMP conditions.

Workload Designer SLES 10 & SLES 11

If you are migrating to TD 14.0 with SLES 11, the PSF settings and workload management schemes used in earlier releases will no longer work.

The following figure highlights the enhancements to the Teradata Viewpoint Workload Designer, and indicates whether the enhancement is available for SLES 10 and/or SLES 11.

TD 14 Capability	SLES 10	SLES 11
You can classify workloads based on the estimated memory use of queries. This allows you to provide memory-intensive workloads with more memory by restricting similar competing jogs from running concurrently. It also controls the amount of memory available for XML operations and can prevent runaway queries from degrading system performance by consuming too many resources.	Y	Y
You can classify workloads, filters, throttles, utility sessions or query sessions by either Function or Method. This allows you to group multiple UDFs into a single rule.	Y	Y
You can create a workload group throttle, which is a collective throttle for a group of Workload Definitions. This allows you to limit the number of queries the group can submit at one time.	Y	Y
There is a STATS manager portlet to automate and collect statistical data using COLLECT STATS. You can control the schedule and scope of each collect job.	Y	Y
You can set a hard limit on CPU and I/O at the Virtual Partition or workload level. A hard limit at the partition level does not affect the hard limit set at the workload level. A hard maximum limit for CPU and I/O resources that	N	Y

can be used by SLG Tier workloads prevents them from benefiting from the inactivity of other workloads on the same or higher tiers.		
You can expedite individual SLG Tier 1 workloads. You can specify the number of AWTs to be reserved for use by the system for each environment.	N	Y
To determine the number of workloads for each UDF or UDM, you can use PM/API TDWM STATISTICS request.	Y	Y
To determine if a query is delayed for a workload throttle, you can use the PM/API TDWM STATISTICS request or the TDWMGetDelayedQueries function.	Y	Y
Priority Scheduler Facility uses Resource Groups, Resource Partitions, and Allocation Groups.	Y	N
Priority Scheduler Facility uses a tiered architecture and virtual partitions.	N	Y

Figure 7.11

Practice Questions

1. Which of the following does not require the user to submit a logon command to their Teradata system?
    a. Single sign-on
    b. General session
    c. Trusted User
    d. General session

2. How many *application_user_names* can be listed in a single GRANT statement?
    a. 15
    b. 20
    c. 25
    d. 30
    e. 35

3. How many workload definitions does the system currently support?
    a. 15
    b. 20
    c. 25
    d. 30
    e. 35

4. Which of the following terms apply to the SLES 11 Priority Scheduler?
    a. Allocation Group
    b. Resource Group
    c. Resource Partition
    d. Virtual Partition

5. Which of the following terms apply to the SLES 10 Priority Scheduler?
    a. Milestone Limit
    b. Timeshare Workload Tier
    c. SLG Workload Tier
    d. Tactical Workload Tier

Chapter Notes

Utilize this space for notes, key points to remember, diagrams, areas of further study, etc.

Chapter 8 - Query Access Logging

Certification Objectives

- ✓ Given a scenario, identify the process to locate a security violation, security breach, or password violation.
- ✓ Given a scenario, identify the Database Query Log (DBQL) tables and logging options that should be used to resolve the problem.
- ✓ Given a scenario, identify the resource that should be used (Access Logging, ResUsage, and DBQL).

Before You Begin

You should be familiar with the following terms and concepts.

Terms	Key Concepts
Access Logging vs. Query Logging	What you can learn from each of these
Access Logging	What commands control this
Query Logging	What commands control this
DBC.LogOnOff	The system view of logging information

Access and Query Logging

While Access Logging can log SQL, it is normally used for auditing purposes (i.e. when a user has tried to access data objects). DBQL can log the actual SQL executed by a user and can therefore be utilized for performance analysis.

Access Logging and Objects Used

How Access Logging Works

Each time a user named in a BEGIN LOGGING statement attempts to perform a specified action against a specified object, an entry is logged in the system table *DBC.AccLogTbl*. Possible entry data includes the type of access, the text of the request, the frequency of access, the action requested, the name of the requesting user, and the referenced objects.

Logging can be ended on any action, user, or object for which logging is currently active through the END LOGGING statement.

A logging entry does not indicate that a statement was performed; rather, it indicates that the system checked the privileges necessary to perform the statement.

Access Logging on Hash and Join Indexes

Because neither hash nor join indexes can be accessed directly, you cannot specify access logging for either type of object. If you need to perform access logging, specify it for the relevant base table.

When a hash or join index is used in a query plan, the access privileges are checked for the base table and logged appropriately.

Here is the BEGIN LOGGING syntax diagram.

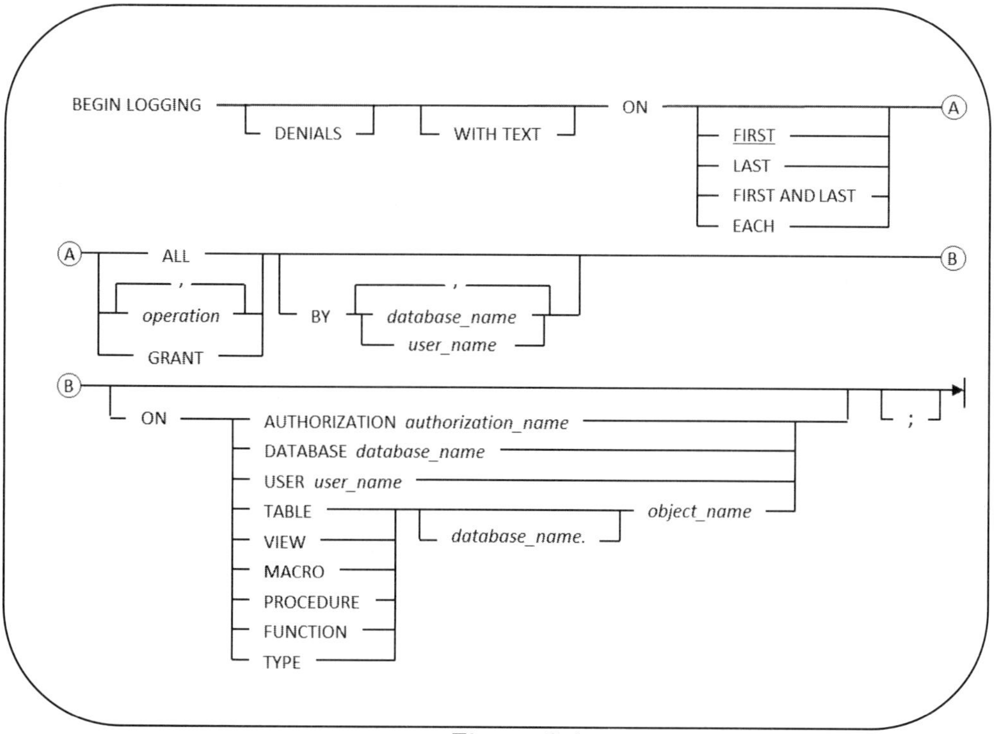

Figure 8.1

Here is the END LOGGING syntax diagram.

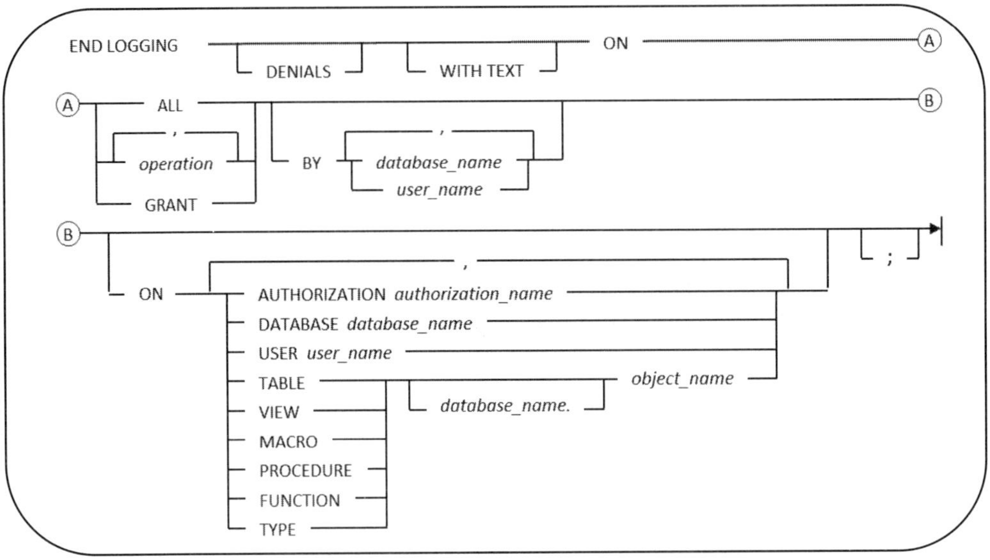

Figure 8.2

Setting up Access Logging

To enable logging of access checks, the DBC.AccLogRule macro must exist and you must have EXECUTE privilege on it. The DBC.AccLogRule macro is an empty macro used only for the privilege check.

```
SHOW VIEW DBC.AccLogRule;

REPLACE MACRO DBC.AccLogRule AS (;);
```

Figure 8.3

You activate access checking by defining the rules in one or more BEGIN LOGGING statements. The rules you specify are stored in system table DBC.AccLogRuleTbl. The GRANT options are the same as for the SQL GRANT statement.

Access Log Views

There are two views associated with access logging, DBC.AccessLogRulesV, and DBC.AccessLogV.

DBC.AccLogRulesV

The AccLogRulesV view provides information about logging rules that are currently in effect on the system. The underlying table, DBC.AccLogRuleTbl, is populated as a result of successfully processed BEGIN LOGGING statements.

DBC.AccLogRulesV

UserName	AcrDropMacro	AcrCreateTrigger
DatabaseName	AcrDropTable	AcrDropTrigger
TVMName	AcrDropUser	AcrCreateRole
AcrAlterFunction	AcrDropView	AcrDropRole
AcrCheckpoint	AcrDropProcedure	AcrCreateProfile
AcrCreateDatabase	AcrDump	AcrDropProfile
AcrCreateFunction	AcrExecute	AcrAlterProcedure
AcrCreateMacro	AcrExecuteFunction	AcrAlterExtProcedure
AcrCreateTable	AcrExecuteProcedure	AcrRepControl
AcrCreateUser	AcrGrant	AcrUDTUsage
AcrCreateView	AcrIndex	AcrUDTType
AcrCreateProcedure	AcrInsert	AcrUDTMethod
AcrCreExtProcedure	AcrReference	AcrCreAuthorization
AcrDelete	AcrRestore	AcrDropAuthorization
AcrDropDatabase	AcrSelect	CreatorName
AcrDropFunction	AcrUpdate	CreateTimeStamp
AcrCreateGLOP	AcrDropGLOP	AcrGLOPMember
AcrConstrDef	AcrConstrAsgn	AcrOverrideIns
AcrOverrideSel	AcrOverrideUpd	AcrOverrideDel
AcrOverrideDump	AcrOverrideRestore	

Figure 8.4

DBC.AccessLogV

Each row that the AccessLogV displays indicates the results of a privilege check. Whether a privilege check is logged or not depends on the presence and the criteria of an access logging rule.

DBC.AccessLogV

LogDate	UserName	DatabaseName
LogTime	AccountName (expanded)	TVMName
LogonDate	OwnerName	ColumnName
LogonTime	AccessType	StatementType
LogicalHostId	Frequency	StatementText
IFPNo	EventCount	QueryBand
SessionNo	AccLogResult	ProxyUser
ConstraintId		

Figure 8.5

DBC.AccessLogV View - Example

```
BEGIN LOGGING ON CREATE TABLE, DROP TABLE
              ON DATABASE csql00;

SELECT UserName, DatabaseName, TVMName, AcrCreateTable,
AcrDropTable FROM DBC.AccLogRulesV;


UserName         DatabaseName  TVMName          CTB  DTB
-------------    ------------- --------------   ---  ---
All              csql00        All              F    F
```

Figure 8.6

```
DROP TABLE logtest;

CREATE TABLE logtest (c1 INT, c2 INT);

SELECT username (CHAR(12)), accesstype(CHAR(12)),
tvmname(CHAR(12)), statementtype(CHAR(12))
FROM dbc.accesslogV;


UserName       AccessType     TVMName        StatementType
------------   ------------   ------------   -------------
CSQL00         DT             logtest        Drop Table
CSQL00         CT             ?              Create Table
```

Figure 8.7

END LOGGING - Example

Here is an example to end the logging started above.

```
END LOGGING ON CREATE TABLE, DROP TABLE
              ON DATABASE csql00;
```

Figure 8.8

The END LOGGING statement erases only the frequency or text flags for the specified actions and user or object. However, if erasing a frequency leaves all logging blank for a particular user, database, and table, then the row is deleted from the *AccLogRuleTbl* table.

You must disable access logging to perform an INITIATE INDEX ANALYSIS or RESTART INDEX ANALYSIS statement. Once the index analysis completes, you can enable access logging once again.

Teradata Administrator – Access Logging

The Teradata Administrator utility provides the ability to manage both Access Logging and Query Logging.

From the main window, click **Tools>Access Logging** or click **Tools>Query Logging**.

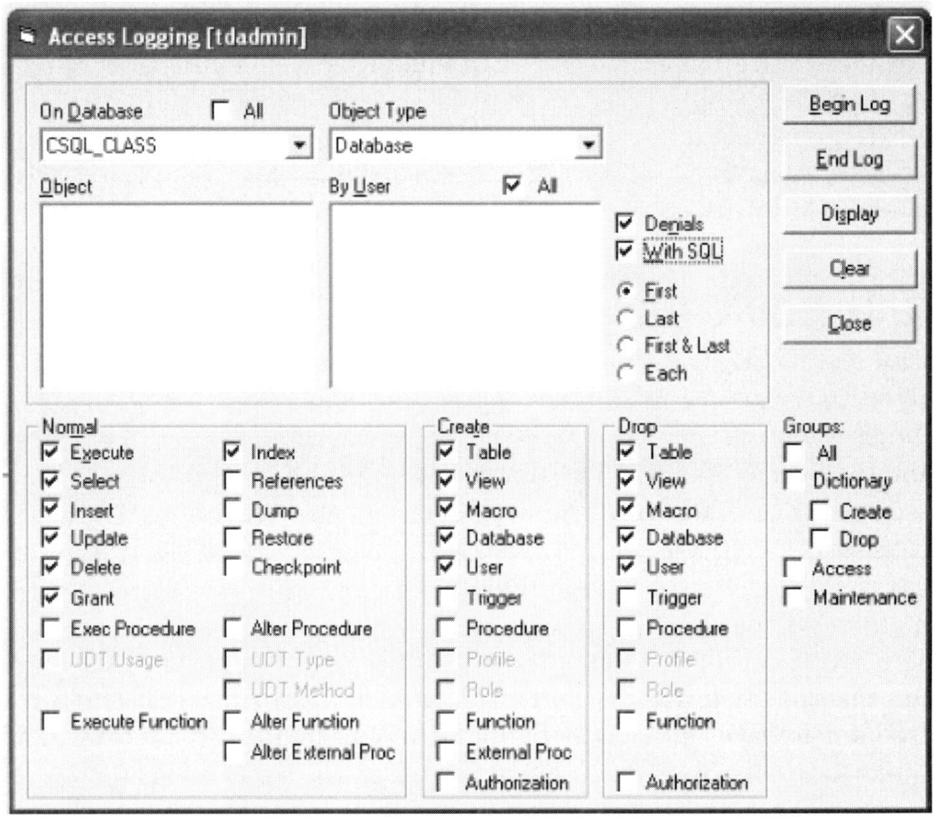

Figure 8.9

Query Logging (DBQL) Concepts

The Database Query Log (DBQL) is an optional feature that you can employ to log query processing activity for later analysis. Query counts and response times can be charted and SQL text and processing steps can be compared to fine-tune your applications for optimum performance.

DBQL collects information based on rules you specify and flushes the DBQL cache as defined by the DBQLFlushRate field in the DBSControl record (the default is 10 minutes), and periodically writes to the DBQL dictionary tables (which are a series of predefined tables also referred to as logs). This information includes historical records of queries and their duration, performance data, and target activity.

DBQL is controlled by the Teradata SQL statements BEGIN QUERY LOGGING and END QUERY LOGGING. Only a user with EXECUTE privilege on DBC.DBQLAccessMacro can invoke the statements.

You cannot issue a BEGIN/END QUERY LOGGING statement while running in ANSI session mode. In Teradata session mode, you cannot issue a BEGIN/END QUERY LOGGING statement within a BT/ET transaction. Instead, use these statements outside a BT/ET transaction or, for ANSI session mode, log off and set the transaction mode to Teradata session mode.

Objects used in Defining Rules for DBQL

The following chart summarizes the dictionary tables and views used by DBQL.

Dictionary Object Name	Object Type	Description
DBC.DBQLExplainTbl	Table	Stores the unformatted EXPLAIN text for a query.
DBC.DBQLRuleTbl		Stores the rules for the Database Query Log.
DBC.DBQLRuleCountTbl		Stores the cardinality of *DBQLRuleTbl*.
DBC.DBQLogTbl		Stores default rows for the Database Query Log, including Query Band information.
DBC.DBQLObjTbl		Stores query object information.
DBC.DBQLSummaryTbl		Stores summary and threshold information for the logged query.
DBC.DBQLStepTbl		Stores query step information.
DBC.DBQLSqlTbl		Stores SQL query text.
DBC.DBQLXMLTbl		Stores query plans and statistics usage information in an XML document.
DBC.DBQLXMLLockTbl		Stores a record of lock delays. The table has no primary index (NOPI) and no fallback.
DBC.DBQLRulesV	View	A view onto *DBC.DBQLRuleTbl*.

Dictionary Object Name	Object Type	Description
DBC.QryLogV		A view onto *DBC.DBQLogTbl.*
DBC.QryLogEventHisV		A view into *DBC.TDWMEventHistory*
DBC.QryLogEventsV		A view into *DBC.TDWMEventLog*
DBC.QryLogExceptionsV		A view into *DBC.TDWMExceptionLog*
DBC.QryLogExplainV		A view onto DBC.*DBQLExplainTbl.*
DBC.QryLogObjectsV		A view onto DBC.*DBQLObjTbl.*
DBC.QryLogSummaryV		A view onto DBC.*DBQLSummaryTbl.*
DBC.QryLogStepsV		A view onto DBC.*DBQLStepTbl.*
DBC.QryLogSQLV		A view onto DBC.*DBQLSQLTbl.*
DBC.QryLogTDWMV		A view onto DBC.*DBQLogTbl.*
DBC.QryLogTdwmSumV		A view into *DBC.TDWMSummarryLog*
DBC.QryLogXMLV		A view into *DBC.DBQLXMLTbl*
DBC.QryLockLogXMLV		A view into *DBC.DBQLXMLLockTbl*

Figure 8.10

BEGIN QUERY LOGGING Statement

The following is the syntax diagram for the BEGIN QUERY LOGGING statement.

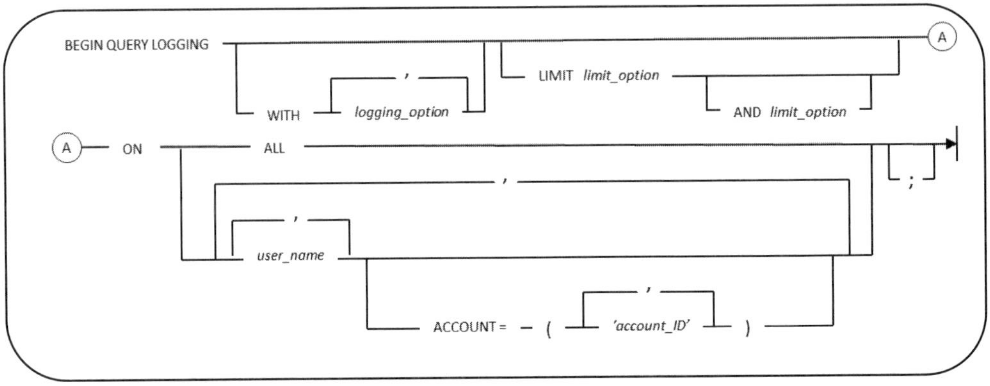

Figure 8.11

BEGIN QUERY LOGGING WITH logging_option

Table 8.12 illustrates the options for logging the objects used by a query, the AMP steps produced to perform the query, the EXPLAIN text for the query, or the SQL query text. Specifying any of the logging options can have a performance impact on your system.

If you do not specify a logging option, then only the default set of query information is logged in a defined default row for each query for each specified user.

Option	Description
ALL	Log query object information, step information, EXPLAIN text, and all SQL statements for all logged on users. This is equivalent to specifying OBJECTS, STEPINFO, EXPLAIN, and SQL individually. This option does *not* log XMLPLAN, LOCK, or STATSUSAGE. If you specify ALL, then you should also specify a value of 0 for SQLTEXT to ensure that the text for the SQL statement is not logged in both the *DBQLogTbl* and *DBQLSqlTbl* tables.

Option	Description
	If you specify ALL, then you cannot specify other logging options.
EXPLAIN	Log the unformatted EXPLAIN text for the query. This option generates and logs the unformatted EXPLAIN text for each query. It does *not* generate EXPLAIN text for queries preceded by the EXPLAIN modifier. You should be cautious about specifying this option because the performance cost of generating the EXPLAIN text for a query can be expensive.
[DETAILED] STATSUSAGE	Capture query optimizer statistics and usage recommendations.
LOCK = n	Logs lock contentions longer than the specified centiseconds.
NONE	This disables logging.
OBJECTS	Log information about databases, tables, columns, and indexes accessed by SQL queries for the specified user set. This option does not log activity for macros or views, nor does it log activity for dictionary tables and columns.
SQL	Log the full text of all SQL statements performed by the specified user set in system table *DBQLSqlTbl*. This option does not log SQL statements within stored procedures, macros, views, or triggers.
STEPINFO	Log AMP step-level information for all SQL queries performed by the specified user set in system table *DBQLStepTbl*.
USECOUNT	Logs use count for a database or a user. If specified for a database, no other options can be used.
[VERBOSE]	Logs the query plan in XML format.

Option	Description
XMLPLAN	

Figure 8.12

The default row stored by DBQL is available through the view DBC.QryLogTDWMV.

DBC.QryLogTDWMV

AcctString	CollectTimeStamp	DefaultDatabase
DelayTime	ExceptionValue	FinalWDID
InternalRequestNum	LastStateChange	LogicalHostID
LSN	NoClassification	OpEnvID
ProcID	QueryID	RequestNum
ResponseTimeMet	SessionID	SessionWDID
StatementGroup	SysConID	TDWMAllAmpFlag
TDWMConfLevelUsed	TDWMEstLastRows	TDWMEstMaxRows
TDWMEstTotalTime	TDWMRuleID	UserID
UserName	WDDelayTime	WDID
WDOverride		

Figure 8.13

BEGIN QUERY LOGGING Examples

The following are some examples of the BEGIN QUERY LOGGING statement.

```
/* Log everything but do not create a second copy of the SQL */

BEGIN QUERY LOGGING WITH ALL LIMIT SQLTEXT = 0 ON CSQL01;
```

Figure 8.14

```
/* Do full logging of queries that exceed the threshold limit,
   otherwise simply count them  */

BEGIN QUERY LOGGING LIMIT THRESHOLD = 10 IOCOUNT
ON CSQL02;
```

Figure 8.15

```
/* Log information about databases, tables, columns, and indexes
   accessed by SQL queries for all users and accounts */

BEGIN QUERY LOGGING WITH OBJECTS ON ALL;
```

Figure 8.16

END QUERY LOGGING Statement

The following is the syntax diagram for the END QUERY LOGGING statement.

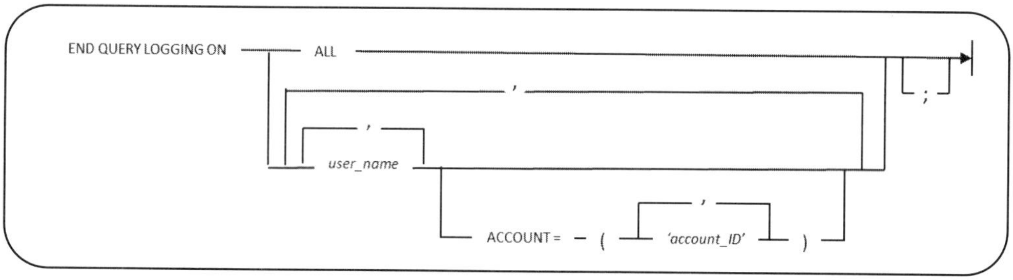

Figure 8.17

DBC.DBQLRulesV View

Here are the columns comprising the DBC.DBQLRulesV view.

DBC.DBQLRulesV

AccountString	ApplName	ExplainFlag
ObjFlag	SqlFlag	StatsUsageFlag
StepFlag	SummaryFlag	SummaryVal1
SummaryVal2	SummaryVal3	TextSizeLimit
ThresholdFlag	TypeOfCriterion	TypeOfRule
UserName	XMLPlanFlag	

Figure 8.18

The following is an example of the content of the Rules tables for the first example given above.

SELECT * FROM DBC.DBQLRULESV WHERE USERNAME = 'CSQL01';

```
 *** Query completed.  One row found.  13 columns returned.
 *** Total elapsed time was 1 second.

        UserName  CSQL01
         Account
         Explain  T
          Object  T
             SQL  T
            Step  T
         Summary  F
       Threshold  F
        TextSize        0
    Summary//Low        ?
             Med        ?
            High        ?
Threshold//Value        ?
```

Figure 8.19

DBC.QryLogV View

Here are the columns comprising the DBC.QryLogV view.

DBC.QryLogV

AbortFlag	AcctString	AcctStringDate
AcctStringHour	AcctStringTime	AMPCPUTime
AMPCPUTimeNorm	AppID	CacheFlag
CalendarName	CallNestingLevel	ClientAddr
ClientID	CollectTimeStamp	CPUDecayLevel
DataCollectAlg	DefaultDatabase	ElapsedTime
ErrorCode	ErrorText	EstMaxRowCount
EstProcTime	EstResultRows	ExpandAcctString
FirstRespTime	FirstStepTime	InternalRequestNum
IODecayLevel	KeepFlag	LogicalHostID
LogonDateTime	LogonSource	LSN
MaxAMPCPUTime	MaxAMPCPUTimeNorm	MaxAmpIO
MaxCPUAmpNumber	MaxCPUAmpNumberNorm	MaxIOAmpNumber
MaxStepsInPar	MinAmpCPUTime	MinAmpCPUTimeNorm
MinAmpIO	NumOfActiveAMPs	NumRequestCtx
NumResultRows	NumSteps	NumStepswPar
ParserCPUTime	ParserCPUTimeNorm	ParserExpReq
ProcID	ProfileID	ProxyRole
ProxyUser	QueryBand	QueryID
QueryRedriven	QueryText	ReDriveKind
ReqIOKB	ReqPhysIO	ReqPhysIOKB
RequestNum	SeqRespTime	SessionID
SessionTemporalQualifier	SpoolUsage	StartTime
StatementGroup	StatementType	TacticalCPUException
TacticalIOException	TotalIOCount	UserID
UserName	UtilityRowCount	WarningOnly

Figure 8.20

DBC.QryLogSummaryV View

Here are the columns of the DBC.QryLogSummaryV view. This view is populated only if summary information is requested or a threshold value is used.

DBC.QryLogSummaryV

AcctString	AMPCPUTime	AMPCPUTimeNorm
AppID	AverageAmpCPU	AverageAmpCPUNorm
AverageIO	AverageParserCPU	AverageParserCPUNorm
AverageTime	ClientAddr	ClientID
CollectTimeStamp	HighHist	LogicalHostID
LowHist	ParserCPUTime	ParserCPUTimeNorm
ProcID	ProfileID	QueryCount
QuerySeconds	SessionID	TotalIOCount
UserID	ValueType	

Figure 8.21

Teradata Administrator - Query Logging

Here is the window in Teradata Administrator that allows you to establish the query log rules mentioned above. It's found under **Tools->Query Logging.**

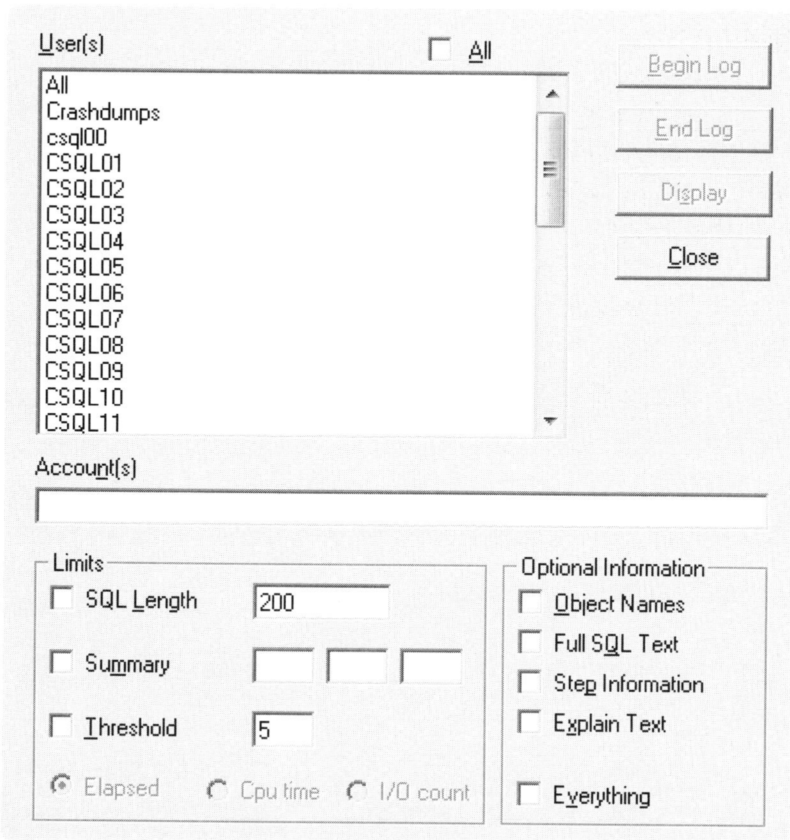

Figure 8.22

Practice Questions

1. Which of the following should be used for performance analysis?
    a. Access Logging
    b. DBQL
    c. DBC.LogOnOffV
    d. Teradata Administrator

2. Which of the following cannot appear on a BEGIN LOGGING command?
    a. FUNCTION
    b. PROCEDURE
    c. TRIGGER
    d. VIEW

3. Which of the following objects cannot have access logged directly?
    a. TYPE
    b. JOIN INDEX
    c. FUNCTION
    d. PROCEDURE

4. Which table also includes Query Band information?
    a. DBC.DBQLogTbl
    b. DBC.DBQLObjTbl
    c. DBC.DBQLStepTbl
    d. DBC.DBQLSumaryTbl

5. Which table has no primary index (NoPI) and is not fallback protected?
    a. DBC.DBQLExplainTbl
    b. DBC.DBQLStepTbl
    c. DBC.DBQLXMLTbl
    d. DBC.DBQLXMLLockTbl

6. In the BEGIN QUERY LOGGING statement, the LOCK = *n* option specifies time in which of the following increments?
    a. Seconds
    b. Tenths of a second
    c. Centiseconds
    d. Milliseconds

Chapter Notes

Utilize this space for notes, key points to remember, diagrams, areas of further study, etc.

Chapter 9 - System Administration Tools

Certification Objectives

- ✓ Given a scenario, identify the management and maintenance tool that should be used (Teradata Administrator, Viewpoint, Teradata Multi-System Manager (TMSM), etc.).
- ✓ Given a scenario, identify the analysis tool that should be used (Show Locks, Recovery Manager, Teradata Index Wizard, Teradata Statistics Wizard, Teradata System Emulation Tool, Teradata Visual Explain, Locking Logger, etc.
- ✓ Identify the actions taken using object use count.

Before You Begin

You should be familiar with the following terms and concepts.

Terms	Key Concepts
Statistics	How they help the Optimizer
Indexes	How various indexes work
Explain	How to explain both single and multi-statement requests

Teradata Administrator

Teradata Administrator is a Windows-based GUI interface to perform a multitude of database administration tasks.

After logging on, here is the initial screen.

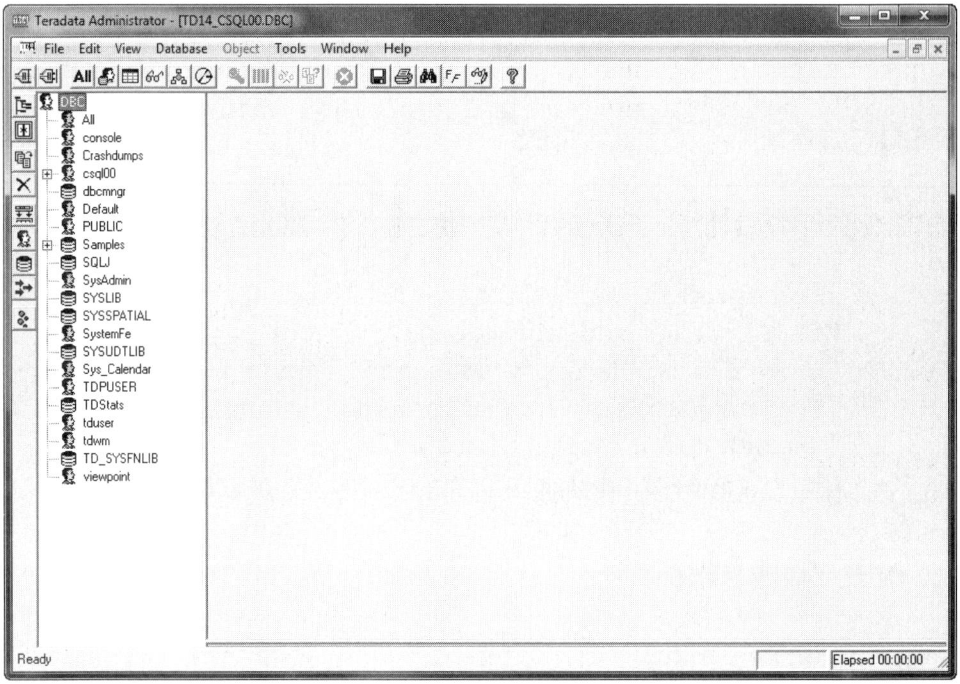

Figure 9.1

With Teradata Administrator, you can perform the following tasks.

- Copy Table, View or Macro definitions to another database, or to another system
- Create Tables (using ANSI or Teradata syntax)
- Create, Modify and Drop Databases, Users, Roles, Profiles, and User-Defined Types
- Display information about a Database, or Users
- Display information about a Table, View, or Macro
- Drop or Rename Tables, Views, or Macros
- Grant or Revoke access and system rights
- Move space from one database to another
- Run an SQL query
- Set up the rules for Query and Access Logging

Teradata Administrator keeps a record of all the actions taken, and that record can be copied to a file. This history contains a timestamp, the SQL that is executed, and additional information such as the statements' success or failure.

Teradata Multi-System Manager (TMSM)

Teradata Multi-System Manager (TMSM) is part of the Teradata Dual Active Solution and is designed to handle multiple Teradata systems. TMSM enables coordination between systems and enables the database administrator to manage their data warehouse environments from a single console from both a system and application level. The following are the features of TMSM:

- Unified View - A multi-system environment includes supporting servers for data loading, query routing and applications. A centralized console enables a view of the system's status and key events within the environment with a drill-down feature to determine which processes are running or have been completed on each system. It also provides feedback on the health and operational status of all components.

- Monitoring - Beyond a unified view, intelligent monitoring of numerous events within the environment is provided, including detection of system operational status and the per-system completion status of processes such as load jobs.

- Simplified User Interface - A graphical user interface portal with easy-to-use controls to manage query routing rules, engage or disengage a system for planned maintenance, or bring a system back online and up to date after an unplanned outage.

- Application routing - Sophisticated controls manage which applications and users can access which system, based on its particular data currency and process completion. This capability ensures that a system is available and has current data before allowing application and user access.

- Thresholds and discrepancy reporting - Managing multiple systems simultaneously requires a level of control as to how current the data is between the systems. Depending on how the systems are used and which users are accessing them, some amount of data-drift can be tolerated. Anything beyond this acceptable amount will require the synchronization lag to be tightened. Alerts will indicate when the thresholds are crossed. The system can also be programmed to take pre-defined actions when this occurs.

- Failover and failback - When the objective is continuous access for users, one of the most valuable features in managing a dual-system environment is the coordination of events to handle system outages. This requires shifting workloads and users between systems during planned and unplanned outages.

Teradata Viewpoint

Teradata Viewpoint is a portal-based system management solution that enables DBAs and system administrators to access Teradata system performance information from a web browser. Teradata Viewpoint offers the following benefits:

- Allows for real-time, proactive and historical monitoring
- Provides self-service tools to end-users through a standard web browser
- Enables broader access to vital decision making data
- Simplifies update and upgrade processes

- Manages multiple Teradata server instances from a single location
- Provides flexibility to deploy your own customized portlets

The major components of Teradata Viewpoint are:

- **Viewpoint Server:** The hardware platform on which the solution stack is installed.

- **Viewpoint Portal:** A web portal framework for delivering client applications.

- **Collection Server:** A daemon process that collects statistics and data from the Teradata system or systems being monitored.

- **Portlet Bundles:** All new client applications are being delivered as portlet(s) (a portlet is a small, reusable Web component). Portlets with a similar subject area are being packaged and delivered as a bundle for easier and more logical packaging and administration.

Teradata Analyst Pack

There is a suite of software tools called the Teradata Analyst Pack. This suite of tools targets query or workload-based analysis and focuses on the execution performance at the individual query level. Tools include:

- Teradata Index Wizard
- Teradata Statistics Wizard
- Teradata Visual Explain
- Teradata System Emulation Tool

Teradata Analyst Pack should be used at a time that will not impact Production. Keeping the query workload set to 15 – 20 queries is a manageable size for in-depth analysis by the tool and the database administrator. Execute against different workloads for optimal results. We will begin our discussion with Teradata Index Wizard.

Teradata Index Wizard

Teradata Index Wizard is a front-end GUI client application that works the Parsing Engine optimizer component that enables this tool to compute, simulate, and evaluate candidates for index selection. This tool, which is installed with Microsoft Windows, empowers users with easy-to-use steps to define workload definitions, index analysis along with providing and reports for both operations. This interface is illustrated in Figure 9.2.

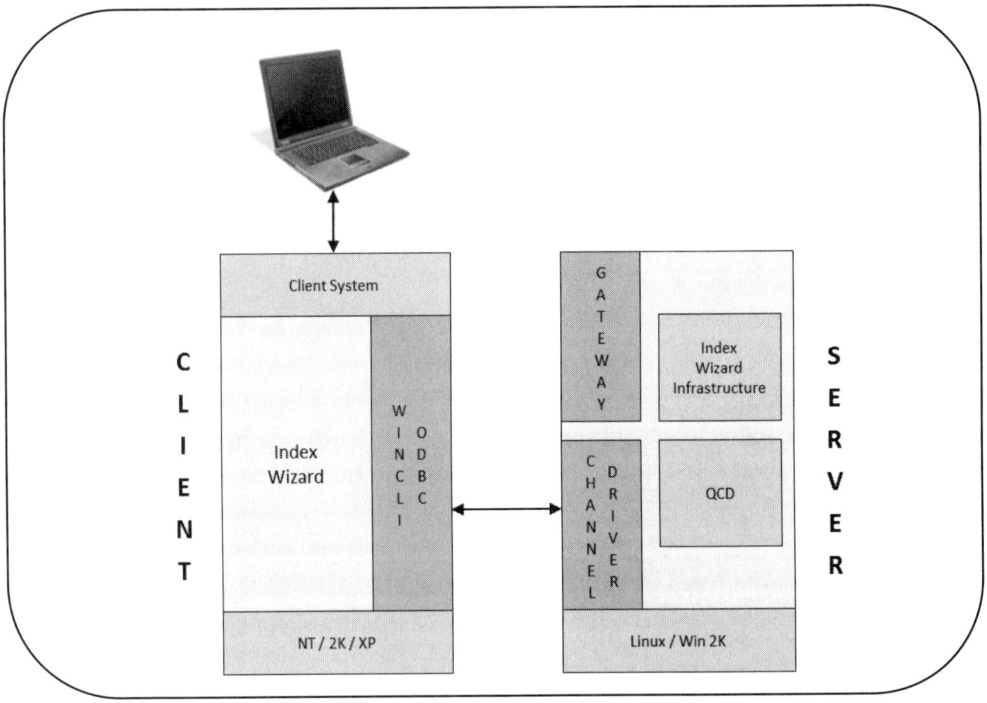

Figure 9.2

In addition, Teradata Index Wizard is integrated with the Database Query Log (DBQL). With this feature, you have the ability to analyze SQL statements that are collected in the query log, and based on the analysis; you can start to define workloads.

DBQL works with other client tools such as Teradata Statistics Wizard, Teradata System Emulation Tool, and Teradata Visual Explain. However, before you can create and analyze a workload using these tools, you must configure a Query Capture Database (QCD). Please see the Teradata Visual Explain section in this chapter for setup and configuration steps.

Once defined, workloads can be imported for analysis on a test or development system before they are promoted to production. It can also be utilized to evaluate and simulate index recommendations on the production system before implementing.

Basic Index Wizard Steps

The following steps describe what you do:

1. Define a workload.

   A workload is a set of SQL statements created or defined using the workload definition dialog box. Index Wizard creates several workload reports after a workload is defined.

   - Using Database Query Log (DBQL)
   - Using statement text
   - From QCD statements
   - Importing workload
   - From an existing workload

2. Workload is analyzed.

After the workload is defined, it is analyzed and a new set of indexes are recommended. Index Wizard may also recommend that indexes be added or dropped to enhance system performance.

There are four types of analysis:

- Index analysis
- Partition analysis
- Restarting an analysis
- What-if analysis

3. Indexes are recommended.

   Index Wizard creates several reports about workloads and indexes. Some reports are created when a workload is defined. Others are created when a workload is analyzed.

4. Index recommendations are validated (optional).

   Index Wizard validates index recommendations on a production system without actually updating the production table index. This feature is optional, but highly recommended because it ensures the index recommendation will help database performance before actually adding the indexes.

   The execution plans obtained with the recommendation can be compared with the original query plans (those without the index recommendations) using Teradata Visual Explain's Compare feature. Index Wizard interfaces with Teradata Visual Explain to provide a query-by-query compare.

5. Index recommendations are applied to the production system.

After an index recommendation is validated, Index Wizard allows you to apply (execute) the index to the production system. You can execute an index immediately or schedule the execution to occur at a different time and day.

Here is the main Teradata Index Wizard window.

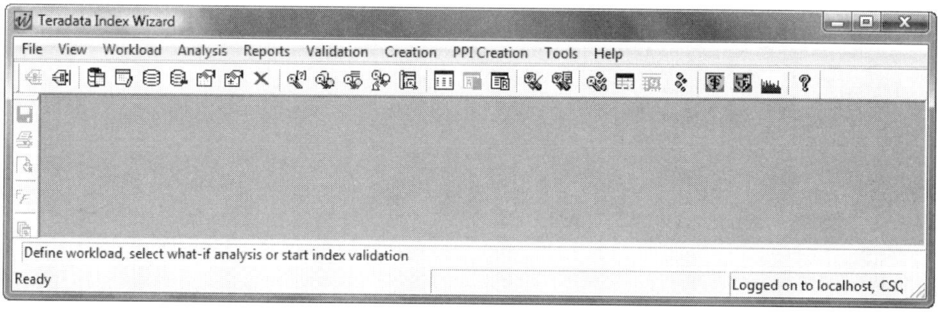

Figure 9.3

The following is an example of a table, a query, and the index analysis report created.

```
CREATE SET TABLE CSQL_CLASS.phcall ,NO FALLBACK ,
     NO BEFORE JOURNAL,
     NO AFTER JOURNAL,
     CHECKSUM = DEFAULT
     (
      area_code SMALLINT,
      phone_no INTEGER,
      call_st TIMESTAMP(0),
      call_et TIMESTAMP(0),
      call_ac SMALLINT,
      call_ph INTEGER)
PRIMARY INDEX ( area_code ,phone_no )
INDEX ( area_code );
```

Figure 9.4

The following window appears under **Workload->Create->Using Statement Text**

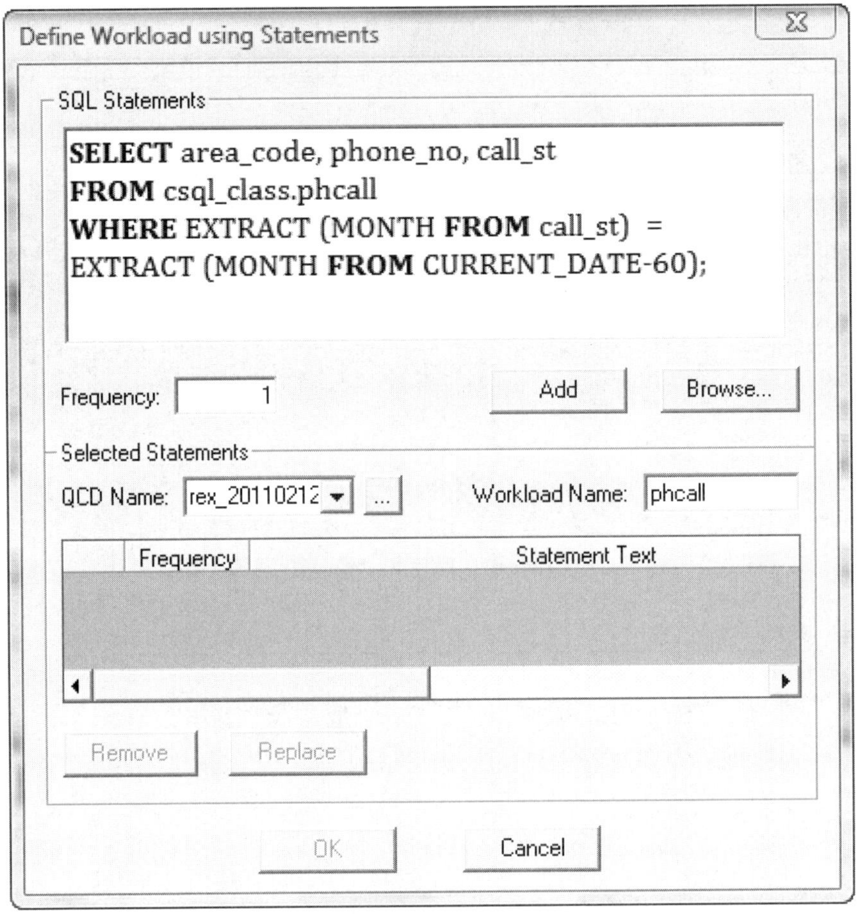

Figure 9.5

The next window appears under **Analysis->Index Analysis**

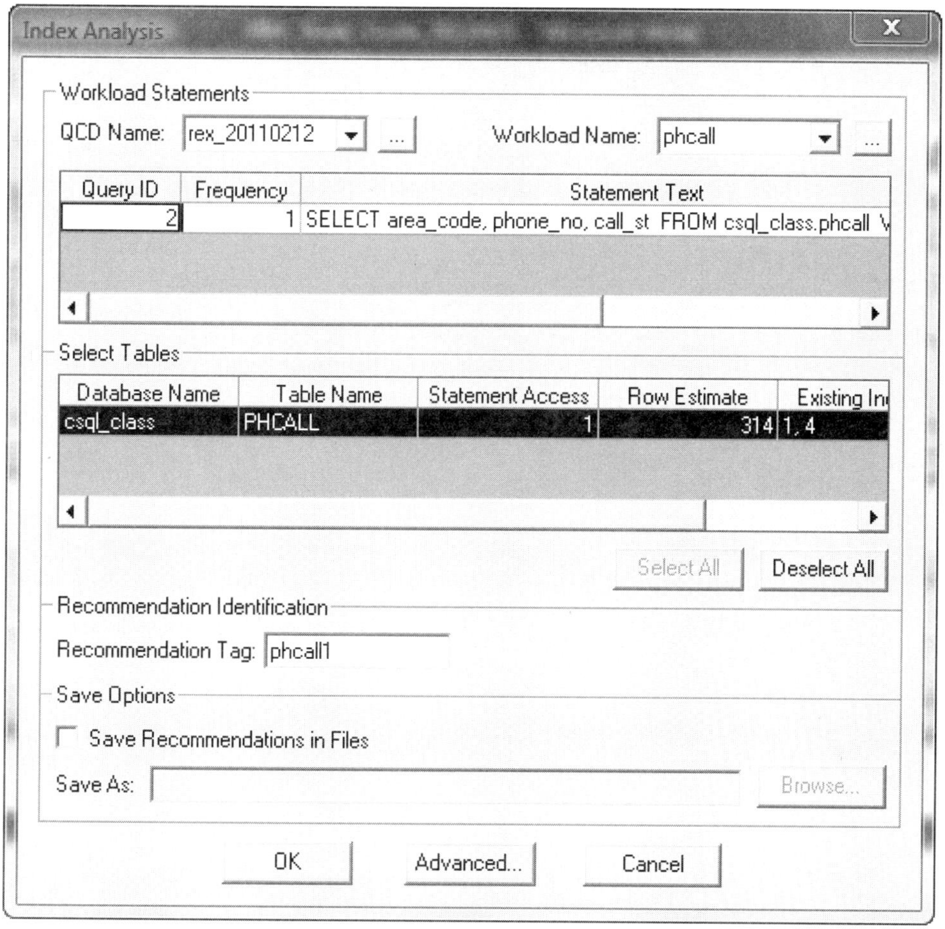

Figure 9.6

The next window appears under **Reports->Current Workload->Index Recommendations**

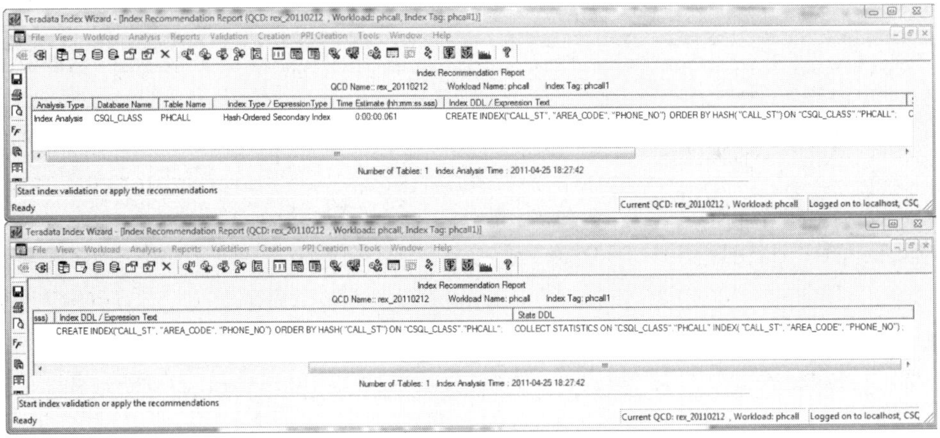

Figure 9.7

Notice the recommendation to create a Hash-Ordered NUSI, followed by the appropriate Collect Statistics statement in the following two (left/right) displays.

The reports that are available are Workload Reports and Analysis Reports.

This Workload Report	**Shows**
Existing Indexes Report	This view displays information about the tables such as index types, unique flags, and index names.
Update Frequency Report	Provides percentage information on UPDATE statements on tables.
Table Usage Analysis Report	Information based on frequency in which the table is accessed within the workload.
Table Scan Report	This view displays usage information of a table. Parameters

This Workload Report	Shows
	include cardinality, AMP usage, and geography information in the workload.
Workload Analysis Report	Provides estimates based on the cost of a workload as it compares to the entire workload including statement text, frequency, and column types.
Object Global Use Count Report	Count information that identifies the objects that are most frequently accessed.

Figure 9.8

This Analysis Report	Shows
Index Recommendation Report	Offers suggestions for Secondary indexes based on analysis.
Query Cost Analysis Report	Analyzes the cost associated with specific types of statements (SELECT, INSERT, DELETE) as it compares to the original index to the proposed recommended index.
Disk Space Analysis Report	Estimates the storage required to create the recommended indexes
Summary Report	Provides secondary index counts and recommendations for all tables in the workload.
Index Maintenance Cost Report	Estimates cost of maintaining indexes based on a particular recommendationID for a specific workload.

Figure 9.9

Index validation verifies if the recommended indexes will actually improve system performance. However, it does not execute the recommended indexes, but instead, uses the Parsing Engine Optimizer component to generate new plans with the recommended indexes.

Note: Index Wizard sample statistics saves them in the QCD. The sampled statistics are used for the index validation process.

The validation is conducted during the simulated session mode. This is where the recommendations for the indexes are tested for the plan generation. These recommendations are compared, analyzed, and validated on the set of SQL statements. The statements are submitted in a “no execute” phase, and the plans are saved into the QCD.

Validation can be done several ways:

Analysis performed on	Validation performed on
Production System	Production System
Test System	Production System
Production System	Test System (not recommended)
Test System	Test System (not recommended)

Figure 9.10

Once validation is complete, Index Wizard has an execute recommendation feature that allows you to execute index recommendations immediately or schedule them for a later time.

Here is an example using the phcall table. The window appears under **Creation->Execute Immediately**

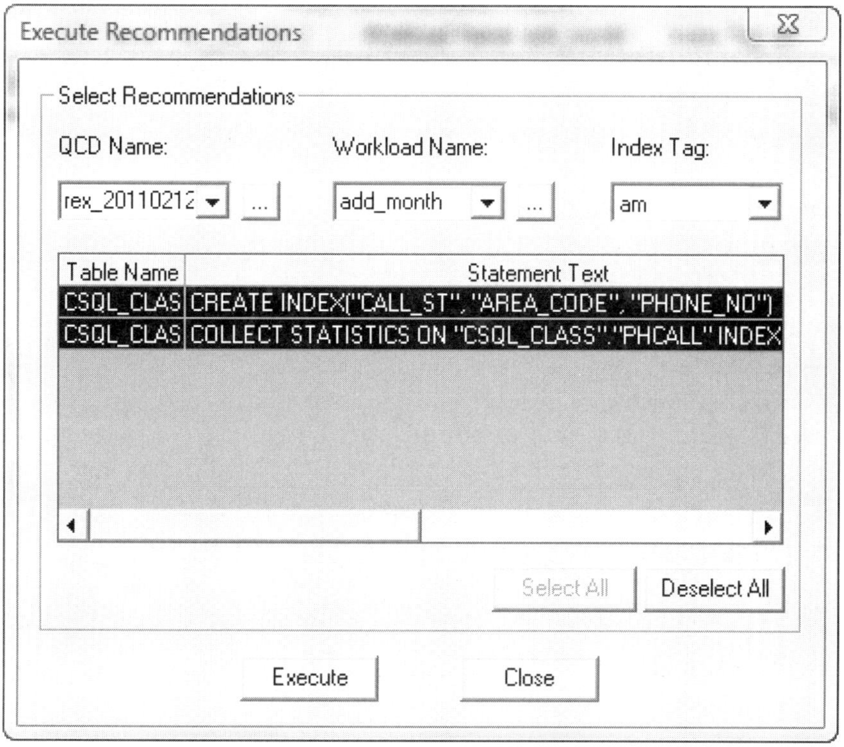

Figure 9.11

Here is the Show Table after execution of the recommendation.

```
CREATE SET TABLE CSQL_CLASS.phcall ,NO FALLBACK ,
   NO BEFORE JOURNAL,
   NO AFTER JOURNAL,
   CHECKSUM = DEFAULT
   (
    area_code SMALLINT,
    phone_no INTEGER,
    call_st TIMESTAMP(0),
    call_et TIMESTAMP(0),
    call_ac SMALLINT,
    call_ph INTEGER)
PRIMARY INDEX ( area_code ,phone_no )
INDEX ( area_code )
INDEX ( area_code ,phone_no ,call_st ) ORDER BY HASH ( call_st );
```

Figure 9.12

Teradata Statistics Wizard

Statistics Wizard can be utilized in automating the process of collecting statistics for a particular workload, indexes, and/or columns identified for collection/re-collection. You can also validate recommended statistics on the production system before applying in order to verify the performance of the proposed statistics.

Using the Explorer Tree, Statistics Wizard displays all of the tables in the selected database.

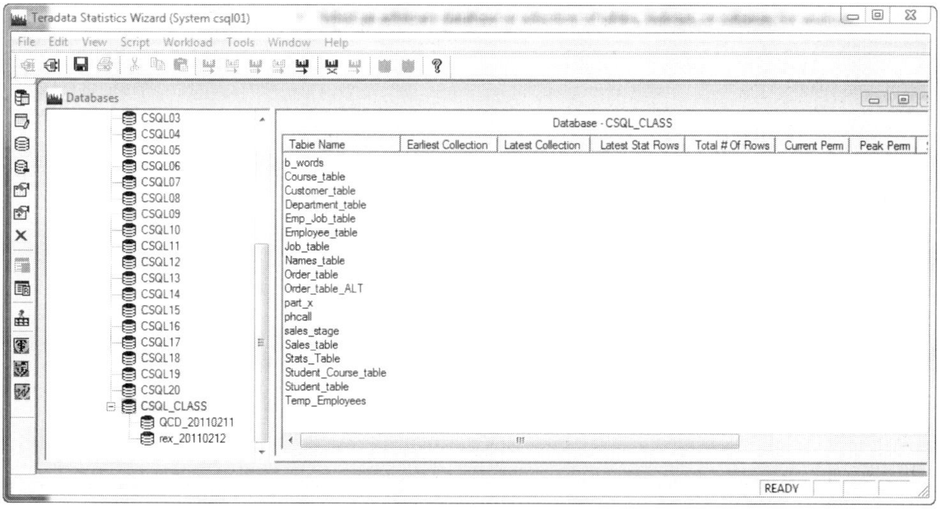

Figure 9.13

Statistics Wizard provides the database administrator (DBA) with the following:

- Analyze a specified workload for recommendations to improve query performance in a workload.
- Select tables, indexes, or columns for arbitrary analysis, collection, or re-collection of statistics.
- Provide recommendations on specific workloads, table demographics, and basic heuristics.
- Schedule collection and dropping of statistics.
- Modify the interval for statistics collection on column or index.

As the database changes, Statistics Wizard can continue to provide analysis and recommendations on tables where statistics are needed. These are based on a number of data demographics such as age of data, table growth; along with identify columns/indexes that would improve with statistics for a specific workload. Finally, the DBA can either accept or reject the recommendations.

The steps for Best Practices are:

- Identify the set of SQL statements that must be analyzed for performance improvements.
- Define the identified set of SQL statements. This will be known as a workload.
- Run the statistics analysis.
- Validate the statistics.
- Apply or schedule the execution of the recommendations.

Like the Index Wizard, the first step is to define a workload. This can be done in the following ways.

- From DBQL Statements
- Using Statement Text
- From QCD Statements
- Importing a Workload
- From an Existing Workload

Double-clicking on a table produces the current statistics information, as shown in the following two (left/right) displays.

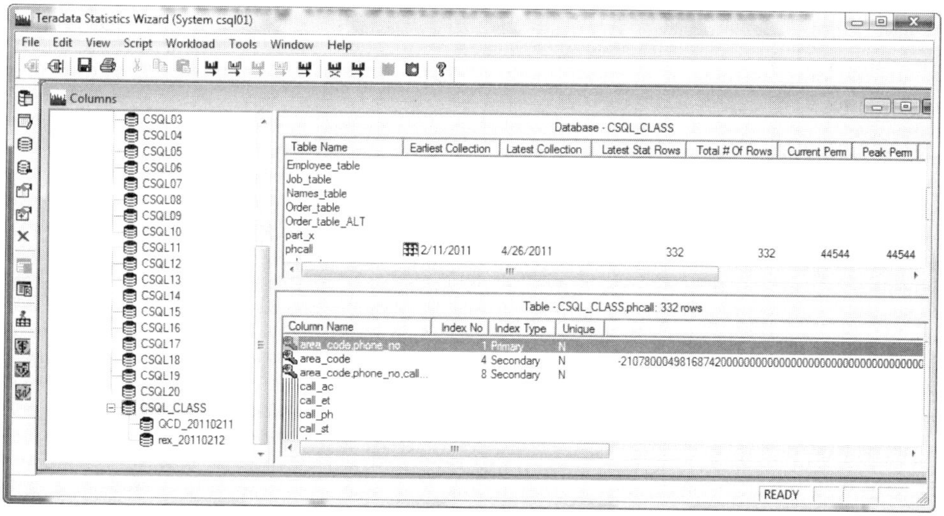

Figure 9.14

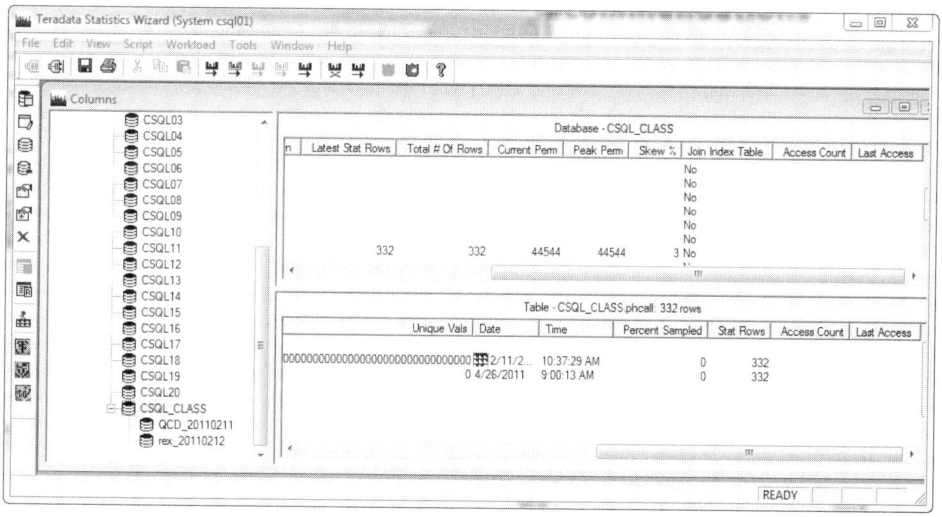

Figure 9.15

Once you define a workload, then generate the recommendations by clicking on **Workload>Reports>Current Workload>Statistics Recommendations**

The reports available are:

This Report	Shows
Statistics Recommendations Report	Provides recommended statistics in the workload for tables.
Update Cost Analysis Report	The total number of statements within the workload based on a percentage that are UPDATE statements.
Table Usage Report	Show the frequency of access for a table within the workload.
Table Scan Report	Displays workload statistics on how a table is used based cardinality, AMP usage, and geography information.
Workload Analysis Report	Offers comparative cost estimates of a relative workload to the entire workload, statement text, frequency, and column types.

Figure 9.16

After examining the recommendations, then click on **Workload>Execute/Schedule Recommendations**, and select the recommendation(s) you want to implement.

By clicking on Tools->Options, you can set parameters that will guide Statistics Wizard. In the Recommendations tab (below), the allowable skew for NUPIs set to 5%. The rest are current defaults.

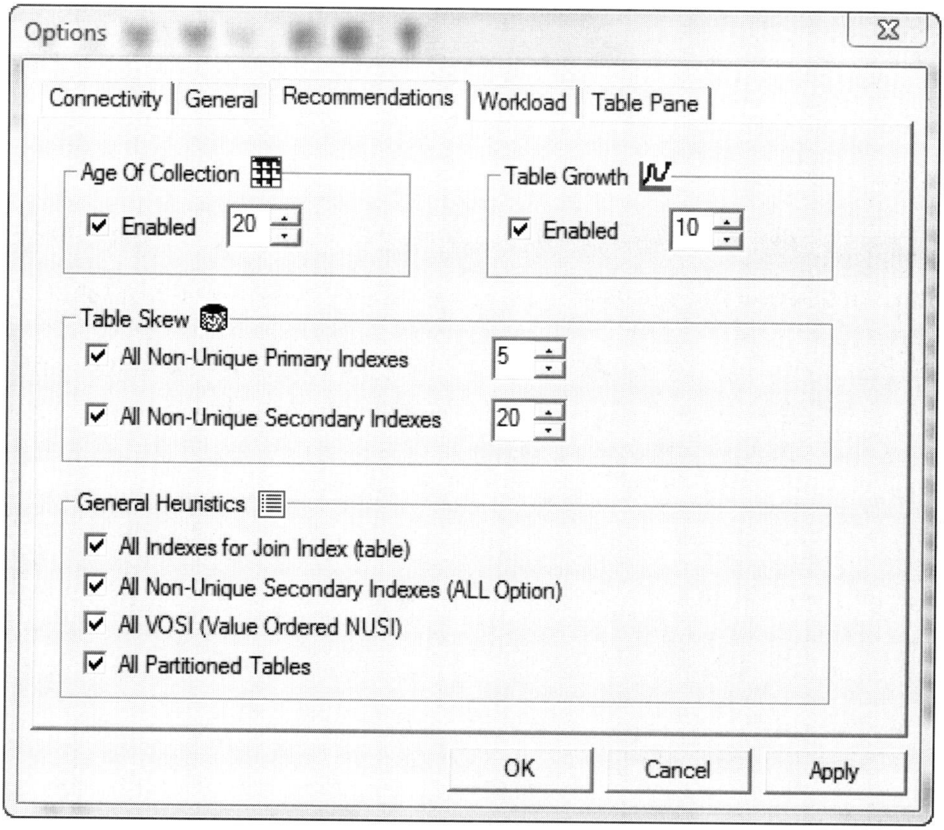

Figure 9.17

In the Table Pane tab in the next example, the first three options were selected.

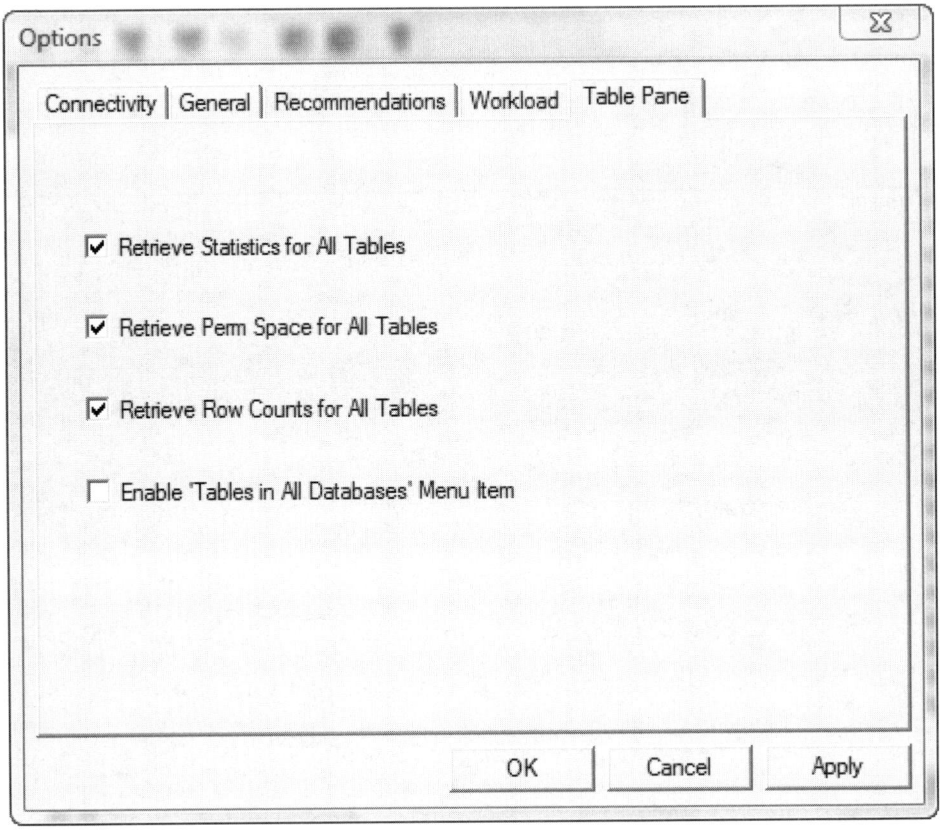

Figure 9.18

Then, using the Explorer Tree, a different database was selected, with the following results.

Note: In the display below, notice the three tables that were flagged because their skew is => 5%.

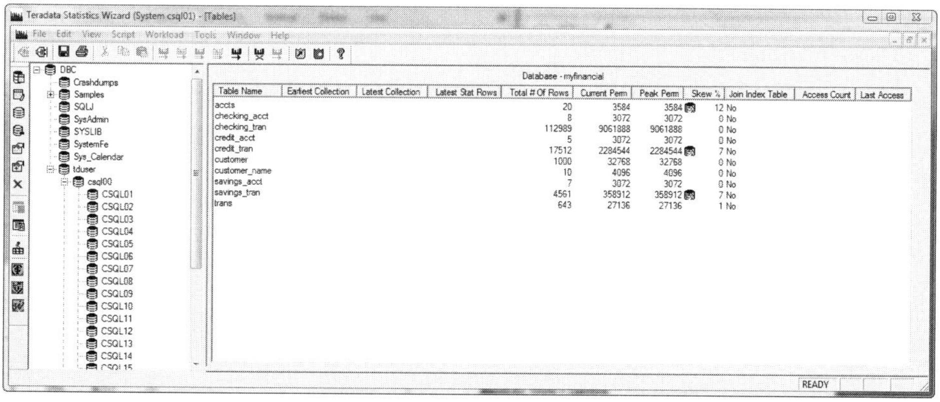

Figure 9.19

Teradata System Emulation Tool

Teradata SET (TSET) enables you to emulate a production system using a test system. Basically, system-level data is captured from the production system, and then imported into the test system. The Teradata Optimizer gathers information from the tables, along with appropriate column and index statistics, in order to build query plans on a test system that can simulate as the production environment.

The following diagram illustrates the relationship between TSET, target systems, and test systems.

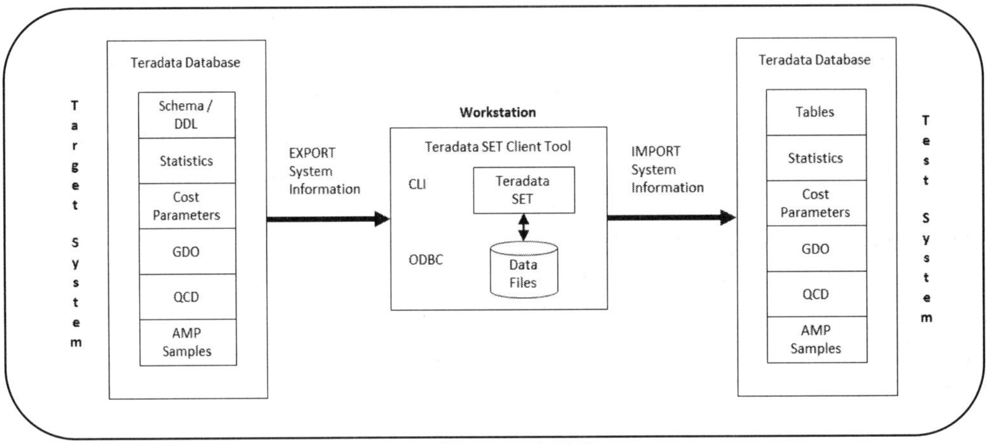

Figure 9.20

Imported data is used to:

- Simulate Optimizer performance of the production system. Execution plans are generated based on several factors including indexes, primary and secondary keys, and available statistics and resources. These factors provide the Optimizer with a accurate execution plan.
- Create query plans that emulate the target system under a variety of conditions. A small test system can be used to create query plans that simulate a production system.
- Conduct *what-if scenarios*.
- Resolve and test Optimizer-related performance scenarios that might occur on the production system.

Note: Teradata Visual Explain can use TSET to simulate how a production system will perform under specific conditions and workloads.

TSET also synchronizes all of the configuration settings, databases, data models, and data dependencies to maintain the correct relationships when exported and imported. In addition, database objects such as tables, views, macros, triggers, join indexes, and stored procedures are duplicated on the test system and function as if they were on the production system. The use of TSET enables users to thoroughly debug and optimize queries in a safe, but equivalent simulated environment before integrating them into production.

Prior to performing export operations, make sure the access rights are set. The SHOW QUALIFIED SQL statement and configuration data (Random AMP Sample (RAS), statistics, object definitions) is required in order for these objects to be returned from this statement and exported.

The following table lists the access rights required to export each type of information.

Exported Information	Required Rights
Cost parameters	INSERT, SELECT, and DELETE on *SystemFE.Opt_Cost_Table* and *SystemFE.Opt_DBSCtl_Table*.
Execution plans	For an existing plan: • SELECT on the QCD tables or on the QCD • EXECUTE on QCD macros DUMP EXPLAIN right for a new query. For a new plans with accompanied demographics: • INSERT EXPLAIN statement for the given query • EXECUTE on the QCD macros.
Object definitions	SHOW statement for join indexes, macros,

Exported Information	Required Rights
	tables, triggers, stored procedures, and User-Defined Types (UDTs). SELECT and SHOW QUALIFIED to export object definitions for a view statement. SELECT on DBC.ColumnsV and DBC.TablesV to export databases and referenced UDTs.
Machine configuration	MONRESOURCE on the database.
RAS	SELECT for tables for export. INSERT, SELECT, and DELETE on *SystemFE.Opt_RAS_Table*.
Statistics	HELP STATISTICS on the tables or join index referenced. SELECT on the DBC.IndexStatsV, DBC.ColumnStatsV, and DBC.MultiColumnStatsV views.
Demographics	SELECT on the data demographics table and related views of the table. COLLECT DEMOGRAPHICS statement on the tables indentified, SELECT on QCD views. EXECUTE on QCD macros.
QCD data	SELECT on QCD tables and views. EXECUTE on QCD macros.
Workloads	SELECT on QCD tables and views. EXECUTE on QCD macros.

Exported Information	Required Rights
Cost profiles	SELECT on the DBC.CostProfiles_v and DBC.CostProfileValues_v views.

Figure 9.21

Set access rights prior to performing import operations. The following table lists the access rights required to import each type of information.

Imported Information	Required Rights
Cost parameters	INSERT access on *SystemFE.Opt_Cost_Table* and *SystemFE.Opt_DBSCtl_Table*.
Execution plans	INSERT, SELECT, and UPDATE on tables and views for the QCD database.
Object definitions	CREATE access on the user or database for objects being imported. CREATE PROCEDURE WITH GRANT OPTION for the stored procedures on the database. UDTTYPE access on the SYSUDTLIB database for creating the UDT. UDTUSAGE access to CREATE TABLE statement for the UDT.
RAS	INSERT on *SystemFE.Opt_RAS_Table*.
Statistics	COLLECT STATISTICS privileges for all tables or join indexes referenced.
Demographics	INSERT, SELECT, and UPDATE on the table and associated views. EXECUTE for macros.
QCD data	INSERT, SELECT, and UPDATE on QCD tables.

Imported Information	Required Rights
	SELECT on QCD views.
Workloads	INSERT, SELECT, and UPDATE on QCD tables. SELECT on QCD views.
Cost profiles	EXECUTE on the DBC.CreateNewCostProfile and DBC.InsertConstantValue macros.

Figure 9.22

The next table lists the access rights required in order to restore the default test system environment (also known as *undo-import* or *cleanup* operations).

Undo-Import Information	Required Rights
Cost parameters	DELETE on *SystemFE.Opt_Cost_Table* and *SystemFE.Opt_DBSCtl_Table* or on the SystemFE object.
Execution plans	DELETE on the tables or on the QCD database. EXECUTE on QCD macros.
Object definitions	DROP or DELETE rights on the parent database or object.
RAS	DELETE on *SystemFE.Opt_RAS_Table* or on the SystemFE database.
Statistics	DROP STATISTICS privileges for the tables or join indexes referenced.
Demographics	DELETE on the tables and the associated views of the table. EXECUTE on macros.

Undo-Import Information	Required Rights
QCD data	DELETE on tables and views. EXECUTE on macros.
Workloads	DELETE on tables and views. EXECUTE on macros.
Cost profiles	EXECUTE on the DBC.DeleteCostProfile macro.

Figure 9.23

Below is the main SET window.

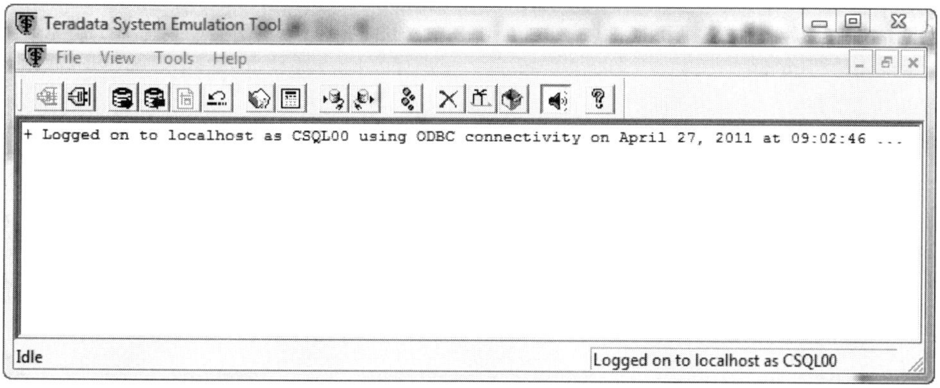

Figure 9.24

The following are the menu items and their function.

MENU	COMMAND	DESCRIPTION
File	Connect	Log onto the Teradata Database.
	Disconnect	Log off the Teradata Database.
	Exit	Exits TSET and returns to the Microsoft Windows desktop.
View	Log File	Open or close a log file.
	Summary Report	Provides a report that summarizes the successes / failures of an import, export, or undo import (cleanup) operation.
	Font	Enables you to change the font style, size, or color for text displayed in the main window (i.e. modify the font used when displaying the log file or summary report.
	Toolbar	Option to show or hide the main window toolbar.
	Status Bar	Option to show or hide the status bar in the main / **Import** windows.
Tools	Export	Capture information from a target system during the simulation.
	Import	Import edit exported emulation information, and then load that onto a test system.
	Undo Import	**Opens** a dialog box and enables you to specify a single *.undo* file and remove it from a test system.
	Customize Data	Provides a window to select an *.mcf* file so you can edit the simulation information without being connected to Teradata Database.
	Set TLE	Opens **Set Target Level Emulation** dialog box to enable you to specify RAS,

MENU	COMMAND	DESCRIPTION
		cost parameters, and cost profiles that are simulated on the connected system.
	Reset TLE	Opens the **Reset Target Level Emulation** dialog box to enable you to reset RAS, cost parameters, and cost profiles to default values.
	Delete Files	Opens the **Delete** dialog box to remove selected TSET files. The *.mcf* files are read and based on the export options specified, the associated file types (i.e. *.ddl* and *.opt*) are deleted.
	Pack	Opens the **Pack** dialog box and combines the *.mcf* file and its corresponding files into one file (*.pack*).
	Unpack	Opens the **Unpack** dialog box to separate the files in the *.pack* file.
	Define Data Source	Opens the **ODBC Database Administrator** dialog box to enable you to specify or edit the ODBC data sources.
	Execute SQL	Displays the query editor (SQL Assistant or Execute SQL) to execute queries. Click **Tools>Options** to open the editor.
	Options	Opens the **Options** dialog box to enable you to customize TSET features.
Help	Help Topics	Open online help.
	About Teradata System Emulation Tool	Shows version and copyright information.

Figure 9.25

Clicking on **Tools->Import** brings up a new window with the following menu items.

MENU	COMMAND	DESCRIPTION
File	Save As	Opens the **Save As** dialog box to enable you to rename an edited file.
	Import	Import simulation information to a target system.
	Exit	Close the **Import** window and return to the main window.
Edit	Undo	Undo the last edit.
	Cut	Enables selected text to move to the Clipboard.
	Copy	Copy specified text to the Clipboard.
	Paste	Inserts text from the Clipboard.
	Find	Opens the **Find** dialog box to search for text in the left or right pane.
	Replace	Replace selected text.
	Select All	Select all of the text in the window.
	Allow Edit	Toggles to edit mode so you can modify object definitions, RAS, statistics, cost parameters, and cost profiles in the **Import** window.
	Apply Changes	Saves edits to the definitions, RAS, statistic, cost parameter, or cost profile.
View	Tool Bar	Display or minimize the **Import** window toolbar.
	Status Bar	Display or minimize the status bar in the main *and* **Import** windows.
	Font	Opens the **Font** dialog box so you can modify the font style, size, or color for text displayed under **Object Definitions Information** and **Explain Text Information** in the **Import** window.

MENU	COMMAND	DESCRIPTION
	Source Machine Configuration	Opens the **Source Machine Configuration** dialog box to view the configuration characteristics of the system from the simulation information that was exported (the target system).
	Estimate Time	Opens the **Estimated Time** dialog box to view the estimated time required for the import operation.
Options	Existing Databases	Opens the **Existing Databases** dialog box to list the existing databases.
	Import Options	Opens the **Import Options** dialog box to specify the databases and simulation information for an import operation.
	Order Databases	Provides the reordering of databases at the same level in the left pane of the **Import** window.
	Set TLE	Opens the **Set Target Level Emulation** dialog box to list the RAS, cost parameters, and cost profiles exported from a target system. Use the dialog box to define the simulation information imported to a target system.
	Change PermSpace	Opens the **Change PermSpace** dialog box to define different permanent space than the automatic calculated value by TSET. Permanent space is required in order to import objects on a target system.
Help	Help Topics	Open online help.
	About TSET	Shows version and copyright information.

Figure 9.26

The Export feature of TSET can be customized to ensure that the test system imitates the features of the target system being analyzed. The following topics explain how to capture information from a target system.

Export by Query

This export option identifies database objects to export via DML statements. The export-by-query, through the use of DML statements as input, uses the SHOW QUALIFIED statement.

Note: Data Definition Language (DDL) statements are not used with the export-by-query option.

The SHOW QUALIFIED command returns the CREATE VIEW text and the CREATE TABLE text of any tables referenced by the view. The same holds true for macros. Here's a view example.

SHOW QUALIFIED SELECT * FROM csql_views.sales_table;

```
*** Text of DDL statement returned.
 *** Total elapsed time was 1 second.

-------------------------------------------------------------
CREATE SET TABLE CSQL_CLASS.sales_table ,NO FALLBACK ,
     NO BEFORE JOURNAL,
     NO AFTER JOURNAL,
     CHECKSUM = DEFAULT
     (
      Product_ID INTEGER NOT NULL,
      Sale_Date DATE FORMAT 'YYYY-MM-DD',
      Daily_Sales DECIMAL(9,2))
PRIMARY INDEX ( Product_ID )
INDEX ( Sale_Date );


 *** Text of DDL statement returned.
-------------------------------------------------------------
CREATE VIEW "CSQL_VIEWS"."Sales_Table" AS
SELECT "CSQL_CLASS"."sales_table"."Product_ID"
,"CSQL_CLASS"."sales_table"."Sale_Date"
,"CSQL_CLASS"."sales_table"."Daily_Sales"
FROM "CSQL_CLASS"."sales_table" ;
```

Figure 9.27

Here's a macro example.

SHOW QUALIFIED EXEC empjob;

```
*** Text of DDL statement returned.
*** Total elapsed time was 1 second.

-----------------------------------------------------------
CREATE SET TABLE CSQL_CLASS.employee_table ,NO FALLBACK ,
     NO BEFORE JOURNAL,
     NO AFTER JOURNAL,
     CHECKSUM = DEFAULT
     (
      Employee_No INTEGER NOT NULL,
      Dept_No SMALLINT,
      Mgr_employee_no INTEGER,
      Last_name CHAR(20) CHARACTER SET LATIN NOT
CASESPECIFIC,
      First_name VARCHAR(12) CHARACTER SET LATIN NOT
CASESPECIFIC,
      Salary DECIMAL(8,2))
UNIQUE PRIMARY INDEX ( Employee_No )
INDEX ( Last_name )
INDEX ( Dept_No );


 *** Text of DDL statement returned.
-----------------------------------------------------------
CREATE SET TABLE CSQL_CLASS.emp_job_table ,NO FALLBACK ,
     NO BEFORE JOURNAL,
     NO AFTER JOURNAL,
     CHECKSUM = DEFAULT
     (
      job_no INTEGER NOT NULL,
      emp_no INTEGER NOT NULL)
PRIMARY INDEX ( job_no )
UNIQUE INDEX ( job_no ,emp_no );
```

Figure 9.28

```
 *** Text of DDL statement returned.
-------------------------------------------------------------
CREATE SET TABLE CSQL_CLASS.job_table ,NO FALLBACK ,
     NO BEFORE JOURNAL,
     NO AFTER JOURNAL,
     CHECKSUM = DEFAULT
     (
      job_no INTEGER NOT NULL,
      job_desc VARCHAR(20) CHARACTER SET LATIN NOT
CASESPECIFIC,
      CONSTRAINT job_no_range CHECK ( job_no <  100000  ))
UNIQUE PRIMARY INDEX ( job_no );


 *** Text of DDL statement returned.
-------------------------------------------------------------
REPLACE MACRO "CSQL_CLASS"."EmpJob" AS (SELECT ((TRIM(BOTH
FROM "CSQL_CLASS"."e"."Last_name" ))||', ')||(TRIM(BOTH
FROM "CSQL_CLASS"."e"."First_name" ))(NAMED "Employee"
),TRIM(BOTH  FROM "CSQL_CLASS"."j"."job_desc" )(NAMED
"JobTitle" ) FROM "CSQL_CLASS"."employee_table"  "e"  INNER
JOIN "CSQL_CLASS"."emp_job_table"  "ej"  ON
"CSQL_CLASS"."e"."Employee_No" =
"CSQL_CLASS"."ej"."emp_no"  INNER JOIN
"CSQL_CLASS"."job_table"  "j"  ON
"CSQL_CLASS"."ej"."job_no" =  "CSQL_CLASS"."j"."job_no"
ORDER BY "CSQL_CLASS"."e"."Last_name" ASC ;);
```

Figure 9.28 - *Continued*

Export by Database

The export-by-database option is used for individual export of database objects selected.

Export by Workload

Export by workload is used to export multiple workloads and the specified QCD database along with capture the definition details for emulation.

Export Options

Under **Export Options**, you have (3) dialog boxes (**Export By Query**, **Export By Database**, and **Export By Workload**) to define the information that can be exported from a production system.

Estimate Export Time

Once the export is defined, TSET can estimate the time required to run the export operation. If the estimate is too long, you can define additional export parameters, or you can run the operation at a different time.

TSET can support multiple versions of the emulation information which enables you to test different scenarios. While offline, the following tasks can be performed to modify the information and create multiple scenarios:

- Open and edit emulation information.
- Change import options.
- Select objects for import.
- Edit import information.

Note: A connection to a Teradata Database or an import operation cannot be performed.

TSET has several administrative functions that enable you to export and import data. These functions are summarized below.

- **Set TLE Parameters**

  Enables the creation of multiple emulation scenarios that cover a variety of ranges for testing possibilities by specifying RAS, cost parameters, and cost profiles at different levels on a separate test system. When completed, the analysis and test system can be reset to their defaults using the **Reset Target Level Emulation** dialog box.

- **Perform Query Testing**

  TSET is used to execute and test SQL statements before they are productionized. This can be done through Execute SQL main window or Teradata SQL Assistant.

- **Perform a File Transfer**

  The Pack feature combines all of the files associated with an export into a single file to easily send them to a location via ftp site or email. Once received, use the Unpack feature to separate the files.

- **Undo Imported Files**

  The Teradata SET Undo Import feature is used to cleanup the imported information after the plan is no longer needed. Every import creates an *.undo* file, which is used to cleanup the files. Only one *.undo* import operation is performed at a time and can remove multiple types of information.

- **Delete Exported Files**

  Once the query plan analysis has been performed and is completed, you can utilize the Delete Files feature to remove the exported files.

- **View Log Files and Summary Reports**

  To troubleshoot an export, import, or undo-import (cleanup) operation, use the log file to view the events in the current TSET session and find the required information. View the summary report for information about failed and successful operations.

- **Retry Failed Import Operations**

  Errors can be encountered when importing objects such as insufficient access rights or permanent space available. If this occurs, use the **SQL Statement Failed** dialog box in order to perform a retry.

- **Disconnect and Close Teradata SET**

  Before connecting to an alternate database, make sure you disconnect from the current database. You can do this by either closing TSET to end the session or disconnect from the current database.

- **Perform File Management**

  Files that are created during export, import, and pack operations are stored in the directory specified under **Export to** in the **Export from Teradata Database** dialog box. Exported parameters are stored with a control (*.mcf*) file that:

  - Tracks elements selected and exported (i.e. object definitions)
  - Stores raw data files with pointers that are created during the export process.
  - Provides version number, release number, and the date and time when the system information was exported from the production system.

Teradata Visual Explain

Teradata Visual Explain (VE) compliments the EXPLAIN by displaying the query plans of SQL statements through a GUI interface. This interface shows the data flow and steps required to excute the query.

Teradata VE, with its ability to do query plan comparisons, provides developers, Database Administrators, and support technicians the ability to optimized queries faster and simpler to ensure queries are executed effectively.

Pictured below is the main screen. Either through the menus or icons, you tell VE what you want to accomplish.

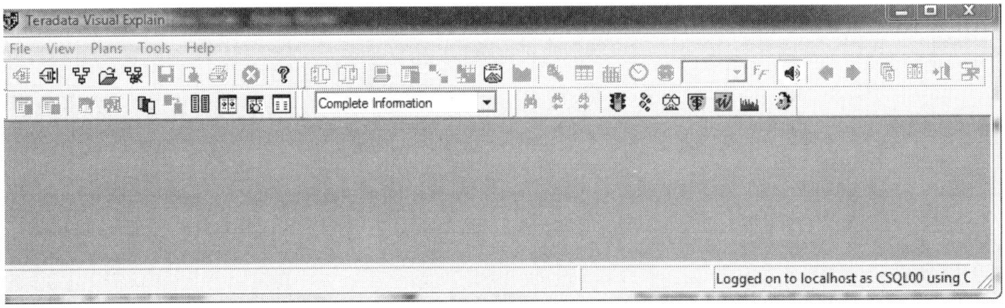

Figure 9.29

Note: VE also provides a command line interface.

The first step is to create a Query Capture Database (QCD). From the main screen, click on **Tools->Control Center** and then click on **Setup QCD**. The screens for each step are pictured below.

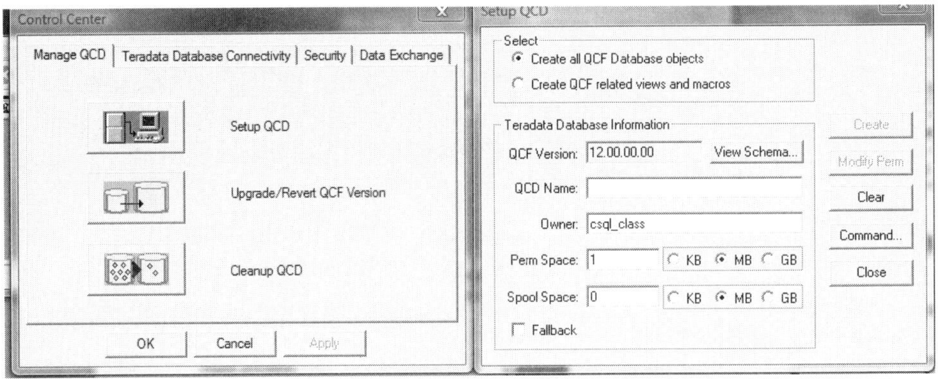

Figure 9.30

Fill in the blanks, and then press Create. The system will then create a QCD.

Once that is accomplished, the next step is to begin capturing queries into the QCD. To begin that process, from the main window select **Tools->Launch QCF** as shown next. Also notice that the other applications in the Teradata Analyst Pack are available from the Tools menu.

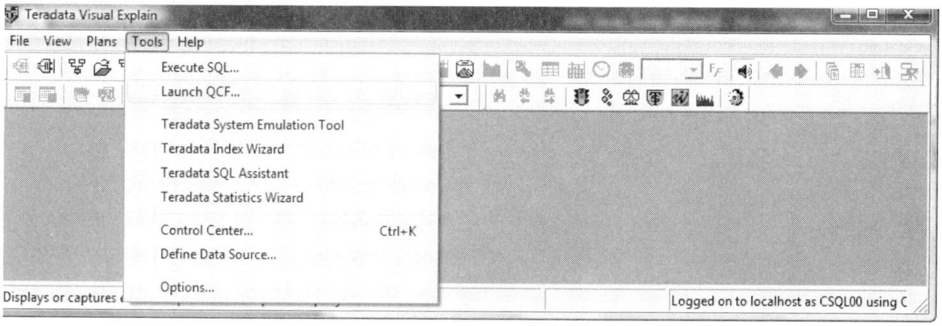

Figure 9.31

When this screen appears, make the appropriate selections and fill in the blanks. If you choose the **Capture Execution Plan (Dump Explain)** button, VE will create a series of QCD INSERT statements which can be printed, saved to a BTEQ file, or loaded into a QCD. If you choose the **View Execution Plan (Insert Explain)** button (as shown), VE will insert the execution plan into the specified QCD.

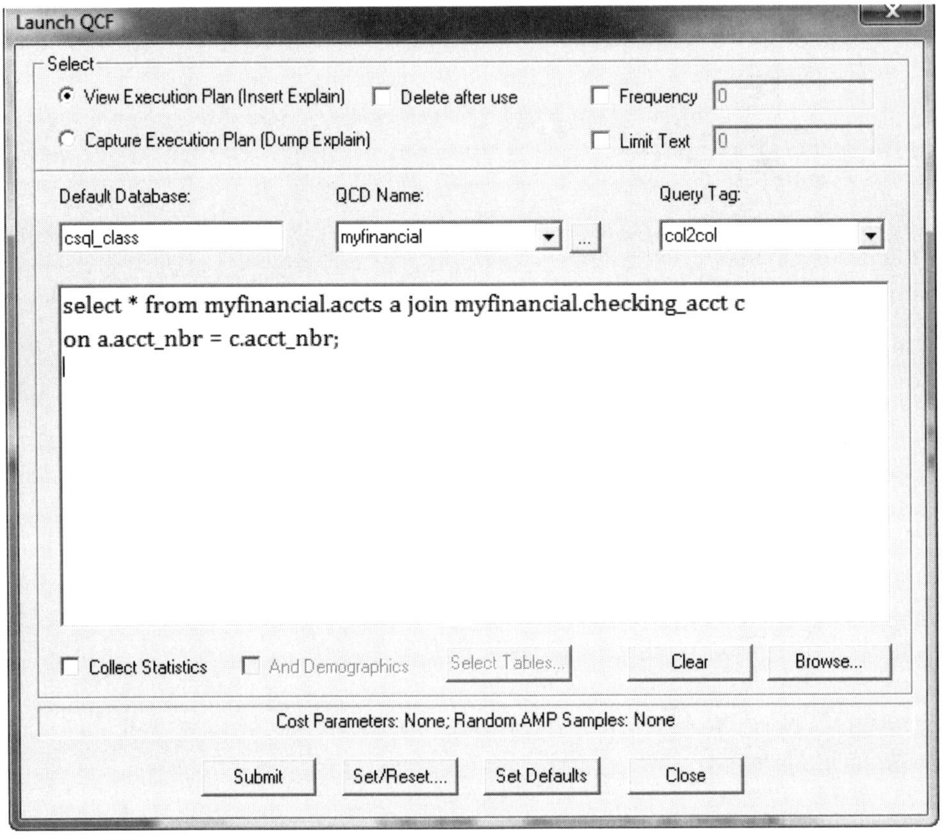

Figure 9.32

In the query shown, the acct_nbr column is not indexed in either table.

Pressing the Submit button will cause VE to display the Explain diagram of the query, as shown next.

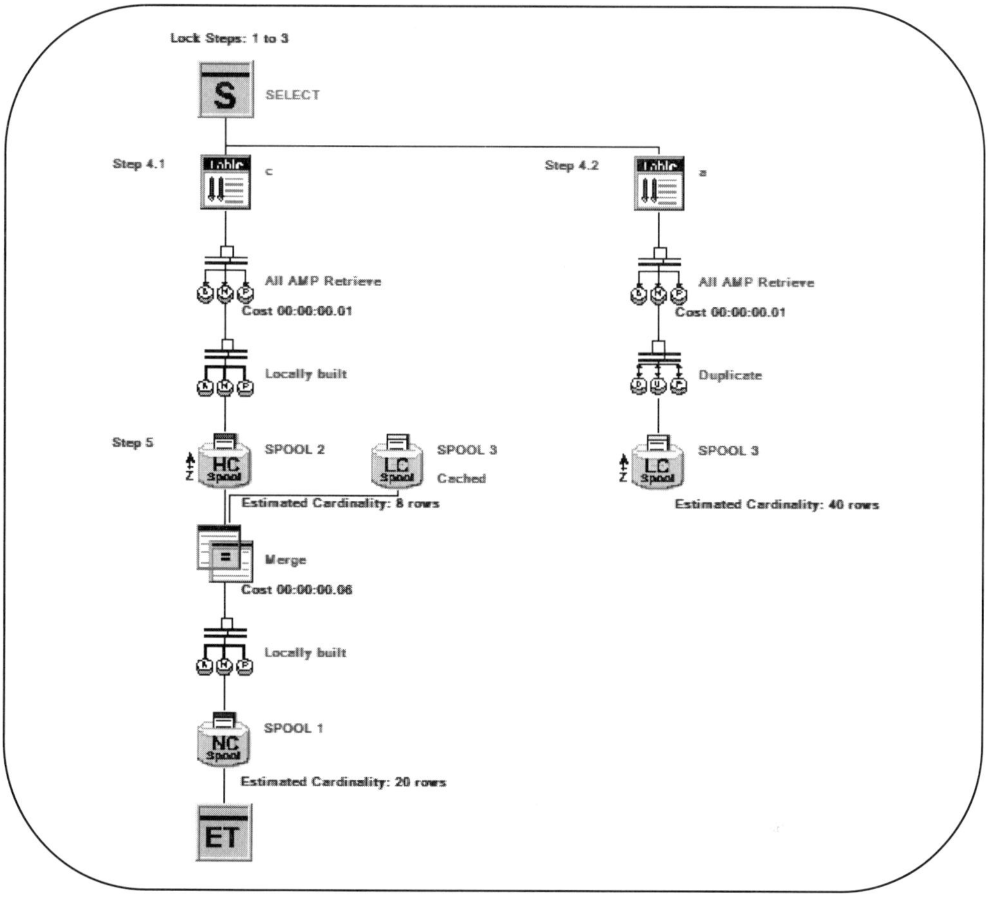

Figure 9.33

Doing a **Right Click** on one of these diagrams will bring up a submenu that allows you to view the Explain text. This is shown in the next two screens.

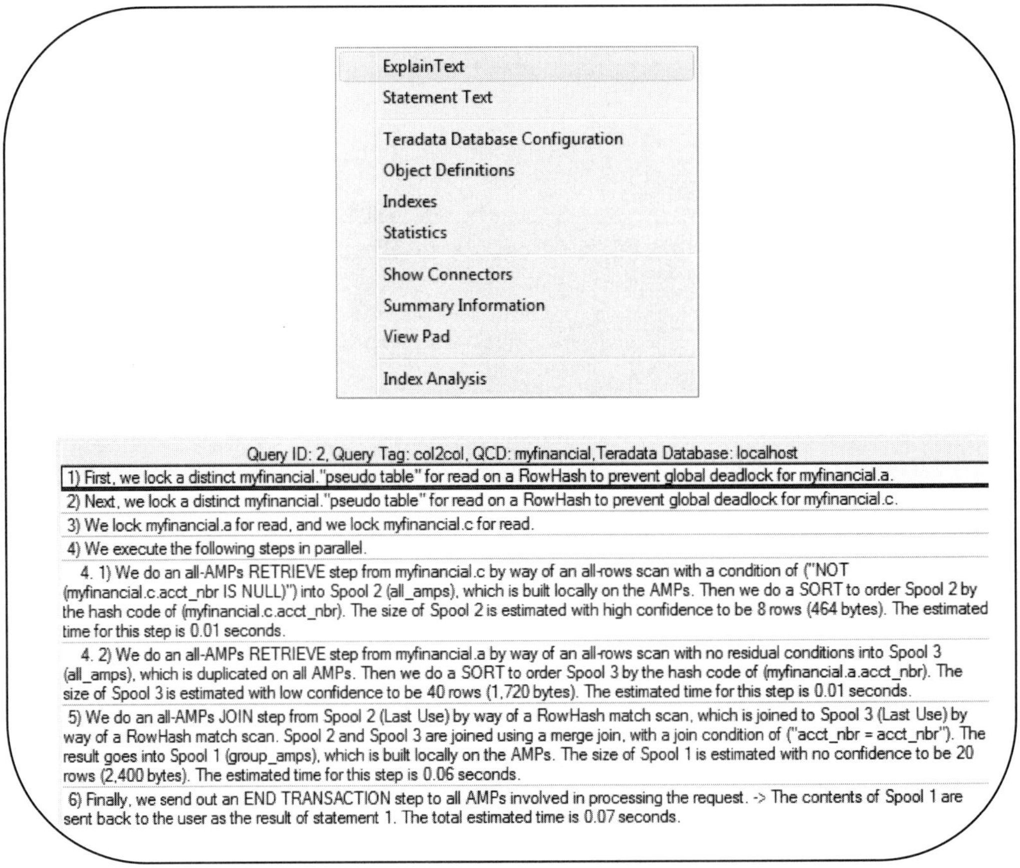

Figure 9.34

A powerful feature of VE allows you to compare different versions of SQL statements. Using QCF, another query was captured into the QCD, as shown next.

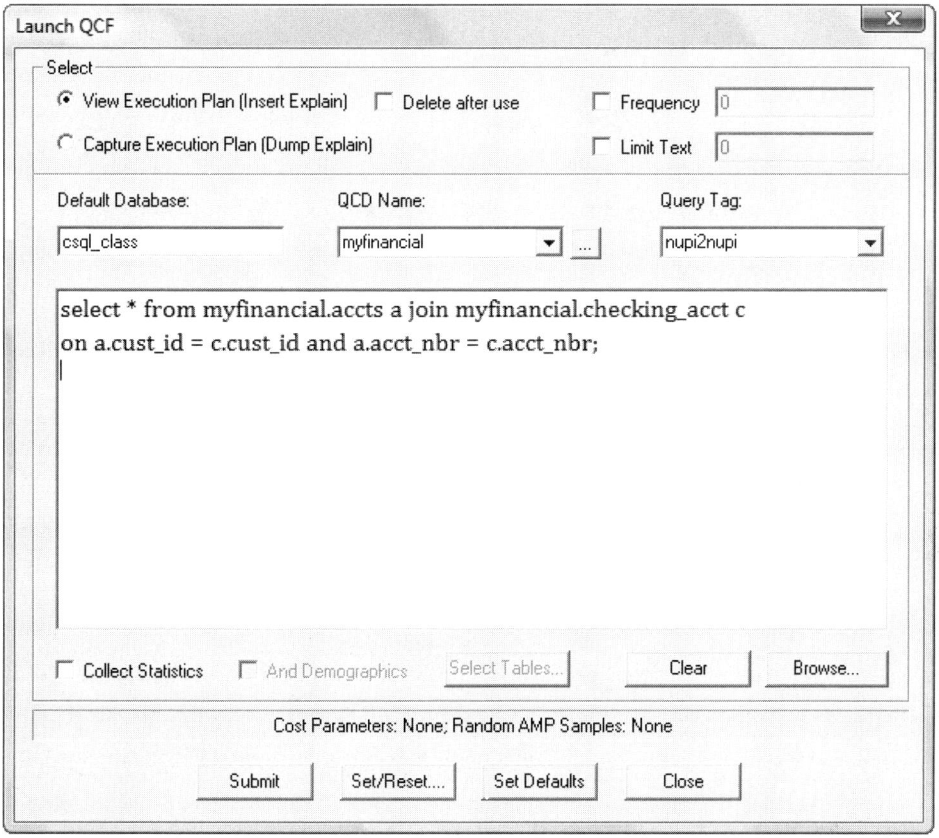

Figure 9.35

In this version of the query, the column cust_id is the NUPI in both tables.

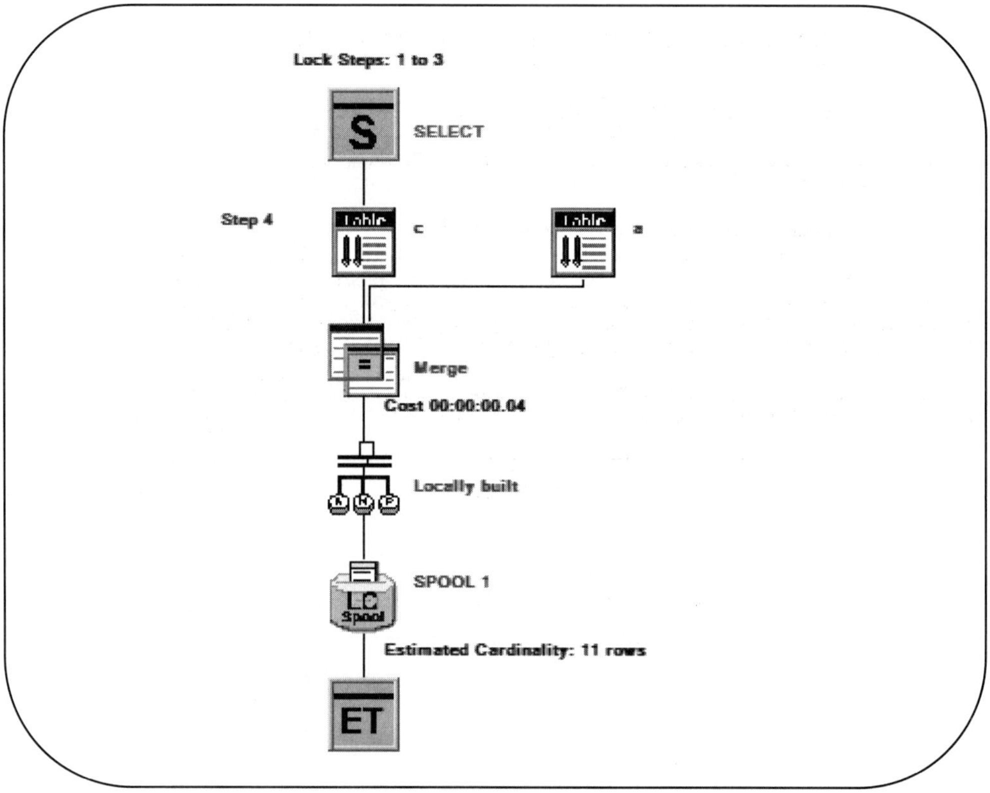

Lock Steps: 1 to 3
S
SELECT
Step 4
c
a
Merge
Cost 00:00:00.04
Locally built
SPOOL 1
Estimated Cardinality: 11 rows
ET

Figure 9.36

Using the right-click submenu, here is the text of the Explain.

```
Query ID: 3, Query Tag: nupi2nupi, QCD: myfinancial,Teradata Database: localhost
1) First, we lock a distinct myfinancial."pseudo table" for read on a RowHash to prevent global deadlock for myfinancial.a.
2) Next, we lock a distinct myfinancial."pseudo table" for read on a RowHash to prevent global deadlock for myfinancial.c.
3) We lock myfinancial.a for read, and we lock myfinancial.c for read.
4) We do an all-AMPs JOIN step from myfinancial.c by way of a RowHash match scan, which is joined to myfinancial.a by way of a RowHash match scan with no residual conditions. myfinancial.c and myfinancial.a are joined using a merge join, with a join condition of ("(myfinancial.a.acct_nbr = myfinancial.c.acct_nbr) AND (myfinancial.a.cust_id = myfinancial.c.cust_id)"). The result goes into Spool 1 (group_amps), which is built locally on the AMPs. The size of Spool 1 is estimated with low confidence to be 11 rows (1,320 bytes). The estimated time for this step is 0.04 seconds.
5) Finally, we send out an END TRANSACTION step to all AMPs involved in processing the request. -> The contents of Spool 1 are sent back to the user as the result of statement 1. The total estimated time is 0.04 seconds.
```

Figure 9.37

Once you have two, or more, queries loaded into the QCD, you can use the **Plans->Compare** menu from the main screen to select which plans to compare, as shown in the next screen.

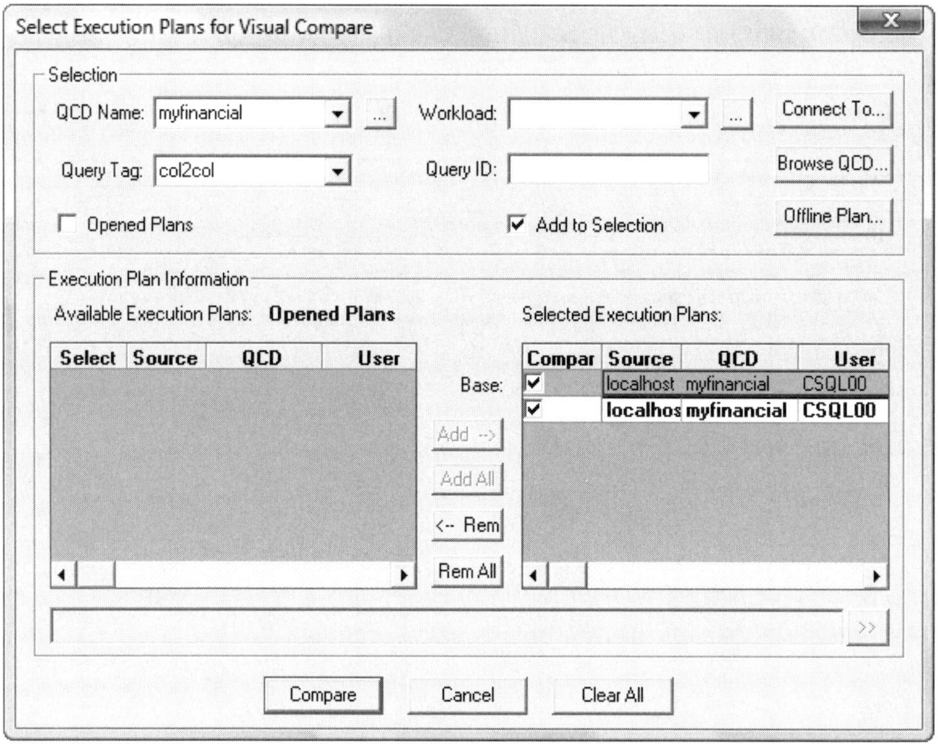

Figure 9.38

VE will display the selected plans side-by-side. It will also display a Summary for each plan.

The Summary for a displayed plan will appear when you click on the plan. The next two screens illustrate this.

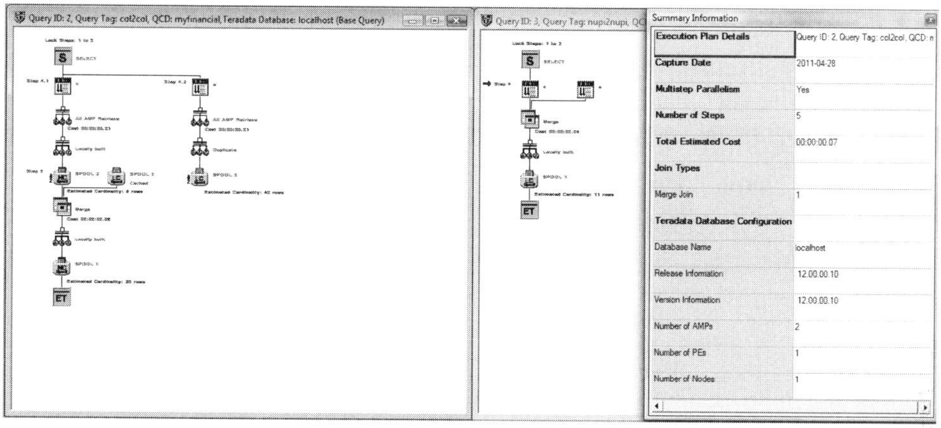

Figure 9.39

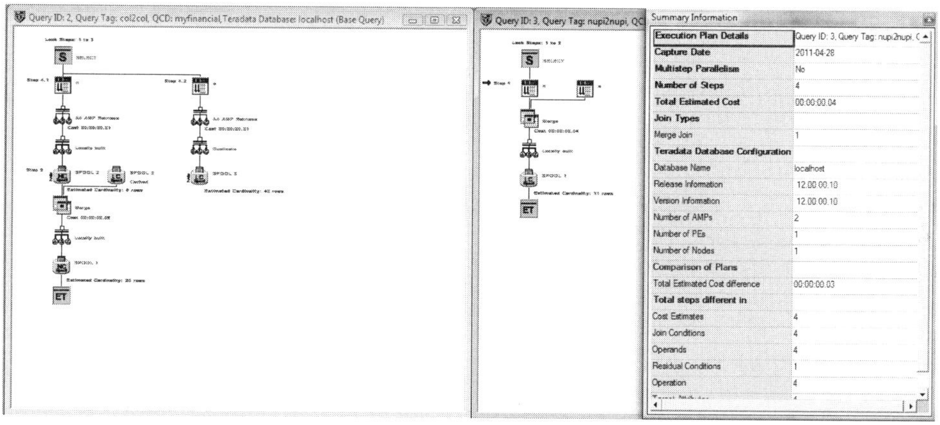

Figure 9.40

Selecting the **Plans->Compare Report** menu will cause VE to produce a series of reports for the chosen plans. The reports are as follows:

- Complete Information Report

- Teradata Database Configuration Report
- Step Information Report
- Estimated Cost Report
- Operation Report
- Operands Report
- Residual Condition Report
- Join Condition Report
- Join Order Report
- Source Attributes Report
- Target Attributes Report
- Indexes Used Report
- Index Condition Report

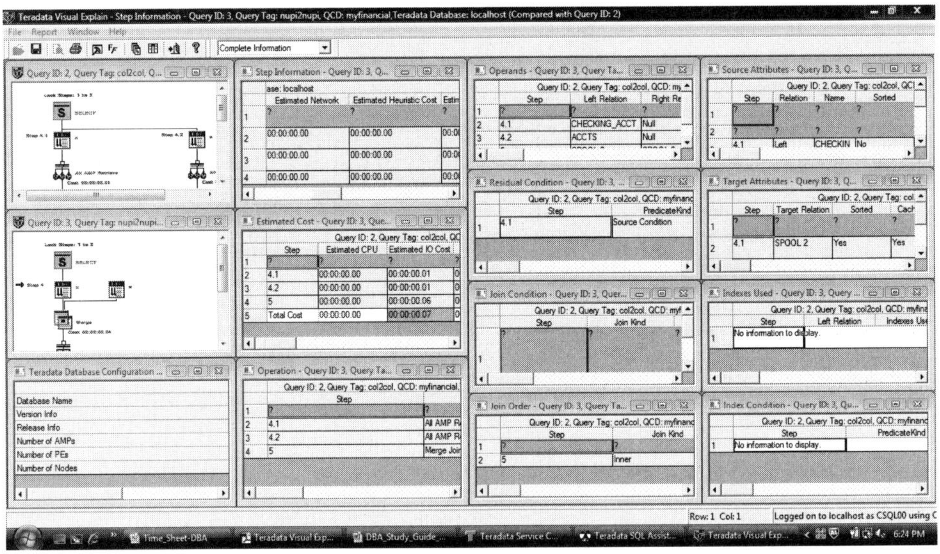

Figure 9.41

Clicking on the Maximize button of any report screen will make its data available for viewing.

Once again, doing a right-click on a diagram and choosing Objects from the pop-up menu will allow you to see any changes in the DDL of the objects. You can also get Index and Statistics information. The following shows the Object screen.

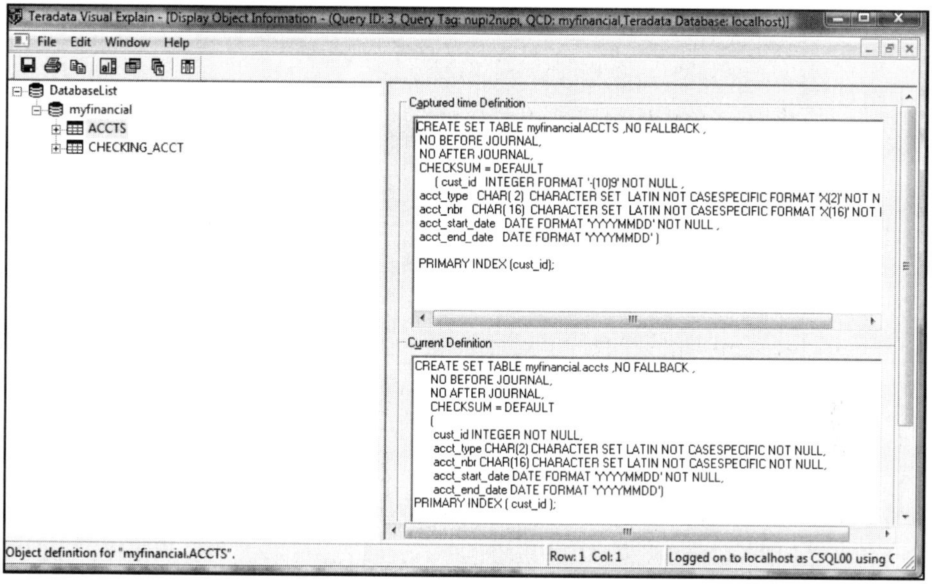

Figure 9.42

Doing a right-click on an object and choosing Table Demographics will bring up a disk space utilization report. Additional reports can be viewed using the same method.

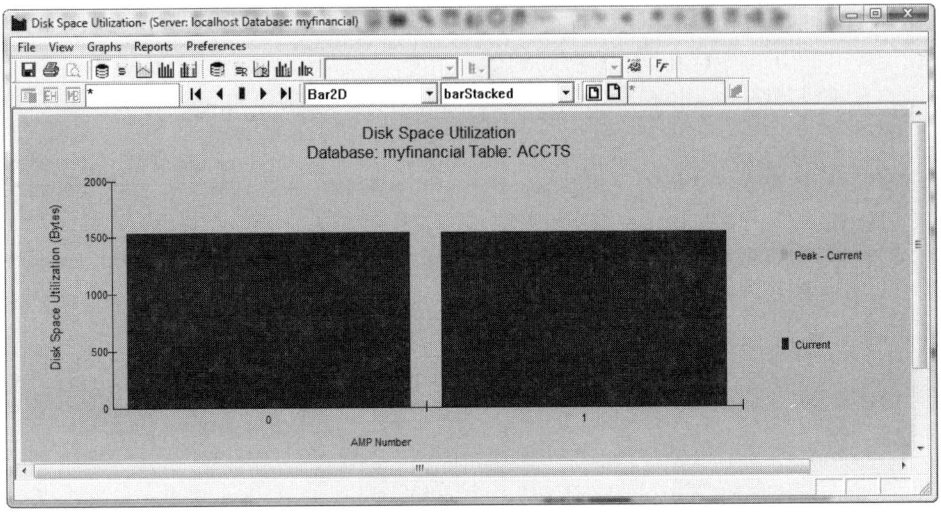

Figure 9.43

One or more execution plans can be saved to a file (*.vec*). Saving an execution plan creates what is referred to as an *offline* plan. Optionally, the corresponding visual plan, Explain text, statement text, or tool tips can be saved.

Click on **File->Save As** to get the following screen. Choose what you want to save, then either have VE create a file name for you using the parameters listed, or create one yourself in the File Name box that will appear if the **Generate file name(s) automatically** box is unchecked.

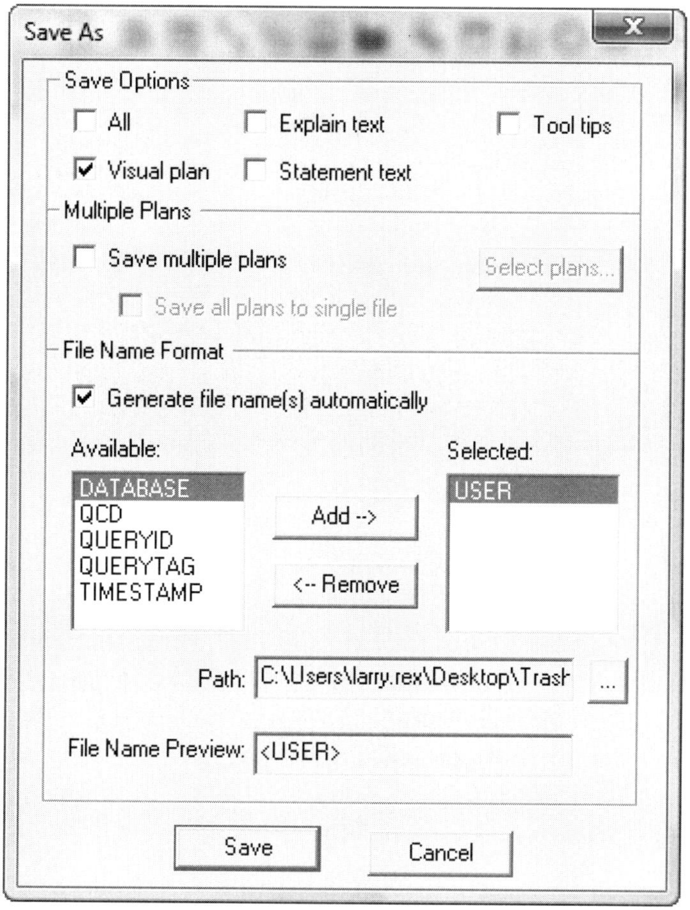
Save As
Save Options
All
Explain text
Tool tips
Visual plan
Statement text
Multiple Plans
Save multiple plans
Select plans...
Save all plans to single file
File Name Format
Generate file name(s) automatically
Available:
Selected:
DATABASE
QCD
QUERYID
QUERYTAG
TIMESTAMP
Add -->
<-- Remove
USER
Path:
C:\Users\larry.rex\Desktop\Trash
...
File Name Preview:
<USER>
Save
Cancel

Figure 9.44

Practice Questions

1. Which of the following is not a function of the Teradata Administrator program?
    a. Create ANSI syntax tables
    b. Grant or revoke privileges
    c. Do performance analysis
    d. Drop or rename objects

2. Which of the following is part of the Teradata Dual Active Solution?
    a. TMSM
    b. TASM
    c. TDWM
    d. TSET

3. Which of the following would help to identify obsolete objects or those with the potential for performance improvements?
    a. Table Usage Analysis Report
    b. Object Global Use Count Report
    c. Table Scan Report
    d. Workload Analysis Report

4. The PACK dialog box of TSET is used to accomplish which of the following?
    a. Combine an .mfc file and its associated files into one .pack file.
    b. Combine an .mfc file and its associated files into one .pck file.
    c. Combine an .mcf file and its associated files into one .pack file.
    d. Combine an .mcf file and its associated files into one .pck file.

5. What will be returned by a SHOW QUALIFIED SELECT * FROM *databasename.viewname*; statement?
    a. An error
    b. The data from the underlying table(s)
    c. The CREATE VIEW text only
    d. The CREATE text for any tables referenced by the view only
    e. The CREATE VIEW text and the CREATE TABLE text of any tables referenced by the view.

Chapter Notes

Utilize this space for notes, key points to remember, diagrams, areas of further study, etc.

Chapter 10 - Monitoring Tools

Certification Objectives

- ✓ Given a scenario including a system bottleneck, identify tools/resources to determine the cause of the bottleneck.
- ✓ Explain the collection and analysis of AMPUsage data in problem resolution.
- ✓ Given a scenario, identify which ResUsage tables to use for problem identification.
- ✓ Given a scenario, identify the Database Query Log (DBQL) tables and logging options that should be used to resolve the problem.

Before You Begin

You should be familiar with the following terms and concepts.

Terms	Key Concepts
Locking	Locking levels (database, table, row hash), lock types (access, read, write, exclusive, HUT), and how they can interfere with one another
ResUsage	Resource consumption tracking
AMP	Access Module (virtual) Processor
Viewpoint	Portlets for monitoring
DBQL	What can and should be logged

Viewpoint

Viewpoint has a Lock Viewer portlet which can be used to display information about resolved lock contentions. Though the report is not real time, it can be used to find out if the performance of the system has been degraded by a lock. Locks that have occurred in the last five minutes, hour, day, or week are shown in the report. You can find locks in a specific database, or in a specified time frame, or locks caused by a specific user, or locks that are blocking a specific user. Some of the information available includes session, transaction, object identifiers, and global deadlocks.

As Teradata systems store more data and users, keeping tabs on everything manually become increasingly difficult. Viewpoint simplifies this by allowing you to set up alerts to notify you when conditions drift outside the desired norm.

The following chart lists the various Alerts that are available, and the metrics of some of them which are monitored and returned.

<table>
<tr><td>Canary Queries – Can be set to alert when the response time exceeds a defined threshold. The options you can specify are as follows;<ul><li>Node ID</li><li>Query Name</li><li>Login Timeout Occurred - Indicated by True and False</li><li>Response Time – Measured in milliseconds. Response time it took for the canary query</li></ul></td></tr>
<tr><td>Data Collectors - Provides an alert when errors occur for the specific data collector(s).</td></tr>
<tr><td>Database Space - When the space utilized exceeds the specified percentage, an alert can be triggered. Options you specify are as follows:<ul><li>Current Perm % - Total percentage of permanent disk space being utilized</li><li>Current Perm Max % - Number of Vprocs / Max Perm</li></ul></td></tr>
</table>

<table>
<tr><td>
<ul>
<li>Current Spool Space % - Total Percentage of spool space currently being utilized</li>
<li>Peak Spool Space % - Total highest percentage of spool space being utilized</li>
</ul>
</td></tr>
<tr><td>Events – Provides an alert when the Teradata Database restarts.</td></tr>
<tr><td>Node - When a node on the Teradata Database reaches the specified performance threshold, an alert can be trigged.</td></tr>
<tr><td>Session – Provides an alert when the Teradata Database (at the session level) exceeds the specified performance threshold. Parameters that can be set are as follows:
<ul>
<li>Account</li>
<li>Active Time – How long the query has been running</li>
<li>AMP CPU - CPU time (in seconds) utilized for executing requests on all AMPs</li>
<li>AMP I/O – Total number of Logical Reads and Writes by session on all AMPs</li>
<li>Blocked Time – Total time the query has been blocked</li>
<li>Connection Time – Total time the session has been connected</li>
<li>CPU delta – Amount of CPU time consumed, in seconds, based on the sampling</li>
<li>CPU Skew</li>
<li>Delta I/O</li>
<li>Host ID - PE Host ID or LAN ID</li>
<li>Hot AMP CPU – Highest AMP based on CPU utilized</li>
<li>Idle Time</li>
<li>Partition – Indicates how the session is connected (SQL, CONSOLE, MONITOR)</li>
<li>Request AMP CPU – Total CPU time, in seconds, on all AMPs by each request</li>
<li>Request AMP I/O – Total count of logical Reads and Writes on all AMPs by request</li>
<li>Sessions Per User – Count of the number of sessions logged by username</li>
<li>Spool Space – Total amount of spool space by the request on all</li>
</ul>
</td></tr>
</table>

AMPs • Utility Session – Used by the Teradata utilities, indicated by **True** and **False**
System – Provides an alert on the Teradata Database when a specific performance threshold is reached. Available settings include: • *A*MP CPU Skew – Delta calculation of busiest AMP to the average AMP • AMP CPU Usage – Percentage of CPU usage of all AMPs • Blocked Sessions • Net A Usage - BYNET utilization • Node CPU Skew – Delta calculation of CPU use on the busiest node to the average node • Node CPU Usage – Percentage of average CPU usage on all active nodes • Node Disk Usage – Percentage of average disk usage across all active nodes in the configuration • PE CPU Usage – Percentage of average CPU usage on all active PEs • Total Sessions - Total count of sessions logged on
System Health – Provides an alert on the Teradata Database when a specific threshold has been exceeded
Table Space – Provides an alert when the DBC.TransientJournal table space exceeds the specified percent. Parameters include: • Current Perm – Total permanent disk space the DBC.TransientJournal table is utilizing • Skew – Based on distribution, this calculates the percent of uneven disk space used by the DBC.TransientJournal table on all AMPs
Vproc – Provides an alert when the Teradata Database reaches a specified performance vproc threshold. Settings include: • System Level AMP CPU Skew – Delta calculation that compares the busiest AMP CPU to the average AMP • System Level AMP CPU Usage – Percentage of average CPU use on all online AMPs on the system

- Available AWT - Total available AMP worker tasks
- CIC Usage - Channel Interface Controller percentage used
- CPU Usage – Non-idle percentage of CPU usage
- Disk I/O
- Disk Out Req Avg - Average count of requests still outstanding
- Disk Usage - Percentage of disk utilized
- Host I/O
- Mem Failures
- Message Count – vproc messages
- Net A Usage - BYNET receiver usage
- System Net A Usage - Total BYNET system utilization
- Sytem Node CPU Skew - Delta of CPU usage based on the busiest node to the average node
- Sytem Node CPU Usage - Percentage of average CPU usage on all nodes
- Sytem Node Disk Usage - Percentage of average disk usage on all nodes
- Sytem PE CPU Usage- Percentage of average CPU usage of all PEs on the system
- Status – Node status, **U** = Node is up and **D** = Node is down
- Swaps – Count of reads and writes swaps
- Total Sessions - Count of logged sessions on the PE

Figure 10.1

Locking Logger

The Locking Logger utility (dumplocklog) creates a table that stores lock information that is extracted from transaction logs on the Teradata Database. This information can be utilized to analyze lock contentions and whether system performance has been degraded by an inappropriate mix of SQL statements.

When logging is enabled, each AMP will create a memory buffer for saving transaction locking information. The locking logger will also capture information for global deadlocks such as Host Utility (HUT) locks.

The lock log buffer default size is 64 KB. When full, the previous log is overwritten. This provides an updated log of the transaction locks encountered on each AMP. This value indicates the size of the locking logger segments. The lock log segment size is divided into two parts: main and partial. The last 32 KB of the lock log segment is the partial part and contains global deadlock information. Both parts contain information about the locks.

Note: This buffer can be changed by modifying the LockLogSegmentSize field in the DBS Control record from 64 to 1024 KB.

When a lock contention delay is encountered by a transaction, the AMP writes an entry into the buffer. The following information concerning the delayed transaction is recorded:

- The date and time of the requested transaction lock
- The length of time the blocked transaction was blocked
- The database and table information which the lock was requested
- The host ID and session number of the requested transaction lock
- The host ID and session number of the transaction that caused the lock
- The AMP vproc where the lock was requested
- The lock level (database, table, row, or range of rows), and type (read, write, exclusive), of the requested lock
- The type of DML statement transaction (INSERT, UPDATE, SELECT, and so forth)
- Indication if the lock caused a deadlock

The lock log table allows you to define the information that you want to retrieve from the lock log buffers. When using Locking Logger to create a lock log table, you must provide the following information:

- User name and password
- Number of SQL sessions Locking Logger will use to perform the INSERT operations. The minimum is one session. The maximum is one session for each online AMP, but is limited by the number of PEs.

If Locking Logger runs in continuous mode then there should be a minimum of one free console session available per PE. There is a limit of 6 console sessions per PE vproc. Depending on what's running, sometimes there are not enough of these sessions per AMP to invoke the Locking Logger utility. Basically, you cannot risk taking console sessions from other more important jobs (i.e. load utilities). However, you are unable to adjust the number of sessions dynamically once the value is set. Therefore, you need to configure this based upon activation. This number should leave enough sessions available for other utilities and provides sufficient parallelism for Locking Logger's to insert rows.

If Locking Logger runs in snapshot mode, then you will need one or more console PE sessions available in order for Locking Logger to run.

Use the Lock Log table along with the DBC.EventLog table to determine the blocked user from the blocking user.

The command-line dumplocklog utility and its associated DBSControl settings are deprecated. You should use DBQL to capture locking information and view it using Viewpoint or by querying DBC.QryLockLogXMLV.

ResUsage Data

Resource usage data is stored on several tables located in the DBC database. There are views and macros available for reporting on the resource usage data that is stored.

You can also write your own queries or macros on resource usage data. As with other database data, you can access resource usage data using SQL.

You need to decide what resource usage data you want to collect and the level of detail you want it to cover. Once you set up your resource usage data collection the way you want, the only maintenance required is to purge old data regularly. The following table is an overview of the information covered by resource usage data:

Resource usage data covers	Which includes
BYNET traffic on a node	Messaging includes point-to-point, broadcast, and merge activities.
client-to-server traffic	Data on each communication link.
CPU utilization	Overhead, user service, and time of session execution.
data tracking	Status of sessions in locking queues.
logical device traffic (SCSI)	Count of reads/writes and amount of data transferred as seen from the SCSI driver.
vdisk logical device traffic	All the cylinders allocated by an AMP.
Priority Scheduler information	Resuage data captured by Performance Group (PG) from Priority Scheduler and reported by Teradata Active System Management (Teradata ASM) workloads (WDs).

Resource usage data covers	Which includes
AMP Worker Task (AWT) Information	AWT statistics.
memory management activity	Memory allocation, aging, paging, and swapping.
summary information	All data collected for a node or vproc.

Figure 10.2

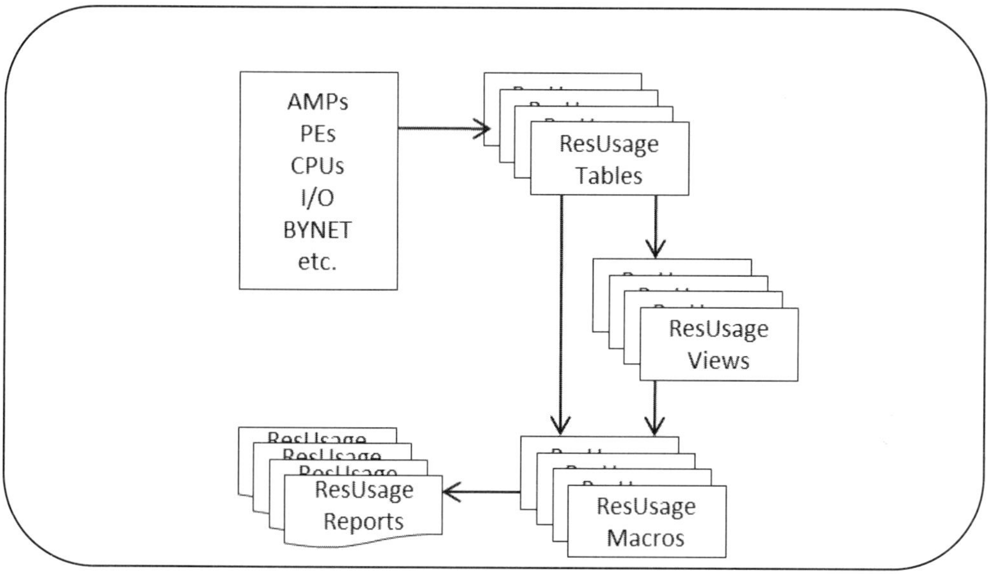

Figure 10.3

ResUsage Tables

Node Resource Usage Tables	
ResUsageSpma *System-wide node information*	**ResUsageScpu** *Information specific to the CPUs within the nodes*

Vproc Resource Usage Tables	
ResUsageSawt *AWT statistics*	**ResUsageShst** *Channel and LAN communication info*
ResUsageSldv *System-wide logical device info*	**ResUsageSpdsk** *Includes Virtual Storage resource usage logs on cylinder I/O, allocation, and migration*
ResUsageSps *Priority Scheduler Performance Group data*	**ResUsageSvdsk** *AMP-level vdisk statistics*
ResUsageSvpr *System-wide vproc information*	

Figure 10.4

Node Resource Usage Tables
The tables in this group are controlled by the RSS Collection Rate and Node logging rate.

Table Name	Covers	When You Should Enable
ResUsageScpu	Statistics on the CPUs within the nodes.	When analysis indicates that the overall performance is limited on an individual processor. For example, a specific CPU on each node or a specific node is active while other CPUs are idle which could indicate a process uses that CPU consistently. Note: When first implemented, you should enable this table to verify

Table Name	Covers	When You Should Enable
		the following: • Verify all CPUs are functioning correctly • Check the load balance among the CPUs
ResUsageSpma	Provided node summary information of overall system-wide utilization. This also integrates information from of the other tables.	This captures the operational history of the system. This table also captures information on BYNET utilization.
ResUsageIpma	System-wide Internal node information	Generally, this table is not used at customer sites. Used by Teradata Engineering.

Figure 10.5

Vproc Resource Usage Tables The tables in this group are controlled by the RSS Collection Rate and the Vproc logging rate.		
Table Name	**Covers**	**When You Should Enable**
ResUsageSawt	Data specific to the AMP worker tasks (AWTs).	Provides the ability to monitor AWTs utilization and whether there is a backlog of work because the AWTs are all being utilized.
ResUsageShst	Channel statistics on the host and LANs that communicate with Teradata Database.	To capture information about the traffic over the IBM Host and LAN channels to determine if

Table Name	Covers	When You Should Enable
		there is a bottleneck.
ResUsageSldv	System-wide, logical device statistics collected from the SCSI bus.	To analyze utilization statistics for disk usage.
ResUsageSps	Data by Performance Group (PG) ID from the Priority Scheduler.	Used to track utilization by the query Workload Definition (WD) level.
ResUsageSvdsk	Statistics collected from the vdisk logical device.	To view the details of the disk usage across the AMPs to look for hot AMPS or other skew issues.
ResUsageSvpr	Data specific to each vpoc and file system.	Provides resource details being utilized by each vproc on the system. Good for investigating hot AMPS or PEs that may be CPU bound.
ResUsageIvpr	System-wide internal vproc processor information,	Generally, this table is not used at customer sites. Used by Teradata Engineering.

Figure 10.6

ResUsage Views

View Name	Description
ResCPUUsageByAMPView	Describes CPU usage per AMP
ResCPUUsageByPEView	Describes CPU usage by each PE
ResSawtView	Based on theResUsageSawt table
ResScpuView	Based on the ResUsageScpu table
ResShstView	Based on the ResUsageShst table
ResSldvView	Based on the ResUsageSldv table

ResSpdskView	Based on the ResUsageSpdsk table
ResSpmaView	Systems operation overview. This replaces the ResGeneralInfoView.
ResSpsView	Utilizes ResUsageSps table information
ResSvdskView	Utilizes ResUsageSvdsk table information
ResSvprView	Reports data on the ResUsageSvpr table
View Name	**Description**
ResCPUUsageByAMPView	Describes CPU usage per AMP
ResCPUUsageByPEView	Describes CPU usage by each PE
ResSawtView	Utilizes the ResUsageSawt table
ResScpuView	Utilizes the ResUsageScpu table
ResShstView	Utilizes the ResUsageShst table
ResSldvView	Utilizes the ResUsageSldv table
ResSpdskView	Utilizes the ResUsageSpdsk table
ResSpmaView	Systems operation overview. This replaces the ResGeneralInfoView.
ResSpsView	Utilizes the ResUsageSps table
ResSvdskView	Utilizes the ResUsageSvdsk table
ResSvprView	Utilizes the ResUsageSvpr table

Figure 10.7

ResUsage Macros

These macros	Provide the following.
ResAWT	Reports the average AMP Worker Task in use for all AMPs in the system.
ResAWTByAMP	Reports the average AMP Worker Task in use for each AMP.
ResAWTByNode	Reports the average AMP Worker Task on all AMPs in each node.
These macros	**Provide the following.**
ResCPUByAMP	Reports how each AMP on each node utilizes the CPUs.

ResCPUByAMPOneNode	Reports how each AMP on a specific node utilizes the CPUs.
ResAmpCpuByGroup	Reports the summary of AMP CPU usage by node grouping.
These macros	**Provide the following.**
ResCPUByPE	Reports how each PE on each node is utilizing the CPUs.
ResCPUByPEOneNode	Reports how each PE on a specific node is utilizing the CPUs.
ResPeCpuByGroup	Reports the PE CPU utilization summarized by a node grouping.
These macros	**Provide the following.**
ResCPUByNode	Reports how each individual node is utilizing its CPUs.
ResCPUOneNode	Reports how a specific node is utilizing its CPUs.
ResCPUByGroup	Reports how a specified Node Group is utilizing the system CPUs.
These macros	**Provide the following.**
ResHostByLink	Reports the host traffic for every communication link in the system.
ResHostOneNode	Reports the host traffic for the communication links of a specific node.
ResHostByGroup	Reports the host traffic for the communication links of a node grouping.
These macros	**Provide the following.**
ResLdvByNode	Reports the logical device traffic channeled through each node by totaling its controller links into one summarized node output line.
ResLdvOneNode	Reports the logical device traffic channeled through a specific node by totaling all of its controller links into one summarized node output line.
ResLdvByGroup	Reports the logical device traffic channeled

	through a node grouping.
These macros	**Provide the following.**
ResMemMgmtByNode	Reports memory management activity for each individual node.
ResMemMgmtOneNode	Reports memory management activity for a specific node.
ResMemByGroup	Reports memory management activity for a node grouping.
These macros	**Provide the following.**
ResNetByNode	Reports net traffic for each node.
ResNetOneNode	Reports net traffic for a specific node.
ResNetByGroup	Reports net traffic for nodes summarized by node groups.
These macros	**Provide the following.**
ResNode	Provides a summary of resource usage averaged across all nodes, excluding any PE-only nodes.
ResOneNode	Provides a summary of resource usage by returning the node requested.
ResNodeByNode	Provides a summary of resource usage by returning the nodes requested.
ResNodeByGroup	Provides a summary of resource usage by defined groups of nodes.
These macros	**Provide the following.**
ResPdskByNode	Reports the device traffic by a physical node.
ResPdskOneNode	Reports the device traffic for a specified node.
ResPdskByGroup	Reports the device traffic node grouping.
These macros	**Provide the following.**
ResPsByNode	Provides a summary of the Priority Scheduler resource usage • By TheDate, TheTime, NodeId, PGId columns on SLES 10 or earlier systems. • By the pWDId column on SLES 11 or later

	systems. The ResPsByNode macro produces one row of data for every set as defined in the GROUP BY clause.
ResPsByGroup	Provides a summary of the Priority Scheduler resource usage by coexistence group, produces one set of rows of data for each node type in the system for each log interval.
These macros	**Provide the following.**
ResVdskByNode	Reports the logical device traffic by a physical node.
ResVdskOneNode	Reports the logical device traffic for a specified node.
ResVdskByGroup	Reports the logical device traffic by a node grouping.

Figure 10.8

Specifying ResUsage Tables and Logging Rates

To record detailed statistics with the ResUsage tables, you need to enable them for logging, along with configuring the logging period to collect the detailed information. It is recommend that you only collect and log data you plan to utilize because this process has additional database system overhead and storage space requirements.

Naturally, the more tables you configure for logging, the more system overhead will be incurred.

You can use the Teradata ctl to enable or disable the ResUsage tables. The following screen capture is for ***ctl***, and the command issued was **screen rss**.

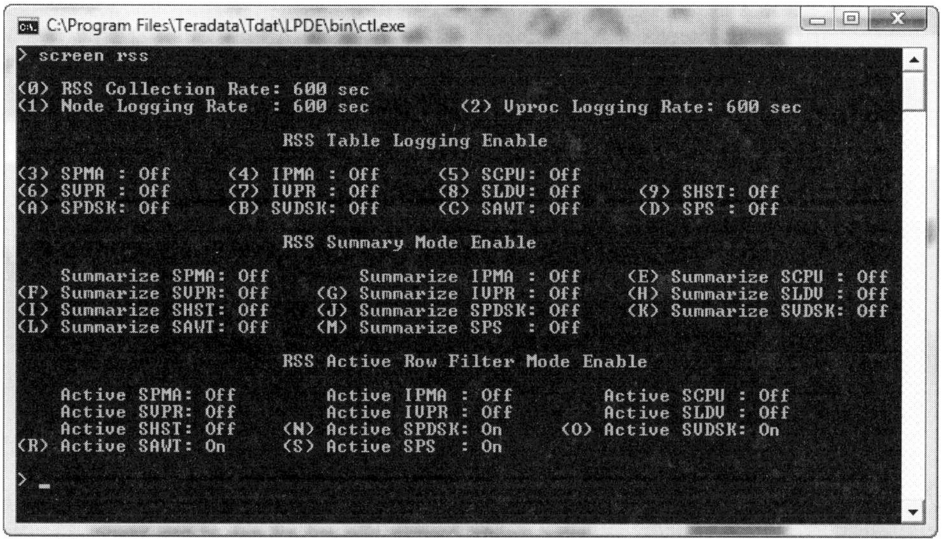

Figure 10.9

At a minimum, consider enabling ResusageSpma, ResUsageSps, and ResusageSawt. All should be enabled at the detail level. ResUsageSps, and ResusageSawt should always have Active Row Filter set to ON.

The default collection and logging settings provides a good start for basic system monitoring. The default results for the ResUsage tables being logged is every 10 minutes (600 seconds). Logging lower than 600 seconds may cause performance issues.

The applications that use the collect buffer generally require more frequent data updates; therefore, the collection rate is typically adjusted to 60 seconds. PMON and other collect buffer based applications: Teradata Manager or PM/API, do not require the logging rate to be changed or any of the tables to be enabled for logging in order to access the RSS data they use.

Populating the ResUsage Tables

Resource usage data gathering is a two-phase process as follows:

- Data collection

  During the data collection phase, the RSS gathers information from the operating system, Parallel Database Extensions (PDE), and Teradata Database.

  Data collection continues for a user-specified period of time, called the collection interval.

- Data logging

  In the logging phase, which occurs at the end of each logging period and consists of one or more complete collect intervals, the RSS writes all gathered data to ResUsage tables and reinitializes the shared data collection buffers for the next log interval.

The following diagram illustrates this.

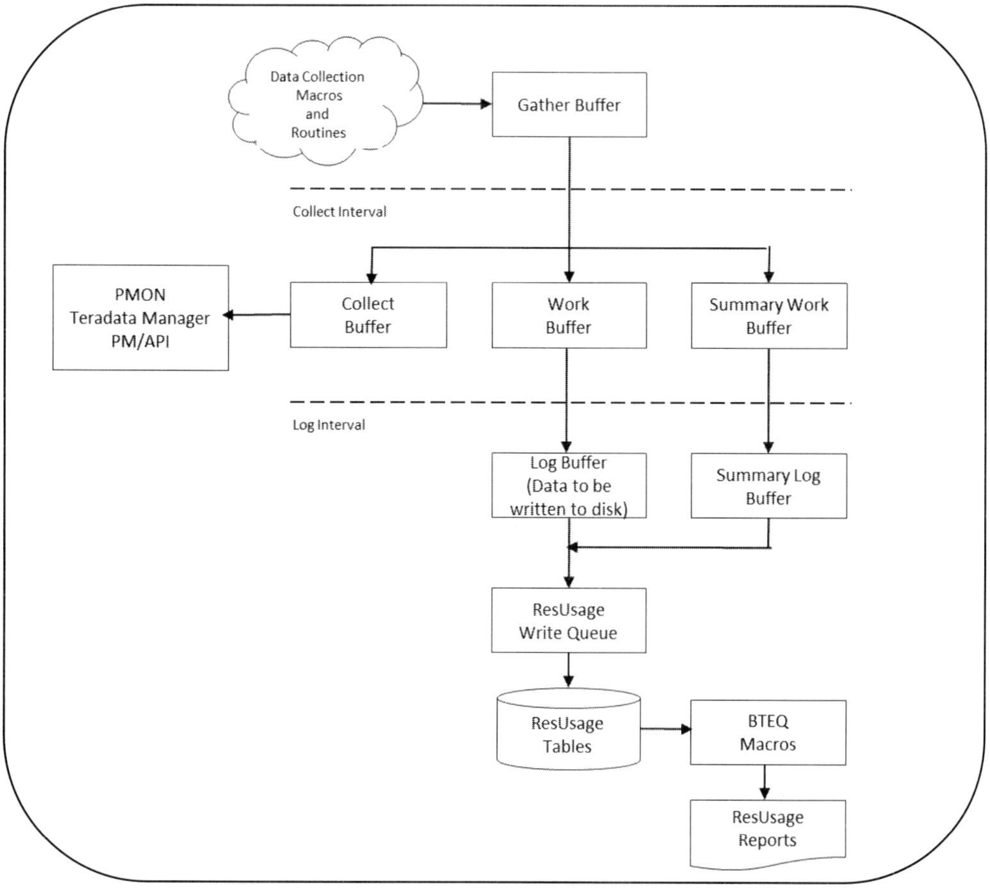

Figure 10.10

AmpUsageV[X]

The DBC.AMPUsageV view displays CPU usage information differently than the way such information is displayed in resource usage data. AmpUsageV can be used to understand individual user characteristics and CPU/IO usage by all users. However, for individual query performance, DBQL should be used.

The following chart summarizes the difference.

This facility	Provides
ResUsage	Metrics on the whole system, without making distinctions by individual user or account ID.
DBC.AMPUsageV view	AMP usage by individual user or account ID. Some CPU used for the system cannot be accounted for in AMPUsage. Therefore, ResUsage CPU metrics will always be larger than AMPUsage metrics. Typically, AMPUsage captures about 70- 90% of ResUsage CPU time.

Figure 10.11

Note: Refer back to Chapter 4 on the AMPUsage view for more information.

DBQL

The recommendation is to identify which SQL requests are to be logged through the use of the account string, rather than the username. You may end up classifying users across 20 or more accounts. This helps to minimize the need to create a log rule every time a new user is created.

As mentioned in Chapter 4, the recommended account string should include the &S&D&H ASE characters. Furthermore, include 4 characters (like *qrst*) to identify a work group. In general, the account string should look like '$*PG*$*qrs*t&S&D&H' where PG = the Performance Group ($R, $H, $M, $L)

Keep in mind that TASM does not use the Performance Group construct in the account string.

The information that should be captured will vary based upon a variety of factors, such as workload characteristics, performance, SLGs, and contention with other workloads.

The table below appeared in Chapter 8, and is repeated for your benefit.

Option	Description
ALL	Log query object information, step information, EXPLAIN text, and all SQL statements for all logged on users. This is equivalent to specifying OBJECTS, STEPINFO, EXPLAIN, and SQL individually. This option does *not* log XMLPLAN, LOCK, or STATSUSAGE. If you specify ALL, then you should also specify a value of 0 for SQLTEXT to ensure that the text for the SQL statement is not logged in both the *DBQLogTbl* and *DBQLSqlTbl* tables. If you specify ALL, then you cannot specify other logging options.
EXPLAIN	Log the unformatted EXPLAIN text for the query. This option generates and logs the unformatted EXPLAIN text for each query. It does *not* generate EXPLAIN text for queries preceded by the EXPLAIN modifier.

Option	Description
	You should be cautious about specifying this option because the performance cost of generating the EXPLAIN text for a query can be expensive.
[DETAILED] STATSUSAGE	Capture query optimizer statistics and usage recommendations.
LOCK = n	Logs lock contentions longer than the specified centiseconds.
NONE	This disables logging.
OBJECTS	Log information about databases, tables, columns, and indexes accessed by SQL queries for the specified user set. This option does not log activity for macros or views, nor does it log activity for dictionary tables and columns.
SQL	Log the full text of all SQL statements performed by the specified user set in system table *DBQLSqlTbl*. This option does not log SQL statements within stored procedures, macros, views, or triggers.
STEPINFO	Log AMP step-level information for all SQL queries performed by the specified user set in system table *DBQLStepTbl*.
USECOUNT	Logs use count for a database or a user. If specified for a database, no other options can be used.
[VERBOSE] XMLPLAN	Logs the query plan in XML format.

Figure 10.12

Practice Questions

1. Which of the following is not a Viewpoint Session alert?
    a. Active Time
    b. AMP CPU
    c. Blocked Time
    d. DBC.TransientJournal skew

2. What is the name of the Locking Logger utility?
    a. locklogger
    b. dumplocklog
    c. locklog
    d. hutlocklog

3. Which ResUsage table contains information about Virtual Storage?
    a. ResUsageSpdsk
    b. ResUsageSvdsk
    c. ResUsageSldv
    d. ResUsageSpma

4. Which of the following should be used for individual query performance?
    a. AmpUsageV
    b. DBQL
    c. ResUsage
    d. LogOnOffV

5. Which of the following should be used for individual user performance?
    a. AmpUsageV
    b. DBQL
    c. ResUsage
    d. LogOnOffV

Chapter Notes

Utilize this space for notes, key points to remember, diagrams, areas of further study, etc.

Chapter 11 - Maintenance Utilities

Certification Objectives

- ✓ Identify the functionality provided by DBSControl.
- ✓ Identify the functionality provided by ctl.
- ✓ Identify the functionality provided by DIP.
- ✓ Identify the functionality of the RECONFIG Utility.
- ✓ Identify the functionality provided by Ferret.
- ✓ Given a scenario of aborting a rollback, identify the impact on the table.
- ✓ Describe the features and functions of the online reconfiguration utility.

Before You Begin

You should be familiar with the following terms and concepts.

Terms	Key Concepts
Data Distribution	How the File System uses Master Index, Cylinder Index, Data Block, Free Space
Recovery	What is meant by Permanent Journaling, Rollback, Rollforward
BTEQ	Know how to run scripts
Reconfiguration	Adding, removing, modifying resources

Maintenance, Diagnostic, and Recovery Utilities

The chart below summarizes the utilities that will be reviewed in this study guide.

Utility	Purpose
Control GDO Editor (ctl)	This displays PDE Control Parameters GDO fields and enables settings to be modified.
Database Initialization Program (DIP)	DIP provides a variety of scripts that can be enabled to create database objects to enhance the functionality of the Teradata Database.
DBS Control (dbscontrol)	Displays the DBS Control Record fields and enables settings to be modified.
Ferret Utility (ferret)	Provides a range of commands that performs an action. For example, moving data to reconfigure data blocks and cylinders, or displaying disk space and cylinder free-space percent.
Reconfiguration Utility (reconfig)	Utility to reconfigure the Teradata Database.
Recovery Manager (rcvmanager)	Monitors the progress of a Teradata Database recovery.

Figure 11.1

FERRET

The Ferret utility provides the ability to view and set disk space utilization attributes of the Teradata Database. Ferret can configure the data in the Teradata file system dynamically while ensuring that data integrity is maintained as changes are being applied. Ferret can be utilized on several data levels such as: vproc, table, subtable, WAL log, disk, and cylinder.

Ferret gives you a wide range of commands that allow you to display specific information about the Teradata Database system, and optimize the system to improve performance.

DEFRAGMENT

Command	Valid SCOPE Options	Function
DEFRAGMENT DEFRAG	Vprocs or tables	Combines free sectors, and moves them to the end of a cylinder.

Figure 11.2

This command combines all of the free sectors of every cylinder, within a defined scope, into a single contiguous block of free space on the cylinder.

The defrag process moves the data blocks of the fragmented cylinder to a new cylinder, packing them close together. This way, all of the free space on the fragmented cylinder occupies a single, contiguous, area on the new cylinder. The fragmented cylinder is then placed on the Free Cylinder list and becomes available for new allocation.

Note: This process does not change the size or the contents of the data blocks.

The FORCE option tells the defrag command to ignore the percentage of free sectors or average block size, and to defrag the cylinder if there is more than one block of free space.

The following is the syntax of the DEFRAGMENT command.

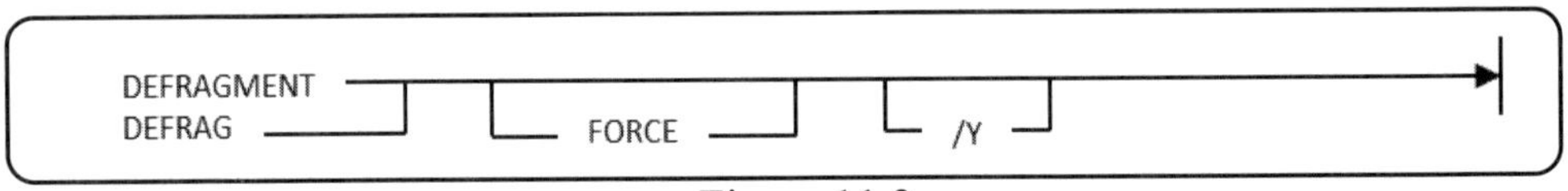

Figure 11.3

FORCE

Command	Valid SCOPE Options	Function
FORCE	None	Sets the cylinders occupied by a table or range of rows, to a specified temperature, regardless of how frequently the data has been historically accessed.

Figure 11.4

Under normal operations, the system gathers statistics on how frequently data is accessed, and determines the data's temperature. The FORCE command can be used to set the temperature for data in a new table, without having to wait for access statistics to be collected.

Using the FORCE command to change infrequently accessed tables or partitions to COLD will cause the system to compress them sooner.

Obviously, this command can be used to override the temperature set by the system if the measured data access frequency differs.

The force command can be used to change the temperature of rows in a non-partitioned table, or one or more partitions of a partitioned table.

The next figure is the syntax for the FORCE command.

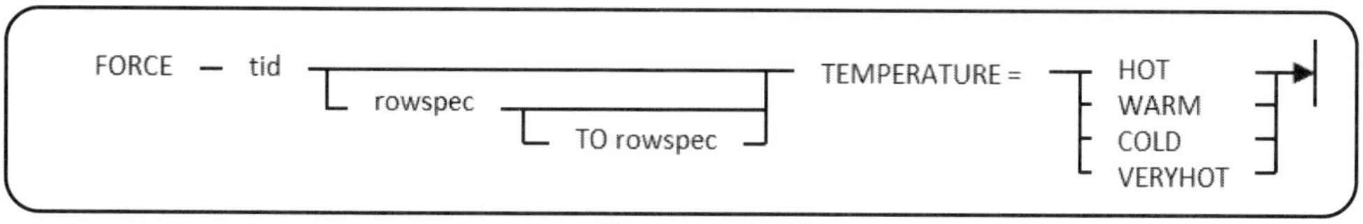

Figure 11.5

PACKDISK

Command	Valid SCOPE options	Function
PACKDISK	Vprocs or Tables	Reconfigures cylinders within a defined scope.

Figure 11.6

The PACKDISK command reconfigures the contents of a disk, leaving a percentage of free space for cylinders within a scope defined by the SCOPE command.

PACKDISK packs either the entire disk or a single table, leaving a specified percentage of the scoped object empty to account for subsequent insert and update operations.

Packing applies only to entire logical cylinders, not to the space inside individual data blocks within those cylinders. Data block sizes are the same before and after the PACKDISK operation.

For a cylinder, the free space percent is a minimum percentage that indicates how much extra free space should be left on each cylinder during a data loading operation. This allows you to reserve space for future updates.

The following is the syntax diagram of the PACKDISK command.

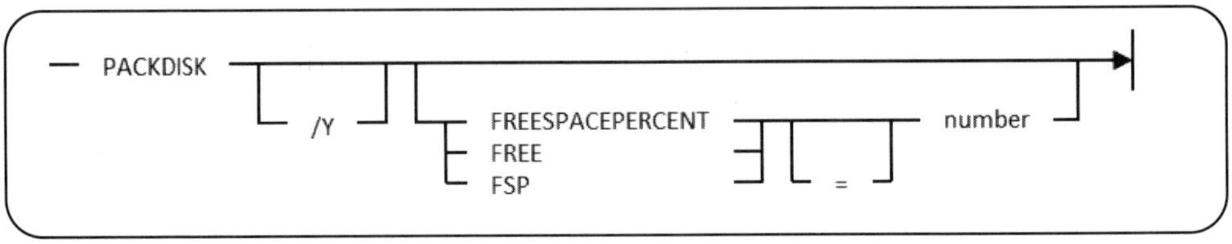

Figure 11.7

SCANDISK

Command	Valid SCOPE Options	Function
SCANDISK	WAL log, vprocs, or tables	Performs a verification of the file system BTree structure.

Figure 11.8

This command validates the physical file system, and reports any errors it encounters during the validation process.

It checks the master index, cylinder index, and data blocks, including the Write-Ahead Logging (WAL) log. It also verifies the ROWIDs and partition numbers for matching key physical rows to those rows in the master index and cylinder index.

For tables with check summing defined, SCANDISK calculates, modifies, and verifies the file system check sums and reports any discrepancies.

SCANDISK can run while the system is online and available for normal operations, though there may be a slight performance impact.

Teradata recommends you run SCANDISK in the following situations:

- To validate data integrity before or after a system upgrade or expansion.
- If you suspect data corruption.
- As a routine data integrity check (perhaps weekly).

Here is the syntax diagram for the SCANDISK command.

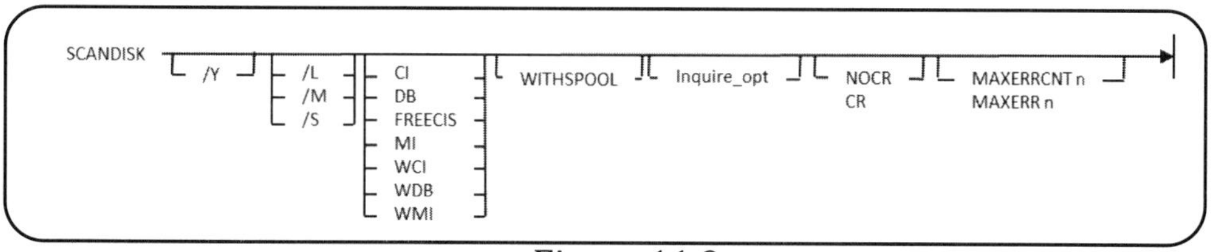

Figure 11.9

SHOWSPACE

Command	Valid SCOPE Options	Function
SHOWSPACE SHOWS	WAL log, vprocs, or tables	Displays storage space utilization for permanent, spool, WAL log, temporary, and journal data, including the amount of free space remaining.

Figure 11.10

The SHOWSPACE command reports on storage space utilization for the defined scope.

It shows:

- The number of allocated cylinders utilized for permanent, journal, temporary, spool, and WAL log data.
- The average per cylinder utilization for permanent, journal, temporary, and spool cylinders.
- The total count and percentage of free cylinders available in the Teradata Database.

The syntax of the SHOWSPACE command is shown in the next diagram.

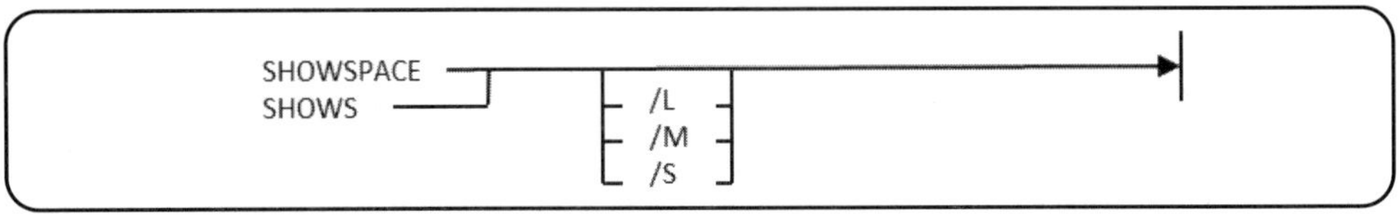

Figure 11.11

SHOWWHERE

Command	Valid SCOPE Options	Function
SHOWWHERE SHOWW	WAL log, vprocs, or tables	Displays information about cylinder allocation and temperature for cylinders in the currently set scope.

Figure 11.12

The SHOWWHERE command is only available for those Teradata Database systems where temperature-based block-level compression is enabled.

The command displays information about cylinder allocation and temperature based upon the current scope. If there is no temperature information available in the current scope, the SHOWWHERE command will return an error.

Here is the syntax of the SHOWWHERE command.

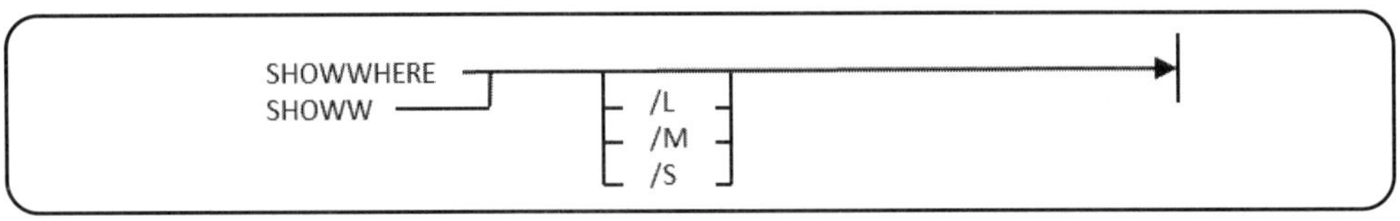

Figure 11.13

Recovery Manager Utility

The Recovery Manager utility, rcvmanager, is used to monitor and provide status information of a Teradata Database system in recovery. The utility also includes information regarding transaction rollbacks if the system experiences a Teradata Database system crash or user abort.

The recovery process includes:

- Online Transaction recovery
- Down AMP recovery of data rows that have changed
- Down AMP recovery of changes at the system level

Also, rcvmanager enables you to do the following:

- Cancel the rollback of one or more specified host and session IDs
- Set the priority level on rollbacks that are in-progress at the host and session ID
- Set priority levels in order to optimize system recovery

List Locks

The LIST LOCKS command shows all locks currently in transaction recovery.

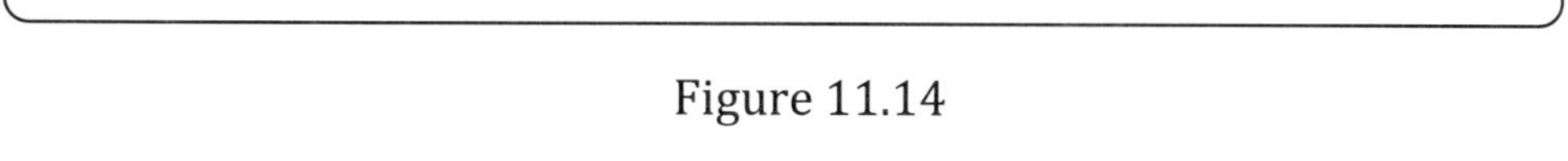

Figure 11.14

The output of the report shows the lock held (i.e. write or exclusive), the object locked (database, table, row range, or row hash) along with the object name.

Note: LIST LOCKS cannot display locks in online or offline catchup mode.

List Rollback Tables

The LIST ROLLBACK TABLES command provides a detailed report of the table(s) that are in the process of a rollback.

Figure 11.15

In order for the LIST ROLLBACK command to show the tables that are in the process of a rollback, it must satisfy the following condition:

- The table must have 10000 (or more) rows remaining on one AMP.
- The transaction status must be aborted.

The output report will only show the column headers if no rollback is in progress, or if no table satisfies the above conditions.

Note: The output report list will not include DBC and Permanent Journal (PJ) tables. The asterisk (*) will only appear next to tables that have Referential Integrity constraints defined. Rollbacks are not allowed on these types of tables.

Cancel Rollback on Table

The CANCEL ROLLBACK ON TABLE command provides the ability to cancel a rollback on a table(s) that is in the process of a recovery, or an online, user-aborted transaction.

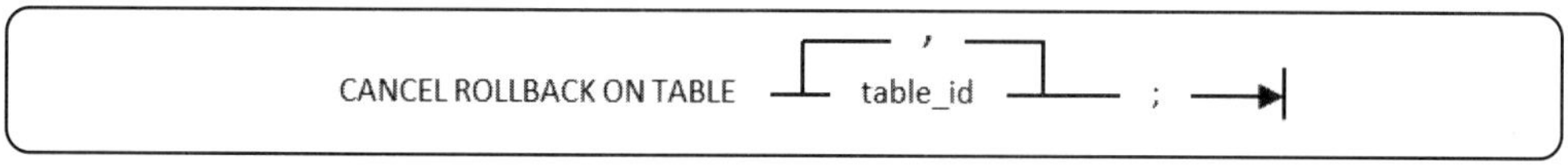

Figure 11.16

It is recommended that you execute a LIST ROLLBACK TABLES command first in order to obtain the table IDs of the table before you issue a CANCEL ROLLBACK ON TABLE. The CANCEL ROLLBACK ON TABLE will fail for tables that are not on the list.

Note: This option should be carefully considered as the table will need to be recovered from backup media.

Reconfig

The Reconfiguration and Configuration utilities are used to define the AMPs and PEs that operate together as a Teradata Database.

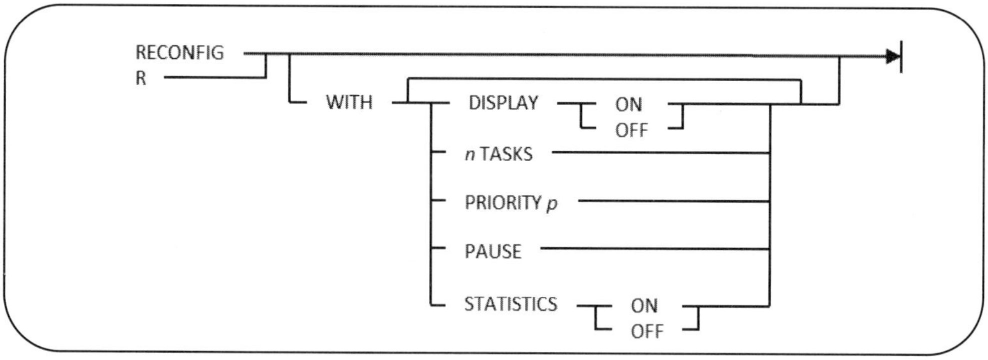

Figure 11.17

Reconfiguration is step two of the configuration and reconfiguration process that configures or modifies a Teradata Database system. Basically, the Reconfiguration utility implements the updated system configuration that is mapped and defined by the Configuration utility.

The Reconfiguration utility is typically utilized when adding new nodes to a current configuration. The Reconfiguration utility can also be used to modify the following:

- Configuration of AMP and PE vprocs and how they relate to nodes
- AMP vprocs cluster specifications

The Reconfiguration process performs the following functions:

- Verifies the system status so the reconfiguration can proceed.

- Verifies disk capacity to ensure that there is adequate storage space available if AMPs are being removed. Reconfiguration will terminate if there is not enough storage capacity.

- Creates a new hash bucket array and configuration maps once the status of the system is verified, .

- Redistributes primary indexes, unique secondary index subtables, and fallback tables if any.

- Deletes and rebuilds non-unique secondary indexes, if any.

- Updates and resets space accounting, hash bucket arrays, and configuration maps.

Before starting Reconfiguration, verify the following:

- Hardware is online and correctly configured.

- All the AMP and PE vprocs are online and ready via the Vproc Manager utility.

- That no tables are in pending status during the PENDINGOP stage by running the CHECK command from the CheckTable utility.

- Logons are disabled, and is in a quiescent state.

- Disable online archive logging for any database object.

Reconfiguration Estimator

The Reconfiguration Estimator utility, *reconfig_estimator*, runs from the Database Window (DBW) or comparable interface to the Teradata Database console subsystem, and should be run before running the Reconfiguration utility.

Its purpose is to estimate the time required based on the number and size of the tables to complete the reconfiguration. The *reconfig_estimator* provides time estimates for the following phases:

- Redistribution
- Deletion
- NUSI building

The utility also validates the existence of the tables in the ordering lists for the deletion and redistribution phases. These lists, DBC.ReconfigRedistOrderTbl and DBC.ReconfigDeleteOrderTbl, specify the order in which Reconfig Estimator and Reconfig should process the tables, and their use is recommended by Teradata. If ordering is not explicitly defined, the tables will be processed in table ID order.

The utility does a sample run of the Reconfiguration utility to determine estimation constants. This process involves inserting and deleting sample data, and requires the user name and password of an exclusive account having CREATE/DROP DATABASE, CREATE/DROP TABLE, INSERT, and DELETE privileges, which has approximately 1 GB/AMP of space.

The time estimates produced by *reconfig_estimator* are affected by how busy the system is when it is running. The best estimates are obtained when *reconfig_estimator* runs for 5-10 minutes on an idle system. The busier the system is, the longer the utility should run, and the more disk space it should have available.

Online and Offline Reconfiguration

The Reconfiguration utility has been enhanced to allow the system to remain available to users during the **redistribution phase** of the reconfiguration process. This allows users to continue to access the system.

Other phases of the reconfiguration process require that logons be disabled and no user sessions are running. The entire process ends with a system restart. Online Reconfiguration dramatically reduces the amount of time the system will be offline.

When the entire reconfiguration process is run offline, the entire process can be completed more rapidly. However, the system will not be available to the users for a longer period of time.

Online reconfiguration cannot be used with move/delete AMP and hash bucket size change operations.

To enable online reconfiguration, do the following:

- Run SCANDISK and CheckTable immediately prior to online reconfiguration
- To specify the order in which the tables should be processed, use the DBC.ReconfigRedistOrderTbl (DBC.ReconfigRedistOrderV) and DBC.ReconfigDeleteOrderTbl (DBC.ReconfigDeleteOrderV) tables.
- Do not change the hash bucket size or delete AMPs

ABORT

Use of the ABORT command depends on whether you are running the Reconfiguration Estimator or Reconfiguration utility. In any event, the ABORT stops the reconfiguration process, all reconfig tasks are aborted, all journaling is stopped, and all checkpoint information is deleted.

If you are running *reconfig_estimator*, it can be stopped during the following phases:

- Entry of the Reconfiguration Estimator parameters
- Pseudo Reconfig, where the utility performs a simulated reconfig to gather processing time estimates
- Table level estimates

If you are running the Reconfiguration utility, the ABORT command can only be used during the redistribution phase of online reconfiguration. The ABORT command is not supported for offline reconfiguration.

ctl

The ctl editors enable you to display and modify PDE configuration settings. The PDE configuration settings affect how the system handles startup, crashes, and the normal operations.

PROGRAM	a.k.a.	PLATFORM	INTERFACES
ctl	Control GDO Editor	Windows	Database Window (DBW)
		Linux	Command line

Figure 11.18

Whether in screen mode or command line mode, the following can be accomplished from either utility.

Screen	Command	Function
Hardware Report	**hardware**	Displays the current system hardware configuration.
DBS	**screen dbs**	Controls how the database software responds to unusual conditions.
Debug	**screen debug**	Controls debugging parameters for PDE and Teradata Database.
RSS	**screen rss**	Permits the following: • Specification and changing of rates at which RSS data is collected and logged into the database • Enabling/disabling the writing of resource data to the specified ResUsage database table(s)
Version	**screen version**	Displays the version numbers of the PDE and database software. Allows specification of other

Screen	Command	Function
		resident software versions that will be installed and run the next time Teradata Database is started.

Figure 11.19

Here again is the **screen rss** output.

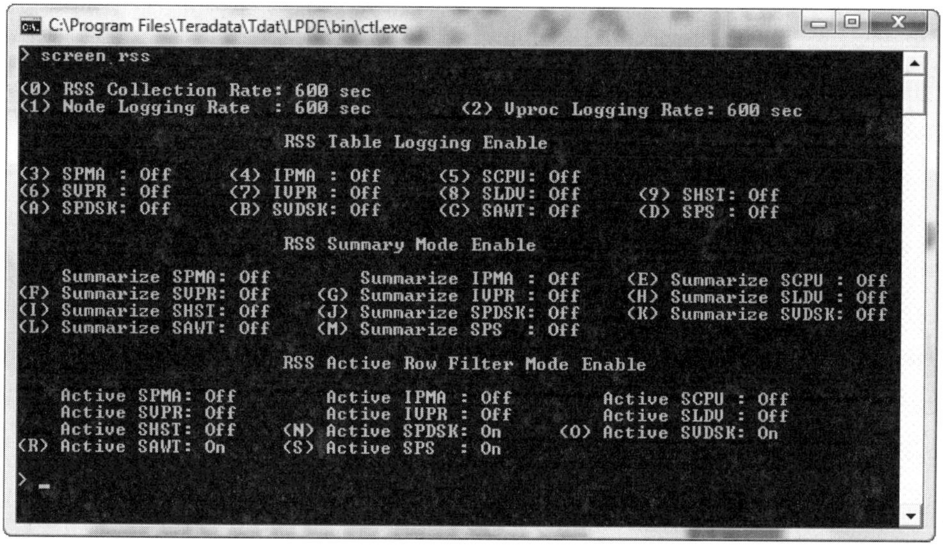

Figure 11.20

DBS Control Utility

The DBS Control utility, dbscontrol, displays and modifies various configuration settings which are stored as DBS Control Record fields in the DBS Control Globally Distributed Object (GDO). GDOs are binary files that store database configuration settings, and are distributed and used by every node in the system.

Use DBS Control to perform the following:

- Display the values of the DBS Control Record fields
- Modify the values of the writable DBS Control Record fields

You can use DBS Control whether or not the Teradata Database is running. DBS Control requires only that PDE and the Database Window are operational.

The DISPLAY command displays the current values for the fields of each of the DBS Control Record groups: GENERAL, FILESYS, PERFORMANCE, and CHECKSUM.

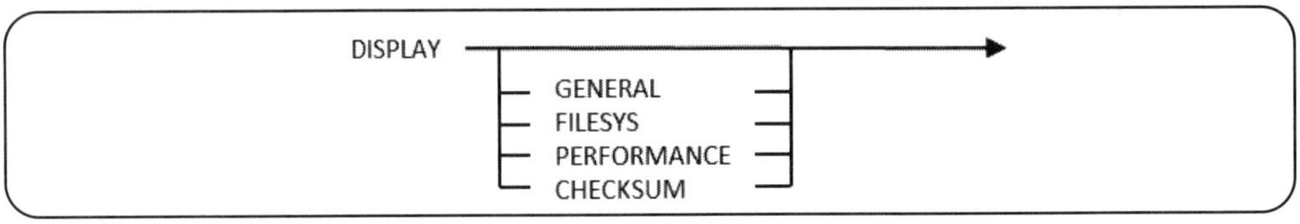

Figure 11.21

Here is a sample output from the DISPLAY command.

```
Enter a command, HELP, or QUIT:
DISPLAY FILESYS
DBS Control Record - File System Fields:
1.  FreeSpacePercent          = 0%
2.  MiniCylPackLowCylProd     = 10 (free cylinders)
3.  PermDBSize                = 127 (sectors)
```

```
4.   JournalDBSize            = 12 (sectors)
5.   DefragLowCylProd         = 100 (free cylinders)
6.   PermDBAllocUnit          = 1 (sectors)
7.   Cylinders Saved for PERM = 10 (cylinders)
8.   DisableWALforDBs         = FALSE
9.   DisableWAL               = FALSE
10.   WAL Buffers             = 20 (WAL log buffers)
11.   MaxSyncWALWrites        = 40 (MaxSyncWalWrites)
12.   SmallDepotCylsPerPdisk  = 2 (cylinders)
13.   LargeDepotCylsPerPdisk  = 1 (cylinders)
14.   WAL Checkpoint Interval = 60 (seconds)
```

The Group Name along with the Field Numbers are used with the MODIFY command.

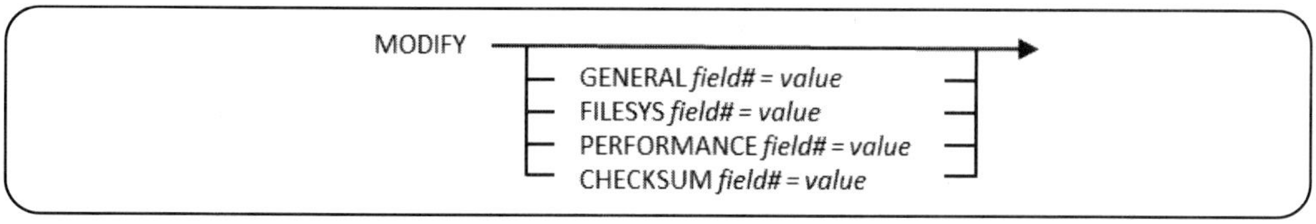

Figure 11.22

After making any allowable changes, you must issue a WRITE command to cause the utility to update the GDO throughout the entire system.

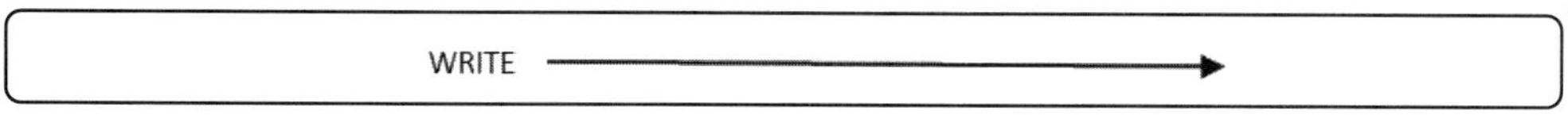

Figure 11.23

If you need help at any time, use the HELP command.

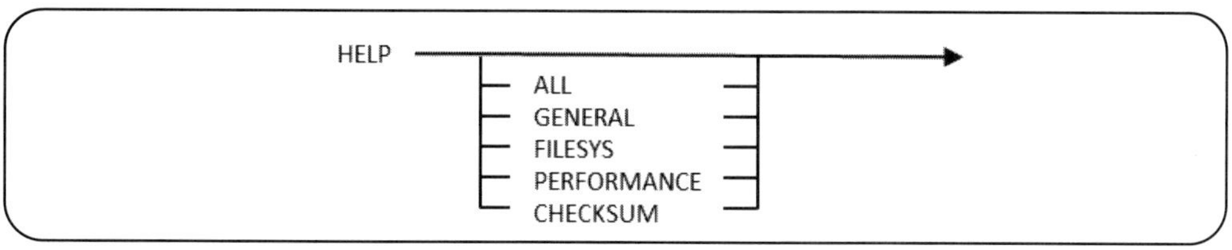

Figure 11.24

When you are finished, the QUIT command will end your session and close the program.

```
QUIT ──────────────────────────────▶
```

Figure 11.25

Free Space

The purpose of Free Space is to reserve an amount of space on each cylinder that is to be left unused during the following operations:

- FastLoad
- MultiLoad into an empty table
- Archive/Recovery RESTORE
- Table Rebuild
- Reconfiguration
- Ferret PACKDISK
- MiniCylPack
- Adding Fallback protection with an ALTER TABLE
- A CREATE INDEX for a secondary index on a populated table
- Configuring Fallback during an INSERT/SELECT into an empty table
- Secondary index creation during an INSERT/SELECT into any empty table

This way, tables can grow without the system having to allocate new free cylinders.

Free space is specified as a percentage (0 – 75) of the space on cylinders during loading operations, and can be set in three different ways:

The amount of free space can be set using the . . .	COMMENTS
FreeSpacePercent field in the DBC Control record	The system uses this global parameter during the loading operations noted above, unless it has been overridden at the table level. You should choose a percentage which reflects the overall system growth rate of your tables (INSERTs minus DELETEs). Typical settings are in the range of 5% to 15%.
FreeSpacePercent parameter of PACKDISK	This operates over the defined SCOPE. It cannot be used to change the FREESPACE value specified by the ALTER/CREATE TABLE. The FREESPACE specified at the table level takes precedence of this value, unless the FORCE option is used. If you use the FORCE option, PACKDISK will pack to the requested FreeSpacePercent, but after that, the AutoCylPack background task will repack the cylinders to the FREESPACE value specified at the table level.
FREESPACE value in the CREATE/ALTER TABLE commands	This overrides the FSP of the DBS Control record. Static tables can be given a very low FSP. Dynamic table will require a higher percentage of free space to minimize CylPacks. How much free space is needed becomes a tradeoff of space versus performance. The system can maintain different levels of FSP on cylinders used to store different tables.

Figure 11.26

AutoCylPack

AutoCylPack is a background task that manages space on cylinders. It finds cylinders with low and high utilization, and returns them to their user-defined FSP. If it finds a cylinder that has less than the desired FSP, it moves some data from the congested cylinder to other cylinders that have more FSP than specified, thereby balancing the space utilization.

The following two parameters control the background task:

PARAMETER	COMMENTS
AutoCylPackThresh	This specifies the difference between the actual amount of free space on a cylinder and the target FSP. A difference smaller than this threshold will cause AutoCylPack to skip the cylinder. The valid range is from 5% - 30%.
AutoCylPackInterval	This specifies the amount of time, in seconds, that AutoCylPack waits between checking for new work. The valid range is from 60 – 600.

Figure 11.27

The amount of free space AutoCylPack maintains for cylinders depends on how the FSP was specified.

- If the FSP was specified in a CREATE/ALTER TABLE command, then AutoCylPack maintains that FSP for the cylinders of that table.
- If FSP was not specified at the CREATE/ALTER TABLE statement, but PACKDISK was run on the table, then the system will maintain the FSP specified for PACKDISK.
- If an FSP has not been specified by a CREATE/ALTER TABLE, and PACKDISK has never been run, then AutoCylPack uses the FSP specified in the DBS Control.

AutoCylPack helps reduce the need to perform regular PACKDISK operations, and reduces the chance of a MiniCylPack. MiniCylPacks are strictly concerned with reclaiming whole cylinders, not maintaining FSP.

MiniCylPack

A MiniCylPack moves data blocks in logical sequence from cylinder to cylinder until the required number of free cylinders is available. The system will start a MiniCylPack when the number of free cylinders drops to the value set in the DBS Control MiniCylPackLowCylProd parameter. If the system needs a free cylinder and none are available, a MiniCylPack occurs automatically. MiniCylPacks are an indication of a severe space shortage. It may be a momentary situation caused by spool files taking up all available space, or it may signal the need for increasing the total disk space on the system. Keep in mind that spool files are never CylPacked.

The following table lists the DBS Control parameters that have an effect on space management.

DBS Control Parameter	Comments
AutoCylPackColdData	This parameter determines whether AutoCylPack should be performed on cylinders storing cold data in addition to cylinders storing more frequently accessed data.
AutoCylPackFreeCylThresh	This specifies the number of free cylinders below which AutoCylPack will not allocate any new cylinders.
AutoCylPackFSP	This parameter specifies the percentage of space within a cylinder that AutoCylPack operations leave free of data to allow for future growth.
AutoCylPackInterval	This specifies the time AutoCylPack

	should wait between checks for new AutoCylPack work.
AutoCylPackIOThresh	This specifies the number of pending I/O operations above which the AutoCylPack task waits for I/Os to complete before continuing.
AutoCylPackStyle	This parameter determines whether the AutoCylPack task is restricted to just packing data more tightly on cylinders, just unpacking data, or if it is unrestricted, and can both pack and unpack data to achieve the target FSP.
AutoCylPackThresh	This determines the threshold difference between actual free space on a cylinder and the target AutoCylPack FSP, below which AutoCylPack will not process the cylinder.
Cylinders saved for PERM	This parameter saves some number of cylinders for permanent data only. This prevents spool and temporary tables from consuming all available free cylinders.
DefragLowCylProd	This parameter determines the number of free cylinders below which cylinder defragmentation can begin.
FreeSpacePercent	This parameter specifies the percentage of free space reserved on cylinders during bulk load operations.
MergeBlockRatio	This parameter specifies the maximum size of a new data block that results from the merging of several smaller blocks.
MiniCylPackLowCylProd	This parameter determines the number of free cylinders below which the File System will start to perform a

	MiniCylPack operation in anticipation of the need for additional free cylinders.

Figure 11.28

Database Initialization Program (DIP)

The Database Initialization Program, DIP, is a series of pre-packaged executable scripts. These scripts will create system users, databases, macros, tables, and views, for the following uses:

- Teradata Database:
    - To configure access logging, character sets, and system calendar arithmetic.
    - Enable the ability to capture and store PDE Crashdumps, resource usage, query text, and error messages.
- Users:
    - Access the Data Dictionary Directory (system catalog) tables
    - Generate reports like resource usage statistics

Note: DIP enables you to execute one, many, or all scripts, which can create a variety of database objects. During the initial Teradata Database installation, all of the DIP scripts required are executed. However, you can implement the DIP utility to add optional features anytime.

The following table lists all of the script files, the objects they create, and their purpose.

SQL Script File	Items Created	Purpose
DIPACC	DBC.AccLogRule macro. Execute this script only if you want to: • Enable null passwords • Implement and log accesschecking	Runs the access logging script. Enables a user who has the EXECUTE privilege on this macro to submit: • GRANT LOGON/REVOKE LOGON statements, used to grant the WITH NULL PASSWORD privilege. (On Windows, this privilege is required to implement external authentication. On channel connected mainframes, null passwords also require TDP exits.) • BEGIN LOGGING/END LOGGING statements, used to enable access rights checking and logging.
DIPACR	Access rights.	Loads and initializes data access rights.
DIPALL	Runs all scripts listed in the DIP screen above its own entry.	Runs all DIP scripts except the following: • DIPACC • DIPPATCH
DIPBAR	• SYSBAR database • BARUSER user • Tables and views to support	Infrastructure to support Data Stream Architecture (DSA) Backup And Recovery (BAR). BAR uses its own subset of DBC views to ensure that when changes are

	BAR	made to mainline views, the impact is minimized. DSA view names are prefaced by BAR_.
DIPCAL	• Sys_Calendar database • CalDates table • Calendar view	Loads the calendar tables and views. Used for date arithmetic in OLAP and other functions.
DIPCCS	Client character sets	• Install client character set definitions. • Install pre-configured translation tables for Unicode, Japanese, and various European non-English languages.
DIPCRASH	Configures Crashdumps database	Crashdumps database and table in database DBC

DIPDEM	• The system database, and SYSLIB database including:
	• Tables
	  • dem
	  • demddl
	  • dempart
	• Stored Procedures
	  • installsp
	  • savepkg
	  • loadpkg
	• External Stored Procedures
	  • Query
		Loads tables, and stored procedures. It also installs a UDF for propagation, backup, and recovery of database extensibility mechanisms (DEMs).
		
		DEMs include stored procedures, UDFs, and UDTs packages.
		
		UDFs and external stored procedures are loaded for Query Banding and Workload Management.

	Banding
	• User-Defined Functions (UDFs)
	  • installpkg
	  • UDFs for Query Banding and Workload Managem ent	

DIPERR	Logs for Error Messages	Error files generated by Teradata Database, software, and client connections are loaded
DIPGLOP	• DBCExtension database objects include: Tables • GLOP_Map • GLOP_Set • GLOP_Data Stored Procedures • GLOP_Add • GLOP_Remove • GLOP_Change • GLOP_Report	Enables and supports global and persistent (GLOP) data. GLOP is a data type available to external routines. **Note:** GLOP data is only available on Linux.
DIPOCES	• Dictionary table with standard cost profile data • View and	Provides OCES metadata support with standard cost profile definitions.

	Macro definitions	
DIPOLH	Online help	Configures online help text messages.
DIPPATCH	Stand-alone patches	Used for loading stand-alone patches.
DIPPDCR	Installs the table definitions, load macros and base table views.	Provides a basic framework for collection of the data. A job(s) would still need to be constructed to do the actual collection.
DIPPOST	Items that must be created near the end of the DIPALL sequence. For example, views that have dependencies on other DIP scripts.	This script is for statements that have multiple DIP dependencies and need to execute near the end of the DIPALL sequence.
DIPPWRSTNS		Ceates a list of restricted words that are restricted from use in new or updated passwords. Initializes the table DBC.PasswordRestrictions automatically.
DIPRCO	• views • secondary indexes	Note: Reserved for future development.

	• check constraints	
DIPRSS	ResUsage tables	Loads stored sample Resource Usage table data.
DIPRUM	ResUsage macros and views	Loads Resource Usage views and macros. Provides you the ability to generate reports from the ResUsage system tables.
DIPSQLJ	• SQLJ system database • Provide support for external stored procedures in the SQLJ database. Modules installed. INSTALL_JAR REPLACE_JAR REMOVE_JAR ALTER_JAVA_PATH SQLJ.REDISTRIBUTE_JAR • The following views in the SQLJ database:	Enables Java-based external stored procedures. The new views and tables in the Data Dictionary.

	SQLJ.JAR_JAR_USAGE SQLJ.JARS SQLJ.ROUTINE_JAR_USAGE	
DIPSTATS	Statistics metadata infrastructure	This script creates the infrastructure required for calling Automated Statistics Open APIs.
DIPSYSFE	• SytemFE • Macros and tables used with Target Level Emulation	• Loads SystemFE macros and Target Level Emulation-related tables. • Generates diagnostic reports used by Teradata support personnel. • Enables implementation of Target Level Emulation for analyzing the performance of your SQL applications.
DIPSYSFNC	• The TD_SYSFNLIB database, if it does not already exist. • System Functions • Calendar views • Calendar macros	Enables database system functions and embedded services. Calendar views and macros that provide custom Teradata, ISO, and COMPATIBLE business calendars.
DIPTDWM	• TDWM database • dbcmngr database Note: If this exists, they will	Creates or upgrades the database infrastructure which is required for Teradata Viewpoint and workload management for alerting.

	be upgraded automatically to the current version.	
DIPUDT	• The SYSUDTLIB • The following macros in this database: HelpDependencies HelpUdtCastMacro HelpUdtCastMacro_Src HelpUdtCastMacro_Dst ShowUdtCastMacro	Creates SYSUDTLIB, the system database for all User Defined Types (UDTs), User Defined Methods (UDMs), and the User Defined Functions (UDFs) that are used by UDTs as Cast, Ordering, or Transform routines.
DIPVIEWS	• The SYSLIB database that provides User-accessible views defined on the system tables • Includes objects such as control macros, query log	• Creates the SYSLIB for UDFs. • Installs system views in the DBC database to access the content of the system tables in the data dictionary. • Creates DBQL objects.

	tables, and views into the logs	
DIPXML	• TD_SYSXML database • XML Type definition • Stored procedures for XML publishing/ shredding	Enables XML functionality including the XML data type, and associated SQL/XML functions, stored in the TD_SYSFNLIB database. Provides stored procedures for XML publishing and shredding stored in the TD_SYSXML database.

Figure 11.29

Practice Questions

1. If the system needs a free cylinder, and none are available, which of the following will be started automatically?
    a. AUTO CYLPACK
    b. DEFRAG
    c. MINI CYLPACK
    d. PACKDISK

2. Which of the following only moves data within a cylinder?
    a. AUTO CYLPACK
    b. DEFRAG
    c. MINI CYLPACK
    d. PACKDISK

3. Which of the following is only available if temperature-based block-level compression is enabled?
    a. PACKDISK
    b. SCANDISK
    c. SHOWSPACE
    d. SHOWWHERE

4. Which of the following has the FORCE option?
    a. AUTO CYLPACK
    b. DEFRAG
    c. MINI CYLPACK
    d. PACKDISK

5. Which of the following is concerned with reclaiming whole cylinders, not maintaining FSP?
    a. AUTO CYLPACK
    b. DEFRAG
    c. MINI CYLPACK
    d. PACKDISK

6. If you want to cancel rollback on a table, which of the following statements is false?
    a. The table will have to be recovered from backup media.
    b. The table will be rolled forward to its state prior to initiating the Rollback.
    c. You can't cancel rollback on a table having any referential constraints.
    d. If the table has less than 10000 rows yet to rollback on all AMPs, you cannot cancel the rollback.

7. What are the names of the tables *reconfig* and *reconfig_estimator* use to determine the redistribution and deletion processing order for tables?
    a. DBC.ReconfigRedistributeOrderTbl and DBC.ReconfigDeleteOrderTbl
    b. DBC.ReconfigRedistOrder and DBC.ReconfigDeleteOrder
    c. DBC.ReconfigRedistOrderTbl and DBC.ReconfigDeleteOrderTbl
    d. DBC.ReconfigRedTbl and DBC.ReconfigDelOrderTbl

8. Which DIP script should be used to load UDFs and external stored procedures for use with Query Banding and Workload Management?
    a. DIPACR
    b. DIPCCS
    c. DIPDEM
    d. DIPPDCR

Chapter Notes

Utilize this space for notes, key points to remember, diagrams, areas of further study, etc.

Chapter 12 - Capacity Planning

Certification Objectives

- ✓ Identify the inputs that need to be collected for future capacity planning.
- ✓ Identify what is monitored to diagnose immediate capacity shortfalls.
- ✓ Identify the causes of a system running out of disk space.
- ✓ Given a scenario, identify potential solutions to capacity shortages.
- ✓ Calculate the space needed for tables and subtables.
- ✓ Given a scenario, identify the implication of adding compression.
- ✓ Identify methods for conserving disk space.
- ✓ Given a scenario including a type of data protection, identify how the data will be protected or recovered.
- ✓ Given a scenario including a component failure and protection types, identify which data is available.
- ✓ Identify the impact of altering table attributes and constraints.

Before You Begin

You should be familiar with the following terms and concepts.

Terms	Key Concepts
Disk space	What consumes it, how much it consumes, and how long does it retain it
Table design features	What performance impact each might have
Compression	What are the various forms of compression
Spool	Insufficient spool error causes

Table design considerations

NUSI

When using NUPIs, you can define a secondary index for a table to give the Optimizer another option for faster set selection. Although the Optimizer may still choose a full-table scan even if you define an SI, it generally chooses the SI if it is more useful for optimizing repetitive and standardized queries.

Multiple ANDed NUSIs might qualify for NUSI Bit Mapping. Sparse NUSIs can also improve performance.

Partitioned Primary Index

If a table can be partitioned on the column(s) most frequently used for access, the system can perform partition elimination and access a smaller portion of the table instead of doing a full table scan.

Batch inserts, updates, and deletes can be accomplished faster if a table's partitioning expression matches the arrival pattern of the data.

Unless the partitioning column set is part of the primary index, primary index access can be degraded. Defining a secondary index on the primary index will make the access independent of the number of partitions the table has.

Joins between partitioned and non-partitioned tables having the same primary index can be degraded. To overcome this, partition both tables identically and join them on their partitioning column set.

Data Protection

The system offers many forms of data protection:

- Dual systems
- Cliques
- Hot standby node
- Clusters
- Fallback
- Archive/Recovery
- Permanent journaling
- Transient Journal

Dual systems protect against the catastrophic loss of a system.

If a node fails, cliques will reassign the virtual disks of the failed node to other nodes in the same clique. Having a spare hot standby node per clique allows production to resume at normal levels.

Clusters provide protection to fallback tables. Should a single AMP, within a cluster fail, inserts, updates, deletes, and queries can continue completely for fallback protected tables. For non-fallback tables, any operation which references the down AMP will fail. If more than a single AMP in a cluster fails, the system will go down, and then Archive/Recovery will have to be used to recover the data.

Archive/Recovery allows you to recover from a system crash, table corruption, and the like. It can also be used to port data from one system to another.

Permanent journaling can be used to protect non-fallback tables. It can also be used on fallback tables since it allows you to do roll forward and rollback operations.

RI Constraints

Referential Integrity means that every Foreign Key (FK) value matches an existing Primary Key (PK) value. However, Teradata utilizes two different types of RI which are outlined below:

- **Hard Referential Integrity** - is the normal referential integrity that enforces any RI constraints and ensures that any data loaded into the tables meets the RI rules. This type of RI constraint prevents inserting child rows that do not have a parent row. It prevents modifying an FK value to reference a non-existent parent. It prevents deleting a parent that still has children. You should keep in mind that neither MultiLoad nor FastLoad allow the target table to have foreign key references. TPump does allow this. This does add overhead to data maintenance operations.

- **Soft Referential Integrity** - is more about accessing the data than about loading it. Soft RI does not enforce any constraints. However, when you specify soft RI, you are informing the optimizer that the foreign key references do exist. Therefore, you need to make sure that is true.

Altering Attributes

Modifying the primary index value for a row requires the system to delete the current row and all index references to it, rehash the primary index, insert the row at its new location and rebuild all index references to it.

Many operations will cause existing rows to expand. This may cause block splits, which in turn may require the allocation of a new cylinder, which may require a MiniCylPack. If space permits, creating a new table with the desired changes and doing an Insert/Select, will be faster.

Compression

Multi-Value Compression (MVC)

Basically, compression enables more rows to be stored per physical block, which results in less overall blocks to store the data. In turn, this means less work is required during a query operation. Disk I/O is further reduced because the compressed values are more likely to be memory resident and don't require disk access. Compression is great for full table scan operations, and any extra CPU utilization for these efforts is negligible in today's Teradata systems.

The best candidates for compression are fixed-width columns with a small number of frequently occurring values. Even though these column characteristics are for the very best candidates, you may choose to compress other columns just to save space. This is perfectly legitimate.

Here are some general rules and facts about compression:

- Only fixed width columns can be compressed at present.
- Up to 255 values can be compressed per column, including NULL values.
- You cannot compress primary index columns.
- You cannot compress spool tables
- You cannot compress volatile or derived table columns, or PERIOD data types
- Compression is not allowed on Row level security constraint columns
- Referenced primary key columns cannot be compressed
- Referencing foreign key columns for (hard-RI) referential integrity relationships cannot be compressed
- You cannot compress referencing foreign key columns.

- Nulls are automatically compressed when the COMPRESS clause is assigned.
- Compression is case sensitive
- There is a limit of 8,192 character per column

You can only perform multi-value compression for the following data types:

- Nulls
- Zeros
- Blanks
- Constant data types including:
    - BYTE (max 510 bytes)
    - VARBYTE (up to 510 bytes per value)
    - CHARACTER (up to 510 characters per value)
    - VARCHAR (up to 510 characters per value)
    - DATE (COMPRESS as (DATE 'yyyy-mm-dd'))
    - Any numeric data type

To get a rough idea of how much table header space is required for compression; create two tables, one with compression, and one without. Then query DBC.TableSizeV.

Before implementing compression, make sure your data types are as narrow as possible. As an example, don't define a column as INTEGER, when SMALLINT or BYTEINT will suffice. Never code a column as VARCHAR (1).

You can use the TYPE function to determine the most efficient data type. Simply perform the following query with the maximum value expected for a column.

```
SELECT TYPE(102.98) ;
Answer: DECIMAL(5,2)

SELECT TYPE(10998) ;
Answer:  SMALLINT
```

Figure 12.1

The following rules apply when adding or modifying rows with compression:

1. For single-value compression, the default for the compress value is NULL.
2. There is no default for multi-value compression. All values in the compression list must be specified explicitly.
3. NULL does not need to be specified in a multi-value compression statement. If there is a COMPRESS clause, NULLs are compressed automatically.
4. You can modify an existing column to have multi-value compression.
5. You cannot add a compress value to a column if the table header row exceeds its maximum length of 1 MB for Teradata Version 13 & 14.

You should not compress columns where NULL values are subject to change. If NULL values change, the column will expand and you could cause block splits. Additional considerations include:

- Adding a column that is not compressible will most likely expand all rows.
- Adding a column that is compressible where there are no spare presence bits will expand the row size.

- Nullable fields also require a presence bit, even if it is not compressible. Therefore, if there are no spare presence bits, the row header and each row will expand.
- Dropping a column, changes all row sizes where data is present.

Join Index Compression

Join Index compression is a form of logical data compression in which the system stores a repeating column value set only once, while any non-repeating column values that belong to that set are stored as logical segmental extensions of the base repeating set.

Column Container Compression

For column partitioned tables, the system has various compression techniques it can use. The type of autocompression the system chooses to use is chosen on a container by container basis, based on the context for each container.

Algorithmic Compression (ALC)

This option is specified at the column level, just like MVC. It requires two UDF's, one to compress the data, and one to decompress the data. There is CPU overhead required even when reading a column value to determine if the row meets any selection criteria or for join processing.

It can be specified by itself or in conjunction with MVC.

ALC can only be used on columns with the following data types:

BYTE	VARBYTE
CHARACTER	VARCHAR

GRAPHIC	VARGRAPHIC
All Period types except for VALIDTIME and TRANSACTIONTIME columns	All non-LOB-based UDT types

Figure 12.2

Software-Based Block-Level Compression

Block Level Compression (BLC) is defined at the table level, not the column level. When a physical data block is ready to be written to disk, BLC tests to see how much, if any, it can be compressed.

The DBS Control parameter, *BlockLevelCompression*, indicates whether BLC is enabled. Other parameters in the Compression group define the categories of tables that can be compressed, and which compression routine should be used.

Temperature-Based Block-Level Compression

Temperature-based block-level compression is a feature of Teradata Virtual Storage, and only applies to permanent user data tables.

TVS determines what to compress. As an example, COLD or WARM data might be compressed automatically, and HOT data might be decompressed automatically if it was compressed previously.

When a table is created, the BLOCKCOMPRESSION option defines the table's temperature-based compression. The possible options are:

- AUTOTEMP – The table's state of compression can be changed by the file system at any time based on its TVS temperature.
- DEFAULT – The table's compression is determined by the DBS Control parameter *DefaultTableMode*.
- MANUAL – The table is not managed automatically like AUTOTEMP tables are.
- NEVER – The table will never be block-level compressed.

Capacity planning

System saturation and bottleneck identification are interrelated. When Teradata Database is saturated, the bottleneck is usually some key resource, such as a CPU or disk. Use the information obtained from performance monitoring, resource usage, query capture and process tracking tools to find the cause of repeated bottlenecks.

If a resource has been a bottleneck consistently during peak utilization periods and you have determined that your database design, data modeling, and query structures are efficient, consider expanding your Teradata Database configuration to improve performance.

There are several kinds of system performance data that should be collected, including:

- AMPUsage
- Data space, which includes spool, perm, and temporary space
- User counts (that is, concurrent active and logged on sessions)
- Heartbeat response times
- Data Sources
  - ResUsage
  - Heartbeat History
  - AmpUsage (collected at date/hour level)
  - DiskSpace (Historical collection created from Diskspace)
  - SpoolSpace (Historical collection created from Diskspace)
  - DBQL
  - CPU limits for existing configuration
  - Space limits for existing configuration
- Activities
  - Review historical usage of key capacity components

- Trending of overall and peak historical usage of key capacity components
- Assemble capacity projections for new and existing applications
- Trending of new and existing application growth

Expansion involves adding any combination of disk arrays, memory, vprocs, or nodes (with BYNETs), and then running the Parallel Upgrade Tool (PUT) and Configuration and Reconfiguration utilities.

The Reconfiguration utility can provide an estimate of the duration of outage based on parameters you supply interactively.

Shortfalls

A basic rule of the file system, that is frequently overlooked, is: **a cylinder may contain data or spool, but not both at the same time**.

Even if you have established a Spool_Reserve database, that doesn't guarantee it represents empty cylinders. If a cylinder contains even one data block, that cylinder can only be used for data. Implementing MVC, or other forms of compression, can reduce the space required for data. You can use Ferret COMPRESS to free up some space, or do a CylPack.

If there are not enough free cylinders for data maintenance, you can increase the value of the DBS Control field *Cylinders Saved for Perm*.

Teradata Viewpoint has a System Health portlet which can be used to track system-level space usage.

It also has a Space Usage portlet which can be used to identify databases that are running short on space, those that have excess space, and those that have skewed space usage. Skewed space usage results from one or more tables having a poorly designed primary index. That same portlet can also show which users are consuming the most spool. Excessive spool usage may indicate poorly designed queries.

You can also derive the same information by querying various system tables, such as DBC.TableSizeV

Future

It's difficult to know where you're going unless you know where you've been.

Capture space utilization on a regular basis, and save it for analysis over time.

Calculating Space Requirements

Teradata provides a series of forms for you to use in designing your database system. These forms can be found in the Database Design reference book, B035-1094-112A.

Keep in mind that these forms can help you understand not only the size of user data tables, but also spool space and Transient Journal space.

There are two forms for calculating the size of a table row. Two forms are needed since several data types have different storage sizes depending on whether you have byte-packed system, or a 64-bit byte aligned system. Using the correct form minimizes the chances of mistakenly using column size values that are too small or too large.

Keep in mind that a Partitioned Primary Index will increase the row size by 2 or 8 bytes. Partitioned tables are 4 bytes wider if MVC is used.

The easiest way to determine the size of a table is through empirical sizing.

- Create the table
- Load a known percentage of rows into it
- Query DBC.TableSizeV
- Use the result to calculate the table's size

The same approach can be used for secondary indexes, join indexes, and MVC and ALC data compression.

Conserving Disk Space

Both MVC and ALC can help reduce the size of rows, though ALC can add CPU overhead, as mentioned earlier. Additional areas that you can focus on / analyze that will assist in reducing storage space are as follows:

- Fallback protection doubles the space required for tables, secondary indexes.

- Drop any secondary indexes that are infrequently used, and recreate them when necessary to meet an SLG.

- Make join indexes non-Fallback and drop and recreate them if necessary.

- Make tables that are not in the critical path non-Fallback, and use Archive/Recovery to restore them in case of failure.

- Use Explain to analyze workloads for use of spool and Transient Journal space.

Peak spool

In order to minimize or avoid "Insufficient spool" errors, the DBA must track how much spool users consume, and when.

Teradata Viewpoint provides the means to configure spool space collection parameters. You can specify the following:

- Retention period for summary data
- Current Spool Alarm Threshold
- Peak Spool Alarm Threshold
- An action to be triggered when a threshold is exceeded
- Monitor ALL or selected users.

Note: This can also be captured with a nightly collection of dbc.diskspaceV followed by using the reset macro.

Practice Questions

1. Which of the following is not a form of data protection?
   a. Cliques
   b. Clusters
   c. Groups
   d. Fallback

2. Of the following choices, which one has the potential to be the most costly?
   a. Adding a column that is not compressible.
   b. Modifying a NUSI index.
   c. Modifying a USI index.
   d. Modifying a Primary Index

3. Which of the following functions can be used to determine the most narrow data type?
   a. TYPE ( )
   b. FORMAT ( )
   c. CHAR ( )
   d. BYTES ( )

4. Which of the following data types cannot be the object of ALC?
   a. BYTE
   b. CHARACTER
   c. INTEGER
   d. VARGRAPHIC

5. Which of the following must be kept in mind when managing space?
   a. MVC
   b. Creating a Spool Reserve database.
   c. A cylinder may contain data or spool, but not both at the same time.
   d. DBS Control field *Cylinders Reserved for Perm.*

6. Which of the following views can be used to track spool usage?
    a. DBC.DatabaseSpaceV
    b. DBC.DiskSpaceV
    c. DBC.SpoolSpaceV
    d. DBC.TableSizeV

Chapter Notes

Utilize this space for notes, key points to remember, diagrams, areas of further study, etc.

Chapter 13 - Performance Optimization

Certification Objectives

- ✓ Given a scenario, analyze response time and throughput.
- ✓ Given a scenario, identify the resource that should be used to assess the situation (SQL hash functions, Access Logging, Data Dictionary, ResUsage, DBQL, etc.).
- ✓ Describe the benefits of capturing, creating, and maintaining an historical operational repository from Dictionary tables.
- ✓ Identify the benefits, features and utilizations of Extrapolated and propagated statistics.
- ✓ Given a scenario, identify the type of statistics to use.
- ✓ Given a query and the resulting rows in DBQL, identify potential areas for improvement.
- ✓ Identify characteristics of a tactical query.
- ✓ Identify causes of poor query performance.
- ✓ Identify causes of poor system performance.
- ✓ Identify conditions when collecting multiple statistics in a single request would be beneficial.

Before You Begin

You should be familiar with the following terms and concepts.

Terms	Key Concepts
Statistics	How to collect full and partial statistics
Table Design Features	What performance impact each might have

Considerations for keeping and utilizing performance data history

To Maintain Efficient Use of Existing System Resources

Managing the use of existing system resources includes, among other things, job mix tuning and resource scheduling to use available idle cycles effectively.

Managing resources to meet pent-up demand that may peak during prime hours ensures that the system operates efficiently to meet workload-specific goals.

To Help Identify System Problems

Managing performance helps system administrators identify system problems.

Managing performance includes, among other things, monitoring system performance through real-time alerts and tracking performance historically. Being able to react to changes in system performance quickly and knowledgeably ensures the efficient availability of the system. Troubleshooting rests on sound system monitoring.

For Capacity Planning

If performance degradation is a gradual consequence of increased growth or higher performance expectations, all data collected over time can be used for capacity or other proactive planning. Since the onset of growth-related performance degradation can often be insidious, taking measurements and tracking both data and usage growth can be very useful.

Managing performance yields efficient use of existing system resources and can guide capacity planning activities along sound and definable lines.

Recommendations to move DBC data to a historical database

- Copy DBC data to historical database nightly
- Retain a 90-day copy in DBC for Teradata GSC and other tools
- DBC tables are optimized for WRITE, not SELECT, operations
- Table definition changes (Fallback)
- Alter primary indexes for reporting (PPI)
- Compression and Statistics
- Time Dimension Represented (Date, Hour)
- Views for dbcmngr database performanace tables
- Accounts defined to represent key user groups and/or applications
- Archive the data for availability
- Maintain the data
- Capacity Planning requirements
- Audit requirements

Best Practices to capture performance data daily

- Resusage (Collection enabled)
    - ResusageSpma
    - ResusageSps
    - ResusageSawt
- Ampusage (Collection automatic)
- DBQL (Collection enabled)
- Logonoff (Collection automatic)
- Session Info (Collection automatic)
- Database sizes (Collection automatic, history is not)
- Table sizes (Collection automatic, history is not)

- User Spool sizes (Collection automatic, history is not)
- Heartbeat query information for key workloads (Collection enabled)
-

Statistics

Reasons to collect statistics

The purpose of collecting statistics is to compute statistical data that the Optimizer uses to improve table access and join plans. The computed statistical data is retained in a synopsis data structure that is stored in the data dictionary for use during the optimizing phase of SQL statement parsing.

Accurate demographics enable the query optimizer to determine the least costly access and join plans for a query.

It is particularly important for the Optimizer to have accurate table demographic information for those situations in which data to be accessed using a column or index might be skewed.

You can also collect, drop, and view table statistics using the Statistics Collection module of Teradata Manager.

Types of Statistics

Statistics are a critical component in ensuring the Optimizer chooses a good query plan when SQL statements are submitted for processing. There are four approaches to collecting statistics which are as follows:

1. Random (Dynamic) AMP Sampling
2. Full statistics collection
3. Using the SAMPLE option

4. Using the SUMMARY option

Collecting stats provides the Optimizer with a row count in the table(s) being queried. The Optimizer will then utilize this formation to determine the best way to access the data. The benefits of collecting stats are as follows:

- If your data distribution is uneven, then stats can improve in accessing a column or index data during a query operation.
- Statistics provide the Optimizer the ability to use a secondary, hash, or join indexes as opposed to doing full-table scans in queries.
- Provide performance benefits when doing complex queries and join operations.
- Improve the estimates of intermediate spool files based on the conditions specified in an SQL query. This is critical for determining join order for tables along with identifying the type of join to best resolve the query.
- Empower the Optimizer to take advantage of NUSI Bit Mapping when available.
- Statistics information remains intact during reconfiguration operations.

Random AMP Sampling

Dynamic Sampling gathers information from an AMP which is selected from the Table ID. This means that different AMPs will be assigned to gather sample information for different tables. This guarantees no single AMP will be overloaded with sampling requests.

Since this process only uses a single AMP, if the data is not distributed evenly, the Optimizer could make improper choices. In all cases, the Optimizer will choose a conservative path to process queries when this technique is deployed.

It is possible to randomly sample table rows from more than a single AMP. The number of randomly selected AMPs from which the system samples statistics is controlled by an internal flag. The default is one AMP, but it is possible to change this default specification to sample statistics from 2 AMPs, 5 AMPs, all AMPs in a node, or all AMPs on your system. Another internal flag controls the percentage of rows to read.

Dynamic AMP sampling calculates the average size of each index for every AMP based on the following criteria:

- Table cardinality
- The average cardinality per value
- The number of distinct values (indexes)
- The average cardinality for each index

Tables with heavily skewed data will improve greatly with this new option. Because of multiple AMP sampling, the Optimizer will receive better estimates when generating query plans.

Full Statistics

A full COLLECT STATISTICS statement is the most complete method of gathering demographic information about a column or an index. Below are the benefits:

- Best option for columns or indexes where data is highly skewed.
- Recommended for small tables, with fewer than 100 rows per AMP.
- Columns where the number of distinct values is moderate or low.
- For all NUSIs and other access columns used with queries.

- For all columns/indexes where the USING SAMPLE does not provide accurate estimates.

Statistics can now be collected on global temporary tables; however, there is still no support for volatile tables. In order to get as accurate a row count as possible, the more extensive dynamic AMP sampling approach, that samples all AMPs, is used by default for volatile tables.

Because tables are in a constant state of change, it is up to the administrator to keep collected statistics refreshed. It is common practice for many Teradata sites to re-collect statistics on the majority of their tables, or partitions, when they change by 10%.

Sample Statistics

Full table statistics requires scanning the base table in order to sort and calculate the number of occurrences for each distinct value. The process in some cases can be time consuming and the resources required to collect and refresh statistics can create problems especially on large tables.

Using the sample option reduces the resources and time required to perform statistics collection. This should not be utilized as a replacement for full statistics collection. It is recommended that analysis and planning should be conducted utilizing this option.

Sampling is recommended for the following:

- Large tables.
- Resource consumption from the collection process is a serious performance or cost concern.

Sampling is not recommended for the following:

- Small tables.

- To replace all existing full scan collections.
- If the system does not determine the correct sample size which will impact accurate statistics.
- Statistics on a column or index are either sample or full. It cannot be both and the when you refresh statistics, the system will determine if the stats are sample or full.
- Do not use sampling with highly skewed data.
- Multicolumn statistics with system-derived column PARTITION. A partitioning column is the table column referenced in the PARTITION BY clause.

Note: This feature cannot be utilized on global temporary tables or to join indexes.

Summary Statistics

COLLECT SUMMARY STATISTICS specifies that only object-level statistical information such as cardinality, one-AMP and all-AMPs sampling estimates, average row size, average block size, and so on be updated.

If you specify SUMMARY, you cannot specify USING options, column references, or explicit COLUMN or INDEX references.

You cannot specify SUMMARY for volatile tables.

You should collect SUMMARY statistics on unpartitioned tables, because these statistics can be collected very quickly and they are extremely useful to the Optimizer for making cardinality estimates.

You can use the SUMMARY option to copy table-level demographics from a source table to a target table. When you copy statistics without specifying the column list for the source and target tables, Teradata Database implicitly copies the SUMMARY statistics from the source to the target. If the system copies the SUMMARY statistics implicitly, you should recollect those statistics natively when you later refresh them.

Extrapolated Statistics

Extrapolated statistics are intended to reduce frequency of re-collection and are most useful with large tables that are growing and where data distribution is relatively uniform. Extrapolation can offer reasonably accurate estimates if:

- Data is skewed,
    - It is recommended that statistics be re-collected
- When stale statistics are detected, an upward adjustment is made to:
    - Table row count
    - Number of distinct values
    - Number of rows estimated for single table selection

Extrapolation happens automatically if stale statistics are detected. The Optimizer detects stale statistics by looking at table row counts. Table row counts are compared from these two sources:

- Random AMP samples collected at the time of the request
- Row counts from previously collected statistics

Extrapolation only takes place if statistics were previously collected. If table growth is detected but shrinkage is not, you should consider the following for best performance:

- Re-collect full statistics on smaller tables
- Re-collect full statistics in the presence of very skewed data
- Re-collect full statistics after purging rows
- Do not rely on extrapolation indefinitely

Derived Statistics

As a query executes, the cardinality estimates that were used to initially optimize the query are adjusted dynamically throughout the optimization process. This is accomplished by applying information derived from various query predicates, database constraints, join indexes, and hash indexes. Due to the way these statistics are calculated, they are referred to as *derived statistics.*

Derived statistics enable the Optimizer to dynamically reoptimize a request in the middle of a query when it determines the current plan is not optimal, without having to reoptimize the entire query from the beginning.

Derived statistics are dynamic snapshots which are derived from the base table histogram statistics and cardinality estimates, which are adjusted using statistical information from other sources such as constraints, query predicates, CHECK, referential integrity, join indexes, and hash indexes. These derived statistics are adjusted dynamically at each stage of the optimization process, and represent the demographics of column values after applying query predicates and demographic information derived those other sources.

What statistics should be collected

You can collect or refresh statistics on a combined maximum of 512 columns and indexes. Even though this feature may consume more system resources to complete, the benefit is that the Optimizer has better information. The end result is more efficient execution plans, which will reduce system resource consumption during query processing.

The use of statistics assists the Optimizer in making the better execution plans. Collecting statistics on columns not utilized in queries, consumes unnecessary resources with no performance gains.

There are five primary areas where statistics should be collected.

1. Tables
2. Columns
3. Multi-Columns
4. Indexes
5. Partitions

It is recommended that statistics get collected at the column level because indexes can be dropped and recreated quite often. Multi-column stats can be collected at the column level without creating an index first.

The STATISTICS privilege is needed in order to collect statistics. Statistics can also be collected on Global Temporary Tables. When users logoff; the data in these tables will be deleted along with the statistics. The HELP STATS command shown later in this chapter is utilized to review the statistics collected on tables.

Note: Drop table privilege will also let you collect or drop statistics. However, the statistics privilege allows you to grant the right without giving drop table to people. You can also collect and drop statistics with the INDEX privilege.

Multi-Column Statistics

If a frequently used access path (indexed or not) consists of multiple ANDed columns, collecting statistics on the individual columns will not help the Optimizer. The optimizer needs to know what the combined mix of values looks like:

```
SELECT * FROM tname
WHERE col10 = 100 AND col12 = 'abc' ;
         --- or ---
CREATE INDEX (col10, col12) ON tname;
```

Figure 13.1

Multi-Column Statistics Considerations include:

- Order of columns within the collected statistics will be the same order as in the CREATE TABLE statement. The exception is when the INDEX option is specified in the collect statistics statement.
- Gives the optimizer information about correlations among columns of the same table.
- Provides a better estimate if a query has constraints on more than 1 column of a table.
- Query constraints must be in an equal condition.
- Default formulas are used if the query expresses non-equal conditions.
- Interval "Values" are automatically adjusted so long CHAR/VARCHAR columns and combinations of columns that exceed that may be truncated.
- The full-length value range starts at 1, but Max, Mode in detail Intervals are larger then specified, the system will dynamically adjust to the Max size.
- If multiple values share the same 25-byte high-order string, optimizer cannot distinguish among them and makes the statistics unreliable.
- When VARCHAR columns are present they are converted to full length before statistics collection.
- Best when VARCHAR columns appear last in multicolumn statistics.
- Nulls in multi-column statistics.
- Histogram interval 0 has two columns for NULLs:
    - Number of Nulls – Count of all rows which have NULL on any or all columns.
    - Number of all Nulls – Count of rows which have NULL on all columns.
- Can derive number of rows with "Partial NULLs".
- Number of Nulls minus Number of all Nulls.

- Multi-Column Statistics with NULLs may result in an over-count of Distinct Values when there is a high number of partial NULLs.
- Evaluate collecting multi-column statistics when one or more columns have NULLs by testing if it is helping the queries or not.

Note: Secondary index columns may qualify for NUSI Bit Mapping with individual statistics being available.

Enabling a Rollup

Consider the following statement.

```
COLLECT STATISTICS
 COLUMN (first_name, mgr_employee_no)
,COLUMN (first_name)
,COLUMN (mgr_employee_no)
ON employee_table;
```

Figure 13.2

Prior to TD14, the system would have done a full base table read for (first_name, mgr_employee_no), a second full base table read for (first_name), and a third full base table read for (mgr_employee_no).

With TD14, the system executes a full base table read for (first_name, mgr_employee_no) to perform the statistics multicolumn aggregation. It then performs a rollup for (first_name) from the prior multicolumn aggregation instead of reading the base table again. It then performs another rollup (mgr_employee_no) from the prior multicolumn aggregation instead of reading the base table again.

The following pages show the Explain of the COLLECT STATISTICS statement.

```
EXPLAIN
COLLECT STATISTICS
 COLUMN (first_name, mgr_employee_no)
,COLUMN (first_name)
,COLUMN (mgr_employee_no)
ON employee_table;

 *** Help information returned. 53 rows.
 *** Total elapsed time was 1 second.

Explanation
---------------------------------------------------------------
  1) First, we lock CSQL_CLASS.employee_table for access.
  2) Next, we do an all-AMPs SUM step to aggregate from
     CSQL_CLASS.employee_table by way of an all-rows scan
     with no residual conditions , grouping by field1 (
     CSQL_CLASS.employee_table.First_name
     ,CSQL_CLASS.employee_table.Mgr_employee_no). Aggregate
     Intermediate Results are computed globally, then
     placed in Spool 18.  The size of Spool 18 is estimated
     with no confidence to be 7 rows (315 bytes).  The
     estimated time for this step is 0.05 seconds.
  3) Then we save the UPDATED STATISTICS for (
     'First_name,Mgr_employee_no') from Spool 18 into Spool
     4, which is built locally on a single AMP derived from
     the hash of the table id.
  4) We do an all-AMPs SUM step to aggregate from Spool 18
     by way of an all-rows scan , grouping by field1 (
     CSQL_CLASS.employee_table.First_name).  Aggregate
     Intermediate Results are computed globally, then
     placed in Spool 21.  The size of Spool 21 is estimated
     with no confidence to be 6 rows (198 bytes).  The
     estimated time for this step is 0.06 seconds.
  5) Then we save the UPDATED STATISTICS for ('First_name')
     from Spool 21 (Last Use) into Spool 9, which is built
     locally on a single AMP derived from the hash of the
     table id.
  6) We do an all-AMPs SUM step to aggregate from Spool 18
     (Last Use)by way of an all-rows scan , grouping by
     field1 (CSQL_CLASS.employee_table.Mgr_employee_no).
     Aggregate Intermediate Results are computed globally,
     then placed in Spool 24.  The size of Spool 24 is
     estimated with no confidence to be 5 rows (145 bytes).
     The estimated time for this step is 0.06 seconds.
```

```
 7) Then we save the UPDATED STATISTICS for
    ('Mgr_employee_no') from Spool 24 (Last Use) into
    Spool 14, which is built locally on a single AMP
    derived from the hash of the table id.
 8) We compute the table-level summary statistics from
    spool 14 and save them into Spool 16, which is built
    locally on a single AMP derived from the hash of the
    table id.
 9) We lock DBC.StatsTbl for write on a RowHash.
10) We do a single-AMP ABORT test from DBC.StatsTbl by way
    of the primary index with a residual condition of (
    "((DBC.StatsTbl.ExpressionList = 'First_name') OR
    (DBC.StatsTbl.StatsId = 6 )) OR
    ((DBC.StatsTbl.ExpressionList =
    'First_name,Mgr_employee_no') OR (DBC.StatsTbl.StatsId
    = 5 ))").
11) We do a single-AMP MERGE into DBC.StatsTbl from Spool
    4 (Last Use).
12) We do a single-AMP MERGE into DBC.StatsTbl from Spool
    9 (Last Use).
13) We do a Single AMP MERGE Update to DBC.StatsTbl from
    Spool 14 (Last Use) by way of a RowHash match scan.
14) We do a Single AMP MERGE Update to DBC.StatsTbl from
    Spool 16 (Last Use) by way of a RowHash match scan.
15) We spoil the statistics cache for the table, view or
    query.
16) We spoil the parser's dictionary cache for the table.
17) Finally, we send out an END TRANSACTION step to all
    AMPs involved in processing the request.
 -> No rows are returned to the user as the result of
    statement 1.
```

Figure 13.3

Viewing Statistics

HELP STATISTICS Command

The HELP STATISTICS command, shown below, returns the following information:

- The DATE when statistics were last collected or refreshed.

- The TIME when statistics were last collected or refreshed.
- The count of UNIQUE VALUES.
- The COLUMN NAMES over which statistics were collected.

Note: The date and time columns are extremely useful. They assist you in determining when the statistics have been collected, refreshed, or even dropped.

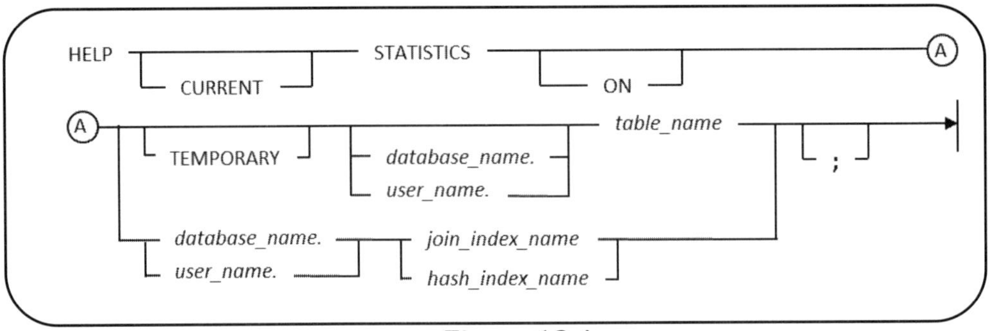

Figure 13.4

You can no longer specify a column or index for a HELP STATISTICS request, nor can you display detailed statistics because HELP STATISTICS now reports only table-level summary statistics.

SHOW STATISTICS Command

With the new DBC.StatsTbl, activated in TD14, you can use the new SHOW STATISTICS command to view summary-level statistics (SHOW STATISTICS) or detail-level statistics (SHOW STATISTICS VALUES). You can also have the information returned in XML format which can be used as input to graphical displays, and other uses.

The following diagram is the syntax for the SHOW STATISTICS command.

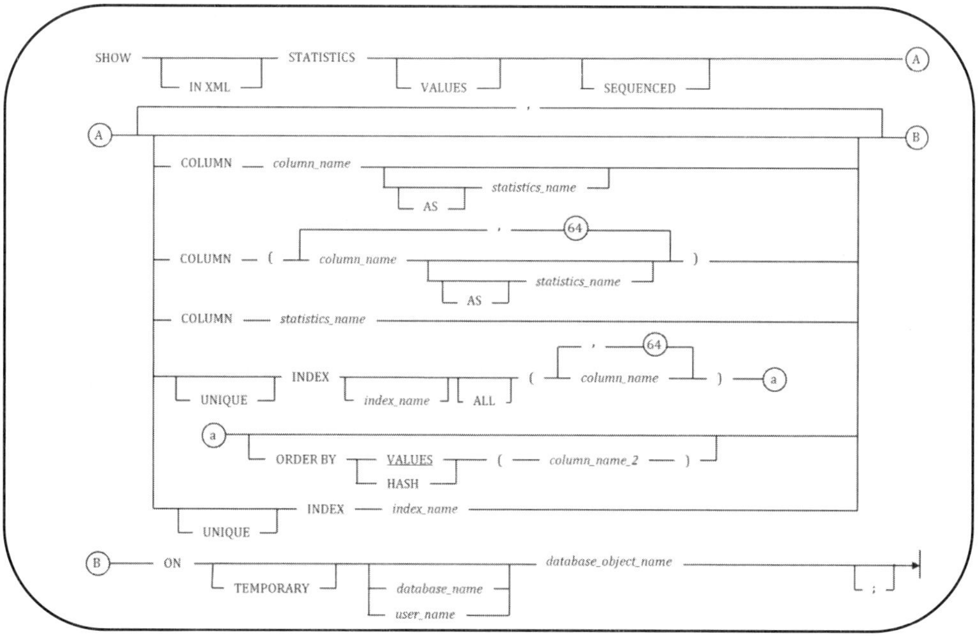

Figure 13.5

The VALUES option reports detailed statistics for all of the columns in the database object. If you do not specify any columns or indexes, this command will report detailed statistics.

The SUMMARY option reports table-level summary statistics for the table or index only.

When utilizing the SHOW STATISTICS command without using the IN XML option, the following things can be utilized with the reported statistics.

- The VALUES option can be used as a backup of those statistics.
- Submit them to the system as reported.
- In dual-active environments, you can transfer them to other systems.

When submitting the SHOW STATISTICS command with the IN XML option, the output can be utilized for processing of statistical data with methods using graphical displays, and transformations.

When statistics are exported, the system shows the date, time and timestamp data in UTC format. No local time zone conversion is done when statistics are exported.

In addition, you can query DBC.StatsTbl, using standard SQL, through four new views:

> **DBC.ColumnStatsV** – returns information about statistics collected on individual indexed and non-indexed columns, including PARTITION statistics.
> **DBC.IndexStatsV** – returns information about statistics collected on indexes for which two or more columns have been defined.
> **DBC.MulticolumnStatsV** – returns information about statistics collected on groups of non-indexed columns.
> **DBC.TempTableStatsV** – returns information about statistics collected on the materialized temporary tables for the current session.

These new system views are not compatible with releases prior to Teradata Database 14.0. Furthermore, these new views do not return statistics information for row level security tables.

Analyzing Response Time and Throughput

Tactical queries

Certain Primary Key (PK) operations can be executed in parallel when submitted as a multi-statement request. Eligible statements are PK operations that do not require USI or RI maintenance. These operations include delete, insert, update, and upsert.

The performance enhancement is achieved by enabling the Dispatcher to increase the number of parallel steps that can be selected for dispatch during each step selection cycle. The Dispatcher, when handling multi-statement requests, selects as many PK operation steps as possible.

This is a runtime optimization as opposed to a Parser optimization. It increases parallel processing by reducing unnecessary synchronization wait time for multi-statement requests involving PK tactical queries. This improves overall transaction response time for tactical queries.

DBQL

As stated in Chapter 8, DBQL can be used to log query processing for later analysis. Query counts, response times, SQL text, and processing steps can be compared to allow you to fine-tune applications.

Review at the detail or step level the following query characteristics:

1. Total CPU used
2. Total IO used
3. CPU Skew
4. IO Skew
5. Product Join Indicator
6. Unnecessary IO Indicator
7. Impact CPU
8. Spool Usage
9. Number of Rows Returned

Refer back to Chapter 8 for more information.

Access Logging

Though access logging can capture SQL, its primary function is to record privilege checks. Refer back to Chapter 8 for information on Access Logging.

ResUsage

Chapter 10 covered ResUsage, its data, and its macros. The following is a summary.

Resource usage data covers	Which includes
BYNET traffic on a node	Messaging includes point-to-point, broadcast, and merge activities.
client-to-server traffic	Data on each communication link.
CPU utilization	Overhead, user service, and time of session execution.
data tracking	Status of sessions in locking queues.
logical device traffic (SCSI)	Count of reads/writes and amount of data transferred as seen from the SCSI driver.
vdisk logical device traffic	All the cylinders allocated by an AMP.
Priority Scheduler information	Data by Performance Group (PG) from the Priority Scheduler and the ability to report resource usage data by Teradata Active System Management (Teradata ASM) workloads (WDs).
AMP Worker Task (AWT) Information	AWT statistics.
memory management activity	Memory allocation, aging, paging, and swapping.
summary information	All data collected for a node or

Resource usage data covers	Which includes
	vproc.

Figure 13.6

Hash Functions

The hash functions can be used to identify uneven distribution, and excessive hash collisions. The hash functions are:

- HASHROW – The 32-bit row hash value
- HASHBUCKET – Which hash map entry the HASHROW value belongs to
- HASHAMP – the AMP that owns the HASHBUCKET
- HASHBACKAMP – the Fallback AMP that owns the HASHBUCKET

The following is an SQL example of how to check for table skew:

```
SELECT COUNT(*),
HASHAMP(HASHBUCKET(HASHROW(employee_no)))
FROM employee_table
GROUP BY 2
ORDER BY 1 DESC;
```

Figure 13.7

Data Dictionary Tables

You can query DBC.TableSizeV to see if the data for a specific table is evenly distributed. This view will return both *currentperm* and *peakperm* values for each AMP.

You can query DBC.DiskSpaceV to see how evenly data is distributed across all of the AMPs. This view returns:

- DatabaseName

- AccountName
- MaxPerm
- MaxSpool
- MaxTemp
- CurrentPerm
- CurrentSpool
- CurrentTemp
- PeakPerm
- PeakSpool
- PeakTemp
- MaxProfileSpool
- MaxProfileTemp

Steps required for analyzing queries for optimization

WHERE clause analysis

Obviously, all JOIN columns should have statistics collected on them.

Columns, whether indexed or not, appearing in a WHERE clause should have statistics collected on them as well.

The Optimizer is not affected by the order of tests in a WHERE clause. As an example, A = 10 AND B = 300, AND C = 'XYZ' is the same as B = 300 AND A = 10 AND C = 'XYZ, which is the same as C = 'XYZ' AND A = 10 AND B = 300.

The important thing is whether statistics on the columns are available. Without statistics, the Parser is very conservative. With statistics, it is far more aggressive.

Though the WHERE clause limits the number of rows appearing in Spool, the number of columns being projected, and their data type size determine the width of Spool rows.

Explains

Use of the EXPLAIN modifier, or Visual Explain, will show the retrieval paths chosen by the Parser.

Modifying the structure of the tables will change performance. As an example:

- Changing a UPI/NUSI to a NUPI/USI
- Creating/dropping SIs
- Collecting/refreshing statistics
- Creating/dropping Join Indexes
- Creating/dropping Partitioned Primary Indexes
- Creating/dropping Hash Indexes
- Using/eliminating temporary (Global/Volatile) tables

You can use the Teradata System Emulation Tool (SET) to test various changes before applying them to the production tables.

Practice Questions

1. Which of the following performance sources must be enabled?
    a. DBQL
    b. AMPUsage
    c. LogOnOff
    d. Session Info

2. Which of the following do you need to capture history manually?
    a. ResUsage
    b. Table sizes
    c. AMPUsage
    d. LogOnOff

3. Which of the following statements about Random AMP Sampling is false?
    a. The sample comes from an AMP based on the Table ID.
    b. Highly skewed data can yield misleading statistics.
    c. It's limited to a single AMP and a fixed percentage of rows.
    d. The Optimizer will choose a conservative path when this technique is used.

4. If statistics have been previously collected, which of the following happens automatically if stale statistics are detected?
    a. Derived statistics
    b. Sample statistics recollection
    c. Full statistics recollection
    d. Statistics extrapolation

5. What is the byte limit on the statistical "Internal Values" of CHAR and VARCHAR columns?
    a. 8
    b. System Adjustable
    c. 16
    d. Values are Truncated

6. Which of the following is not a valid hash function?
    a. HASHROW
    b. HASHBUCKET
    c. HASHBACKBUCKET
    d. HASHBACKAMP
    e. HASHAMP

7. Which of the following is not a valid TD 14 statistics view?
    a. DBC.ColumnStatsV
    b. DBC.IndexStatsV
    c. DBC.MultiColumnStatsV
    d. DBC.VolatileTableStatsV

Chapter Notes

Utilize this space for notes, key points to remember, diagrams, areas of further study, etc.

Chapter 14 - Load Utilities

Certification Objectives

- ✓ Given a scenario, identify which load utility tool to use.
- ✓ Identify the unique features of Teradata Parallel Transporter.
- ✓ Given a scenario, identify how to control utility limits.
- ✓ Given a load utility failure, determine recovery procedures.

Before You Begin

You should be familiar with the following terms and concepts.

Terms	Key Concepts
Loader Slots	How you can adjust the count
Import	Which utilities can be used
Export	Which utilities can be used

BTEQ

To use BTEQ to load rows into the database, you use the normal SQL INSERT command.

When you logon to BTEQ, the default is to send your SQL through a single session. However, BTEQ can log on to Teradata sessions in sets, so that a number of sessions can run in parallel within a given set. This is especially helpful when you need to process a high volume of repetitive tasks whose order does not matter, such as loading a large number of rows onto a database. In this case, having a number of parallel sessions with each handling some of the requests can substantially speed up operations.

Though BTEQ can support a maximum of up to 200 sessions, the actual maximum depends on the configuration of your system and your terminal or workstation. The maximum for your system could be less than 200, and as few as 16 for PC workstations.

You specify the number of sessions in a set by entering the SESSIONS command prior to the LOGON command. The default number of sessions is 1, as stated above.

Through the use of the .IMPORT command, you can specify a data file to be used as input.

Transactions and BTEQ

BTEQ does not recognize BT/ET transactions. BTEQ handles Request Parcels, which may contain 1 or more SQL statements. If certain errors occur, and RETRY is ON (the default), BTEQ will resend the failing request parcel. <u>BTEQ only has RETRY logic, not RESTART logic.</u>

You can create multi-statement requests by proper semicolon placement in your BTEQ script, or you can put the SQL statements in a macro and have BTEQ execute the macro.

You can speed up BTEQ by specifying QUIET ON. If you use the QUIET command with the REPEAT or = command, BTEQ determines the reporting of time statistics by the number of sessions being run. With multiple sessions, BTEQ only reports the summary times for each cycle (start time, finish time, and total time). During a single session, BTEQ reports summary and processing times of queries executed in each cycle.

Typically, the QUIET and REPEAT commands are used together in multi-session data-load operations.

FastLoad

Teradata FastLoad is a command-driven utility that enables you to load large quantities of data into an empty Teradata Database table.

You can load data from:

- Channel-attached disk or files from tape on a client system
- Network-attached PC workstation files
- INMOD routines to preprocess input data
- External devices with source data properly setup for loading

By utilizing multiple sessions to load data, Fastload can increase the throughput for loading operations. However, Fastload can only load data to one table per job. If you want to load data into more than one table in the Teradata Database, you must submit multiple Teradata FastLoad jobs - one for each table.

Full tape support is not available for any function in Teradata FastLoad for network attached client systems. If you want to load data from a tape device, you will need to build a custom access module that communicates with the device.

When you invoke Teradata FastLoad, the utility executes the control commands and along with the SQL statements in your Teradata FastLoad job script. During this operation, the following is done:

1. Logs you on to the Teradata Database with the defined specified number of sessions with your username, password, and tdpid/acctid information.
2. Loads the data into the table on the Teradata Database.
3. Logs you off from the Teradata Database.
4. If successful, the FastLoad utility will return the following information:

- Total records read, skipped, and delivered to the database
- Number of errors inserted FastLoad error tables
- Number of rows inserts and applied
- Count of duplicate rows

As noted above, the table getting loaded with data must be empty and cannot have any secondary indexes defined. In addition, FastLoad does not load duplicate rows (i.e. where every value has the exact same data across all columns of an existing row.) This rule also applies to MULTISET tables. If you want to load duplicate rows, you will have MultiLoad with a MULTISET table.

On network-attached workstations, Teradata FastLoad uses the TCP/IP network protocol for all data transfer operations.

On channel-attached systems, Teradata FastLoad transfers data as either:

- A multi-volume data set or file
- A number of single-volume data sets or files in separate Teradata FastLoad jobs

You can restart serial Teradata FastLoad operations by loading the next tape in a series instead of beginning with the first tape in a set.

In either case, Teradata FastLoad:

- Uses multiple Teradata sessions, at one session per AMP, to transfer data
- Transfers multiple rows of data within a single message

Until you complete the Teradata FastLoad job and have loaded the data into the Teradata FastLoad table:

- There is no journaling or fallback data

- You cannot define the secondary indexes
- Join indexes, hash indexes, or foreign key references are not allowed until the load is completed

Restarting FastLoad

A FastLoad job that has been stopped before completing during a load or end-load phase of the operation is considered to be in a paused state. This condition can be unintentional, intentional, or can be a system failure or error condition.

To pause a job intentionally, use the LOGOFF or QUIT command before the END LOADING command in your script. Unintentional conditions to pause a job are as follows:

- Client workstation or FastLoad failures
- Conditions that cause unrecoverable errors
- Database or table errors
- Database failures

Note: While in a paused state, the target table and the error tables are locked on the database. You cannot access the table until the Fastload job completes; that is, the data is not available until the job is finished.

Restart Procedures

The procedure that you use to restart a paused FastLoad job is dependent on the phase of the job when it was paused.

- You can restart a job that was paused during loading, either from the beginning, or from the most recent checkpoint if the checkpoint option was specified in the BEGIN LOADING command.

- You can also restart a job that was paused during the end-loading phase. This is because checkpointing is done internally by the database in this phase. You generally do not need to do anything in this case because processing after the END LOADING command is executed on the database and does not depend on the FastLoad utility.

To restart the job if paused during the loading phase

1. Remove the CREATE TABLE, DROP TABLE and DELETE statements from the FastLoad job script. You do not want your restarted job to drop the partially loaded FastLoad table or delete the entries in the two error tables.

2. Restart the Teradata FastLoad to start the job. The Teradata FastLoad utility:

   - New sessions are created with the LOGON command.
   - Establishes the restart point by reading the restart.
   - he BEGIN LOADING command will notate that the job will be being restarted.

Note: If a load is using an INMOD routine, the INMOD routine (when restarted) needs to be able to handle restarts and checkpoints. During this restart, the FastLoad job will display a status code of 2 or 4 in a load operation. The INMOD routine will modify the record to read the position of the last checkpoint and then send these data records to be loaded.

To restart the job if paused during the end loading phase

1. The same LOGON command must be used as in the previous job.

2. Use BEGIN LOADING and END LOADING commands, as outlined in the following example:

```
LOGON dbc/ldr,music ;
BEGIN LOADING Fast_Table
ERRORFILES Error_1, Error_2 ;
END LOADING ;
```

Figure 14.1

Note: If you use your FastLoad job script to CREATE, DROP, or DELETE, these commands need to be deleted before restarting the job.

FastExport

Teradata FastExport is a command-driven utility that enables you to unload large quantities of data from tables or views on a Teradata Database. You can export data from any object (i.e. tables, views) as long as you have the SELECT privilege.

The exported data can be offloaded via the following methods:

- To a flat file located on a network-attached PC workstation or channel-attached system
- The Output Modification (OUTMOD) routine is an optional command that enables you to preprocess and verify the exported data before it is stored.

When you invoke FastExport, the utility executes the control commands and SQL statements in the job script. These instruct FastExport to do the following:

1. Logs you on to the database with your defined number of sessions, tdpid/acctid, username, and password for the script.
2. Access the data from the Teradata Database with your defined SQL Statement based on your format requirements.

3. Execute any OUTMOD routine defined to preprocess the data and export the data to the destination file.
4. Log you off the database

Restarting FastExport

A FastExport job that has been stopped before completing during an offload operation, where the restart log table has not been dropped, can be restarted. This condition can be unintentional, intentional, or can be a system failure or error condition.

Unintentional conditions to pause a job are as follows:

- Job script error
- Hardware failures
- Software errors

FastExport can restart some jobs that are stopped automatically. However, and in most cases, jobs will have to be manually restarted.

To manually restart the job, resubmit the entire job making sure that the same restart log table is used.

Once restarted, the FastExport utility will do the following:

1. Reestablish sessions specified in job
2. Access and reads the restart log table to establish the restart point
3. Resumes processing the job script

After a Job Script Error

When an error occurs in a job script, it creates an error message and returns an error code. From there, you can access the job script and make modifications to resolve the problem. Once completed, you can resubmit the job. FastExport will restart based on the last completed statement that was recorded in the restart log.

After Hardware Failures or Software Error Conditions

Automatic restarts of jobs will occur after some hardware failures and software errors after system recovery. These include:

- Down AMP
- CLIv2 errors on your PC workstation
- Network failures
- Nonrecoverable I/O error
- Database restarts

If the failure occurred with a *single* select request, then FastExport will resume processing when the system recovery is completed and by resubmitting a single select request.

If the failure occurred with *multiple* select requests, then FastExport will resume processing after system recovery is completed and by resubmitting the last select statement before the failure occurred based on the restart log.

MultiLoad

MultiLoad is a command-driven utility that enables you to load or maintain large quantities of data from table(s) on a Teradata Database. A single MultiLoad job can perform several different import and delete tasks on database tables and views:

- Import tasks can do INSERTs, and UPDATEs functions on up to five different tables or views.
- A Delete task can remove large numbers of rows from a single table.

You can import data from the following:

- Disk or tape files from a channel-attached client system, which requires a customer access module.
- Files from a network-attached PC workstation.
- Input modules (INMOD) can be utilized to preprocess and validate data before loaded.
- Utilize access modules to connect to other database for loading
- Other device providing source data

Note: In order to load and perform maintenance tasks with MultiLoad, you must have the appropriate access rights.

Multiload does have some restrictions and limitations. For example, the table(s) you are going to load with Multiload cannot have any USI's, referential integrity, or defined triggers. In addition, Multiload does not support loading into a NOPI table. However, NUSi's are allowed.

Just like the Fastlaod, Multiload has two primary loading phases which are as follows:

- **Acquisition Phase** – Data from the input stream is hash-distributed to the appropriate AMPs. When all of the input records have been read and sent to the AMPs, they are then sorted into row hash sequence and written to a work table. The target table is still available to the users during this phase.

- **Application Phase** – The system upgrades the lock to a Write lock. The sorted input records are applied to the table using the appropriate DML command(s). Each target data block is read into memory just once and all changes are applied to it at that time. When the phase successfully ends, the work tables are dropped during a subsequent cleanup phase.

Restarting a Paused MultiLoad Job

A MultiLoad job that has been stopped before completing a load operation, and is still in the acquisition phase of the MultiLoad operation, can be restarted. This condition can be unintentional, intentional, or can be a system failure or error condition.

You can pause a MultiLoad job intentionally by using a PAUSE ACQUISITION command between the BEGIN MLOAD and END MLOAD commands in the MultiLoad job script.

Unintentional conditions to pause a job are as follows:

- A MultiLoad job script error
- An unrecoverable I/O error
- A system that is in down AMP recovery status
- Database restarts
- Job aborts
- Client system failures

Note: MultiLoad permits non-exclusive access to target tables from other users except during the Application Phase. However, once in the acquisition phase, you must have an ACCESS lock to read the table.

After Using the PAUSE ACQUISITION Command

To restart a job that is in a paused stated caused by a PAUSE ACQUISITION command, do the following:

1. Remove the PAUSE ACQUISITION command from the job script.
2. Restart the MultiLoad job.

Once done, MultiLoad will do the following:

1. Reestablishes sessions specified in job
2. Access and reads the restart log table to establish the restart point
3. Resumes processing the job script

After a MultiLoad Job Script Error

When an error occurs in a job script, it creates an error message and returns an error code. From there, you can access the job script and make modifications to resolve the problem. Once completed, you can resubmit the job. MultiLoad will restart based on the last completed statement that was recorded in the restart log.

After an Unrecoverable I/O Error

When experiencing an unrecoverable I/O error while accessing a fallback type table, MultiLoad will automatically attempt to restart the job script.

Note: Some I/O errors can cause an AMP to stop participating in a job. In this occurs, the job will stop with error messages. In addition, if you are conducting a restart operation, error messages may occur as well.

After a Down AMP is Recovered

When MultiLoad is recovered from a down AMP situation and an error occurs with a worktable with fallback on the restart, this could indicate that additional procedures will be required to recover the table.

After a Teradata Database Restart

MultiLoad will automatically restart after the normal recovery operation such database restart. In this case, no intervention is required for this job. However, if the work tables or error tables are mistakenly dropped or missing, the job will abort with an error message.

After a Teradata Database System Reconfiguration

If a MultiLoad job is active and the Reconfiguration program is invoked, you could encounter problems where the error tables are not redistributed. When MultiLoad restarts after the reconfiguration is completed, the MultiLoad script will fail with errors.

In this scenario, when MultiLoad attempts to restart, the following error message will occur:

```
UTY0805 DBC failure, 2563: MLOAD not allowed: DBC had been reconfigured.
```

When this occurs, the tables being loaded cannot be recovered and the target tables must be reloaded.

Note: Do not reconfigure the Teradata Database during an active MultiLoad job.

After a Job Abort or Client System Failure

If the job was halted before or after the application phase due to client failure or an abort command, then you can restart the job as long as no changes were done to the job script. MultiLoad will utilize the restart log table to determine where to resume the job.

Note: If you modify tables or databases that are involved in a multi-step job, you may corrupt them.

TPump

TPump is a stream loading data utility that enables you to load data in near real time into your data warehouse. TPump also supports all the DML commands (i.e. update, delete, insert, and atomic upsert).

TPump, unlike MultiLoad, is a low-volume batch utility tool that can load and perform maintenance on several tables simultaneously. To achieve this, TPump uses native SQL commands to load or maintain data at low, medium, and high rates into the Teradata Database. Throttles such as using multiple sessions and multi-statement requests are utilized to handle the throughput.

TPump achieves this near real-time processing by continuously streaming data into the data warehouse, rather than through traditional batch updates. Continuous loads are achieved by accessing data from the client system in low volumes. The result is more accurate and timely data.

The key difference is that TPump uses row hash locks where the other utilities use table level locks. This enables TPump to simultaneously load data while users are running queries. This feature also enables TPump to be stopped at any time with no failures.

As indicated, the throttling feature which enables TPump to stream when the business is utilizing the system, or load like MultiLoad during batch windows, is a dynamic and key benefit of this utility.

TPump can not only throttle the number of statements to run per minute, you can also determine the amount of data that will be processed per minute. TPump's main benefits include:

- TPump does not require data staging, files, or custom hardware.

- Jobs restart with no interaction. They can run during database restarts, and network slowdowns.
- TPump can transform data in-flight before loading it to Teradata.
- TPump supports native SQL and conditional logic statements, making it unnecessary to customize the utility.

Recovering an Aborted TPump Job

A TPump job that has been stopped before completing a load operation (i.e. database space, abort commands, UNIX kernel panic, error limits exceeded), can be restarted providing the database objects, the restart log table, the error table, and DML macros have not been changed.

Note: An aborted TPump job can be restarted if the same job script is utilized in which case, TPump will perform the recovery.

Recovering from Script Errors

When an error occurs in a job script, it creates an error message and returns an error code. From there, you can access the job script and make modifications to resolve the problem. Once completed, you can resubmit the job. Tpump will restart based on the last completed statement that was recorded in the restart log.

Teradata Parallel Transporter

Teradata Parallel Transporter (TPT) is a client software product that uses a single script language to accomplish tasks that were executed using the traditional ('standalone') utilities of FastLoad, MultiLoad, FastExport, and TPump. Jobs are run using 'producer' operators and 'consumer' operators which define the type of task (load or unload) to be performed.

Though source data may come from a variety of inputs, including any ODBC database, data files or devices, the target for the load operators must always be the Teradata database.

TPT can be invoked via a script, or it can be activated by an API (Application Program Interface). There is also a GUI-based **TPT Wizard** which can be used for script generation.

Major Features of TPT

The following are principal features of TPT:

1. **Single Script Language**
   This simplifies the creation of load/unload operations.
2. **Complex 'Multi-Step' Load Scenarios**
   A TPT script can contain multiple job steps, each of which may be performing a load or unload function.
3. **Increased Throughput**
   TPT permits multiple instances of each operator in a script, thereby eliminating the single input stream of the traditional utilities.
4. **Direct API**
   The Application Program Interface (API) allows customers and vendors to write programs to directly load or unload Teradata tables using C or C++.
5. **Reduced File Storage**

TPT eliminates the need for intermediate file storage by holding data in data buffers (called 'streams').

TPT integrates the traditional utilities (FastlLoad, MultiLoad, TPump, and FastExport) into one platform using a single scripting language that uses 'operators'. To load a table, you now invoke a 'load' operator instead of running FastLoad. To update a table, you invoke an 'update' operator instead of running MultiLoad, and so on. Each operator can, of course, use multiple user sessions for additional parallelism.

Additional TPT Features

Teradata Parallel Transporter replaces the former Teradata Warehouse Builder. It uses the same script language so migration from TWB to TPT is seamless.

Here are some of the features of TPT:

- Concurrent Load from Multiple Sources
  - TPT can simultaneously load data from multiple and dissimilar sources in a single job.
  - It can execute multiple instances of an operator.
  - It can export, transform, and load one or more tables in a single job.
  - It can perform in-line filtering and transformation of data.
- Improved Performance through Parallelism and Scalability
  - TPT automatically distributes input and output data into data streams.
  - Data is streamed between operators without being written to disk.
  - Each data stream can be shared with multiple instances of the operators.
- Checkpoint Restart

  - TPT can automatically resume load jobs from the last checkpoint if the job aborts.
- Directory Scan
  - Permits multiple files in a client directory to be simultaneously processed as source data.
- Improved Throughput
  - Overcome input file I/O and CPU bottlenecks with multiple operator instances, as opposed to single-threaded applications such as MultiLoad or FastLoad.

The following diagram illustrates the TPT architecture. The three tiers represent source, load, and target environments, which can either reside on the same or different servers.

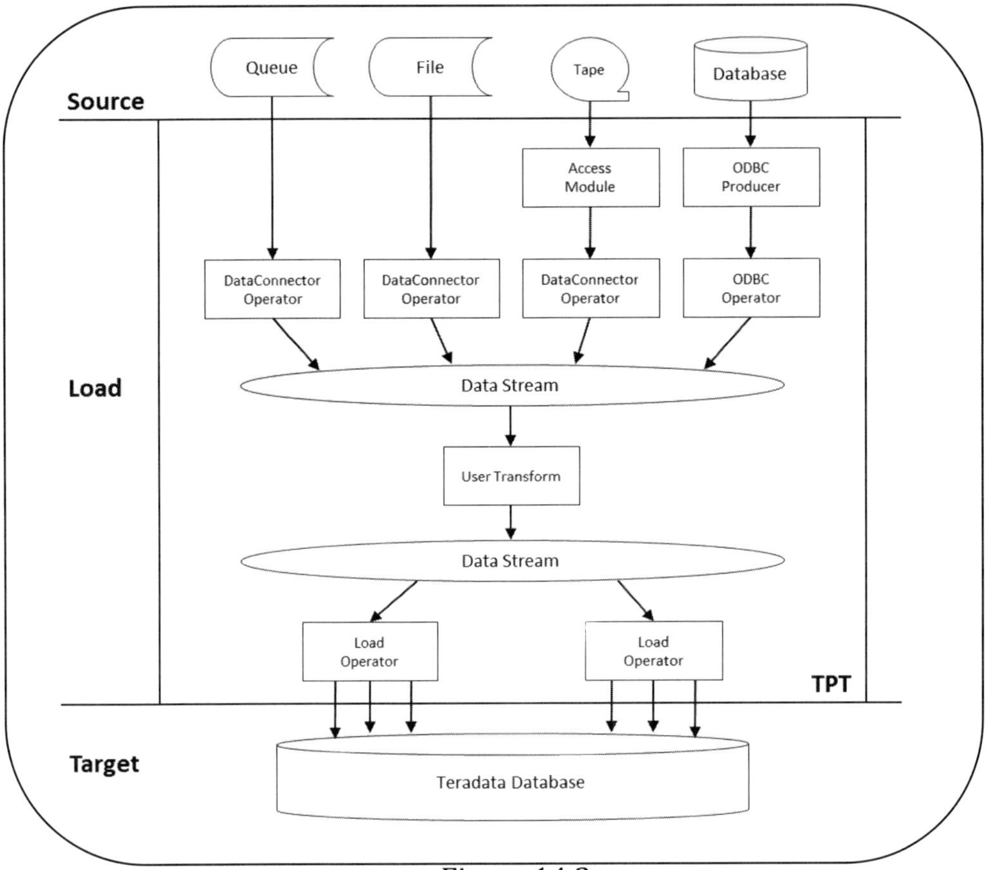

Figure 14.2

TPT achieves pipeline parallelism by connecting operator instances through data streams.

The following chart shows the major components of a TPT job.

COMPONENT	FUNCTION
Input Sources	These can be databases (both relational and non-relational) or database servers, data storage devices (i.e. tape or DVD readers), file objects, such as images, pictures, voice, text, etc.
Producer Operators	These extract data from a source and write it to a data stream. They 'produce' a data stream.
Data Stream	A data buffer in memory used to temporarily hold data. A data stream can accept data from multiple producer instances, and can distribute the data to multiple consumer operator instances.
Consumer Operators	These accept data from a data stream. They 'consume' the data and write it to the output target.
Output Target	These can be databases (both relational and non-relational) or database servers, data storage devices. For a load operator, the target must be a Teradata database.

Figure 14.3

The following chart shows the differences between TPT and the stand-alone utilities.

Operator	Standalone Equivalent	Purpose
DataConnector operator	Data Connector (PIOM)	Read data from and write data to flat files
DataConnector operator with WebSphere MQ Access Module	Data Connector (PIOM)	Read data from IBM WebSphere MQ
DataConnector operator with Named Pipes Access Module	Data Connector (PIOM)	Read data from a named pipe
DDL operator	BTEQ	Execute DDL, DCL, and self-contained DML SQL statements
Export operator	FastExport	High-volume export of data from Teradata Database
FastExport OUTMOD Adapter operator	FastExport OUTMOD Routine	Preprocess exported data with a FastExport OUTMOD routine before writing the data to a file
FastLoad INMOD Adapter Operator	FastLoad INMOD Routine	Read and preprocess data from a FastLoad INMOD data source
Load Operator	FastLoad	High-volume load of an empty table
MultiLoad INMOD Adapter Operator	MultiLoad INMOD Routine	Read and preprocess data from a MultiLoad INMOD data source
ODBC operator	OLE DB Access Module	Export data from any non-Teradata database that has an

Operator	Standalone Equivalent	Purpose
		ODBC driver
OS Command operator	Client host operating system	Execute host operating system commands
SQL Inserter operator	BTEQ	Insert data into a Teradata table using SQL protocol
SQL Selector operator	BTEQ	Select data from a Teradata table using SQL protocol
Stream operator	TPump	Continuous loading of Teradata tables using SQL protocol
Update operator	MultiLoad	Update, insert, and delete rows

Figure 14.4

In addition to producer and consumer operators, TPT also has filter operators and standalone operators.

The follow chart summarizes the operators and their characteristics.

OPERATOR TYPE	FUNCTION
Producer Operators They *Produce* a Data Stream	Get data from the Teradata database or an external data source. Write the data to a data stream. Typically make the data available to other operators.
Consumer Operators They *Consume* a Data Stream	Typically receive data from other operators. Read data from a data stream. Load data into a Teradata database or external data store.
Filter Operators	Perform data selection, data validation, data

OPERATOR TYPE	FUNCTION
They *Consume* and *Produce* Data Streams	cleansing, and data condensing. Filter operators function as both consumers and producers since they consume an input stream, handle the data, and then produce an output data stream.
Standalone Operators No Data Stream action	Used for submitting DDL commands. Also used for doing Delete Tasks (functioning as an update operator). Do not depend on input data from any sources other than the job script. Do not send or receive data from other operators – no data streams.

Figure 14.5

Checkpoint and Restart

Export operator

The Export operator behaves differently from other TPT operators in that it does not support a user-defined restart log table. Instead, it takes a checkpoint only when all data is sent to the data stream. If a restart occurs, the operator either must send all of the data or none of the data depending on whether the checkpoint has taken place.

DDL operator

The DDL operator restarts at the beginning of the group of SQL statements whose execution is interrupted by an abnormal termination. If the interrupted group has only one SQL statement, the DDL operator restarts at that statement.

Because SQL statements are sent to Teradata Database by group in the order in which they are specified in the TPT APPLY statement, the

DDL operator can take a checkpoint after each group is executed. A group can contain one or more SQL statements. A checkpoint, in the case of the DDL operator, marks the last group of DDL/DML SQL statements to execute successfully.

If the last request was successful prior to a restart, the operator can resume at the next request in line. If the last request failed prior to a restart, then the operator resumes at the failed request.

Load operator

TPT can automatically resume load jobs from the last checkpoint if the job aborts.

Update operator

The Update operator cannot be rolled back. Once changes are applied to target tables in the application phase, a job can only move forward. Since a target table cannot be returned to its original state, it is advisable to archive tables prior to running Update operations against them.

Stream operator

Checkpoint options control how often a row is written to the checkpoint file for the purposes of restarting a job. Unless otherwise specified, a checkpoint is taken at the start of and at the end of the input data. Since this process does not provide granular restartability in the case of longer running jobs, checkpoint intervals can be user-specified in terms of minutes or seconds.

Utility Limits

The setting of two control fields, *MaxLoadTasks* and *MaxLoadAWT*, affect how many utilities can run concurrently.

The MaxLoadTasks field specifies the combined number of FastLoad, MultiLoad, and FastExport tasks (jobs), and their TPT counterparts, that are allowed to run concurrently on Teradata Database.

Throttle rules for load utility concurrency set by Teradata Dynamic Workload Manager override the MaxLoadTasks setting.

AMP Worker Tasks (AWTs) are processes (threads on some platforms) dedicated to servicing the database work requests. A Teradata Database has a fixed number of AWTs that were defined during system initialization. Each AWT looks for a work request to arrive in the Teradata Database system, services the request, and then looks for another. An AWT can process requests of any work type.

The number of AWTs required by FastLoad and MultiLoad changes as their jobs run. More AWTs are required in the early phases of the jobs than in the later phases. Teradata Database dynamically calculates the total AWTs required by active jobs, and allows more jobs to start as AWTs become available.

The following chart shows the different number of required AWTs at different phases of execution for FastLoad and MultiLoad.

Load Utility Phase	Number of AWTs Required
FastLoad: Loading	3
FastLoad: End Loading	1
MultiLoad: Acquisition	2
MultiLoad: Application	1 per target table

Figure 14.6

If MaxLoadAWT is greater than zero, new FastLoad and MultiLoad jobs are rejected when the MaxLoadAWT limit is reached, regardless of the MaxLoadTasks setting. Therefore, FastLoad and MultiLoad jobs may be rejected before the MaxLoadTasks limit is reached.

Here is how the MaxLoadTasks field works together with the MaxLoadAWT field.

- If MaxLoadAWT is zero (the default):
  - MaxLoadTasks can be an integer from zero through 15.
  - The MaxLoadTasks field specifies the maximum number of combined FastLoad, MultiLoad, and FastExport jobs that can run concurrently.
  - The system does not consider the number of available AWTs when limiting the number of load utilities that can run concurrently.
- If MaxLoadAWT is greater than zero:
  - MaxLoadTasks is an integer from zero through 30.
  - The MaxLoadTasks field sets the maximum number of combined FastLoad and MultiLoad jobs that can run concurrently. MaxLoadTasks does not directly limit the number of FastExport jobs that can run.
  - The number of combined FastLoad and MultiLoad jobs that can run concurrently is limited by the values of both the MaxLoadTasks field and the MaxLoadAWT field. When either limit is met, no further FastLoad or MultiLoad jobs are allowed to start until the limiting factor is reduced.
  - The maximum number of load utility jobs of any type—FastLoad, MultiLoad, or FastExport—that can run concurrently is 60. Consequently, the number of FastExport jobs allowed to run at any time is 60 minus the number of combined FastLoad and MultiLoad jobs that are running.
  - If MaxLoadAWT is set to anything greater than zero, it can only be reset to zero if MaxLoadTasks is 15 or less.

Practice Questions

1. Which utility is best suited for performing small amounts of data loading?
   a. BTEQ
   b. FastLoad
   c. MultiLoad
   d. TPump

2. Which utility uses standard SQL for data loading?
   a. FastLoad
   b. MultiLoad
   c. TPT Load
   d. TPump

3. Which utility does not have restart logic?
   a. BTEQ
   b. TPump
   c. MultiLoad
   d. FastLoad

4. The following FastLoad script is an example of which of the following?

   ```
   LOGON dbc/usr234,pwd567;
   BEGIN LOADING my_table
   ERRORFILES Error_1, Error_2;
   END LOADING;
   ```

   a. Doing a syntax check of the script.
   b. Restarting after a checkpoint.
   c. Restarting after the end loading phase.
   d. Restarting after the begin loading phase.

5. If maxloadtasks = 5 and *maxloadawt* = 5, which of the following statements is false?
    a. One FastLoad and one MultiLoad job can start
    b. Two FastLoad jobs can start.
    c. Two MultiLoad jobs can start if a FastLoad job is in the end loading phase.
    d. Two MultiLoad jobs can start.

Chapter Notes

Utilize this space for notes, key points to remember, diagrams, areas of further study, etc.

Chapter 15 - Archiving

Certification Objectives

- ✓ Describe the features and functions of Online Archive
- ✓ Describe the features and functions of the archive, recovery, restore, and copy operations
- ✓ Describe the features and functions of Partition Archive and Restore
- ✓ Identify the archive and recovery implications of user defined functions, table functions, user defined types, and stored procedures
- ✓ Identify maintenance implications of triggers

Before You Begin

You should be familiar with the following terms and concepts.

Terms	Key Concepts
Archive	Creating backup copies
Restore	Recovery using backup copies
Partitioned Primary Indexes	How partitions are defined
Sessions	Defining single/multiple sessions
Copy	Copy backup data to the same/different system

Archive and Recovery Utility (ARC)

Teradata Database provides a number of automatic data protection features. However, these features do not cover all types of data loss. The ARC utility provides data protection for situations such as:

- Loss of an AMP for non-fallback tables
- Loss of multiple AMPs in the same cluster
- Failed batch processes
- Accidentally dropped tables, views, or macros
- Miscellaneous user errors
- Disaster recovery

ARC serially writes and reads files on a client system to archive, restore, recover, and copy database table data.

The difference between *copy* and *restore* is in the kind of operation being performed:

- A restore operation moves data from archived files back to the same Teradata Database from which they were archived or to a different Teradata Database *so long as the database DBC is already restored.*
- A copy operation moves data from an archived file back to a Teradata Database, not necessarily to the same system, *and* creates a new table if one does not already exist on the target database. When you copy selected partitions, the table must exist and be a table that was previously copied as a full-table copy.

Teradata ARC creates files when you archive databases, individual data tables, selected partitions of primary partition index (PPI) tables, or permanent journal tables from the Teradata Database. You provide Teradata ARC with such files when you restore databases, individual data tables, partitions of tables, or permanent journal tables back to the Teradata Database.

Teradata ARC also includes recovery with rollback and rollforward functions for data tables defined with a permanent journal option. Moreover, you can checkpoint these journals with a synchronization point across all AMPs, and delete selected portions of the journals.

Archive and Recovery Phases

Archive or recovery jobs always operate in two phases: the Dictionary phase and Data phase. The steps of each phase are described below.

The archive process is intensive. You may want to create a user just for archive activities so that you can log on as the administrative user to perform other actions while the archive is running.

Dictionary Phase Steps

1. Allocate an event number.
2. Issue a BEGIN TRANSACTION statement.
3. Resolve object name.
4. Check privileges.
5. Place utility locks on Data Dictionary rows and data rows.
6. Delete existing tables prior to RESTORE.
7. Issue an END TRANSACTION statement.

Data Phase Steps

1. Issue a BEGIN TRANSACTION statement.
2. Insert rows into RCEVENT and RCCONFIG.
3. Perform the operation.
4. Update RCEVENT.
5. Release locks (if user specified).
6. Issue an END TRANSACTION statement.

Restore versus FastLoad

The FastLoad utility can be an alternate way of loading client data files to empty Teradata tables. To do this, instead of archiving to tape, use the BTEQ EXPORT command or FastExport to store the information in a host file. To load data into more than one table, submit multiple FastLoad jobs.

The ARC utility is great for recovering a very large number of objects and can restore an entire machine with one command. Using FastLoad is an option for also quickly loading recovered data, but can only load into empty tables and load only one table per job.

Session Control

In general, the amount of system resources (memory and processing power) which are required to support the archive or recovery increases with the number of sessions. The impact on a particular system depends on the specific configuration.

Teradata ARC uses two control sessions to control archive and recovery operations. The **LOGON** statement always connects these sessions no matter what type of operation is being performed.

Multiple Sessions

Teradata ARC connects additional data sessions based on the number indicated in the SESSIONS parameter. These sessions are required for the parallel processing that occurs in archive and restore or copy operations.

If additional data sessions are required, Teradata ARC connects them at one time. Teradata ARC calculates the number of parallel sessions it can use, with maximum available being the number of sessions indicated with this parameter. Any connected sessions that are not actually used in the operation result in wasted system resources.

You can specify the number of archive or recover sessions with which to work, or use the default of 4. To set the number, use the SESSIONS runtime parameter.

The number of sessions to use can vary based on a number of factors.

Operation	Data Session Requirements
All-AMPS archive	No more than one session per AMP.
Cluster or specific archive	Teradata ARC calculates the nearest multiple of online AMPs for the operation and assigns tasks evenly among the involved AMPs. For example, if you archive four AMPs with nine sessions specified, Teradata ARC actually uses eight sessions (two per AMP). The extra connected session wastes system resources since it is unused.
Restore/copy	Restore operations use all the sessions specified using the sessions parameter.

Figure 15.1

Although Teradata ARC is able to process up to 350 ARCMAIN jobs at a time, each with up to 1024 sessions, it is highly recommended that you avoid running so many jobs.

ARCHIVE Statement

The following is the ARCHIVE statement syntax diagram.

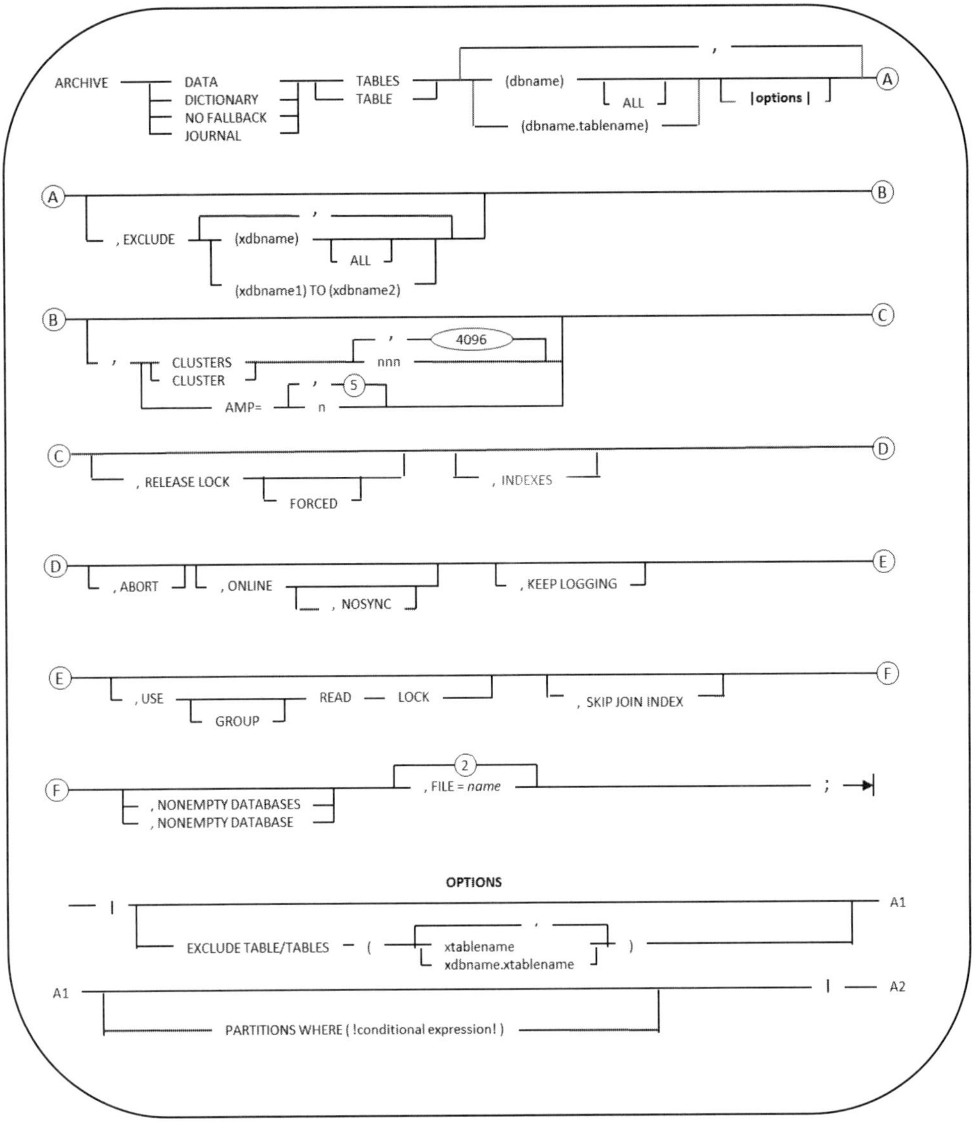

Figure 15.2

ANALYZE Statement

Here is the syntax diagram of the ANALYZE statement.

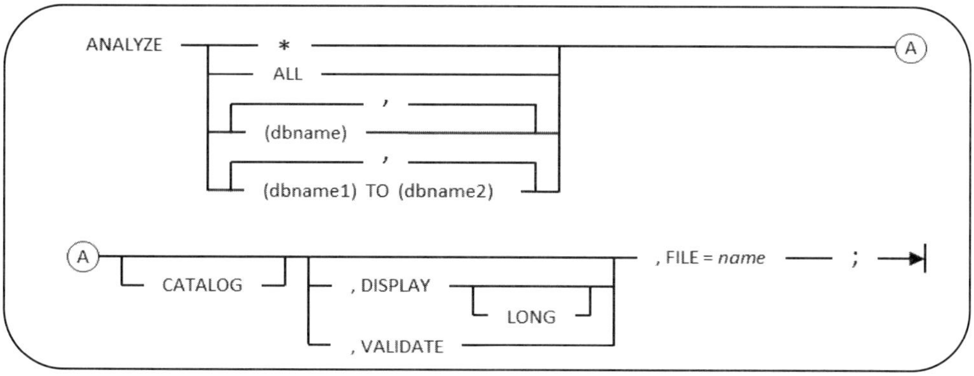

Figure 15.3

The **ANALYZE** statement provides the following information about the specified databases:

- Time and date the archive operation occurred.
- Whether the archive is of all AMPs, clusters of AMPs, or specific AMPs.
- The name of each database, data table, journal table, stored procedure, view and macro in each database, and the fallback status of the tables (if you specify the LONG option).
- The number of bytes and rows in each table (if you specify either the LONG or VALIDATE option).
- If an archive file contains a selected partition archive of a table, the bounding condition used to select the archived partitions is displayed with an indication as to whether the bounding condition is well-defined.
- Online logging information.
- User-Defined Method (UDM) and User-Defined Type (UDT) information.

It is possible to specify both the DISPLAY and VALIDATE options in a single **ANALYZE** statement. The default is DISPLAY.

Types of Archives

Beginning with TTU 13.00.00, there is support for archiving all objects as individual objects. However, triggers can only be restored, not copied.

An archive operation copies database information from the Teradata Database to one or two client resident files. The archive can be from any of the following:

- All AMPs
- Specified clusters of AMPs
- Specified AMPs

In general, Teradata ARC archives have these characteristics:

- If an **ARCHIVE** statement specifies more than one database, Teradata ARC archives the databases (except for DBC and SYSUDTLIB) in alphabetical order. Within each database, all related tables and stored procedures are archived in alphabetical order.
- If the statement specifies multiple individual tables, Teradata ARC archives the tables in alphabetical order according to database and then by table.
- If an archive of database DBC is interrupted for any reason, the entire archive must be performed again. It is not possible to restart an archive operation on database DBC once it has been interrupted.
- Archives cannot contain both data tables and journal tables. A journal table archive contains only the saved portion of the table.

- Journal table archives do not delete change images from the journal table. Therefore, you can accumulate change images for several activity periods by executing a checkpoint with save after each period and then archiving the table without deleting the journal.

The following table lists the archive types.

Archive Type	Table Protection Type	Data Included
All AMP database	Fallback	• Primary data rows and Secondary Indexes (SIs) from all the tables in the database(s) • Data Dictionary rows of the tables/macros/views/ functions/stored procedures • All table/macro/view/stored procedure/triggers/UDF • information • Table structure information
	No fallback	• Available data rows • Data Dictionary rows of the tables/macros/views/functions/ stored procedures/triggers/UDF • All table/macro/view/stored procedures/triggers/UDF information • Table structure information No SIs are included if an AMP is down.
All AMP table	Fallback	• Primary data rows • Secondary Indexes (SIs) • All dictionary information for the table • All table, column, and index definitions
	No fallback	• Available data rows

<table>
<tr><th>Archive Type</th><th>Table Protection Type</th><th>Data Included</th></tr>
<tr><td></td><td></td><td><ul><li>All dictionary information for the table</li><li>All table, column, and index definitions</li></ul>Note that no SIs are included if an AMP is down.</td></tr>
<tr><td>Specific AMP</td><td>No fallback</td><td><ul><li>Available data rows from the table(s) within the database(s)</li><li>Table structure information</li></ul>Note that:<ul><li>No dictionary rows are included. This information is included in the Dictionary archive.</li><li>No SIs are included.</li></ul></td></tr>
<tr><td>Specific cluster</td><td>Fallback or no fallback</td><td><ul><li>Available data rows from the table(s) within the database(s)</li><li>Table structure information</li></ul>Note that:<ul><li>No dictionary rows are included. This information is included in the Dictionary archive.</li><li>No SIs are included.</li></ul></td></tr>
<tr><td>Data Dictionary</td><td></td><td>Dictionary rows for tables/macros/views/ stored procedures/triggers/UDFs. For tables (PJ information is not included):<ul><li>DBC.TVM</li><li>DBC.TVFields</li><li>DBC.Indexes</li><li>DBC.IndexNames</li></ul></td></tr>
</table>

Figure 15.4

Archive Options

The following table describes the ARCHIVE options.

ARCHIVE Option	Description
ABORT	Keyword to abort an all-AMPs or cluster operation for when you archive non-fallback tables or single image journal tables and an AMP goes offline during the operation.
ALL	Include/exclude the named database and its descendants.
DATA TABLES	Archives fallback, non-fallback, or both types of tables from all AMPs or from clusters of AMPs.
DICTIONARY TABLES	Archives only the dictionary rows of a table. A dictionary archive of a database includes all table, view, macro and trigger definitions, and dictionary entries for stored procedures. This option includes the table definition for the specified table in the archive only if you archive a specific table.
EXCLUDE	Keyword to prevent specific databases from being archived.
EXCLUDE TABLES	Keyword to prevent specific tables from being archived.
FORCED	When specified, FORCED will instruct ARC to attempt a release of any placed locks in the event that the ARCHIVE statement fails.
INDEXES	For all-AMP archives only, this option specifies to include secondary indexes with the archive. You will need more time and media to archive objects with their secondary indexes.
JOURNAL TABLES	Archives dictionary rows for journal table and the saved subtable of journal table.

ARCHIVE Option	Description
KEEP LOGGING	Overrides the automatic termination of an online archive that was initiated with the ONLINE option.
NO FALLBACK TABLES	Archives non-fallback table from specific AMPs to complete a previous all-AMPs or cluster archive taken with processors offline.
NONEMPTY DATABASES	Instructs the ARC utility to exclude users/databases without tables, views, or macros from the archive.
PARTITIONS WHERE	Archive selected partitions of a PPI table rather than the entire table.
ONLINE	Archive rows that have update, insert, or delete operations also ongoing on those rows by using the online archive option.
RELEASE LOCK	Automatically releases utility locks when the operation completes successfully.
USE GROUP READ LOCK	Permits you to archive as transactions update locked rows. You must define after image journaling for the table during the time the archive is taking place.
NOSYNC	Enables online archive on all tables involved in the archive but does not require all tables to be enabled before access to those tables is allowed.
SKIP JOIN INDEX	Skip the archive of join and hash indexes.

Figure 15.5

Database DBC Archive

The DBC database stores essential system tables in the Teradata Database.

The following are the tables archived for Database DBC.

AccessRights	AccLogRuleTbl	Accounts
AsgdSecConstraints	BusinessCalendarException	CollationTbl
ConstraintFunctions	ConstraintValues	Dbase
DBQLRuleCountTb1	DBQLRuleTb1	Dependency
Hosts	LogonRuleTbl	Next
OldPasswords	Owners	Parents
PasswordRestrictions	Profiles	RCConfiguration
RCEvent	RCMedia	ReconfigDeleteOrderTbl
ReconfigInfoTbl	ReconfigRedistOrderTbl	RoleGrants
Roles	SecConstraints	SysSecDefaults
Translation	TVFields	TVM
UDFInfo	UDTCast	UDTInfo
UDTTransform		

Figure 15.6

If a DBC table is not listed in the table (above), it will not be archived. If this is the case, use SQL commands to copy the DBC table data into a user-level table in another database. This will allow for the backup.

Note: The above process will not allow for the data to be directly copied back to the DBC table during a restore process.

If database DBC is included in the archive process, it will always be archived first, regardless of order. Also, if database DBC is included in a restore or copy process, then it is always restored or copied first. Refer to the next section for specific instructions on restoring database DBC.

Archiving Selected Partitions of a PPI Table

It is possible to perform an all-AMPs archive on one or more partitions of a table rather than performing a full-table backup and restore. This feature is limited to all-AMP archives.

Use selected partitions to archive only a subset of data and avoid archiving data that has already been backed up. (Minimizing the size of the archive can improve performance.)

Restrictions on Archiving Selected Partitions

These restrictions apply to archiving selected partitions of a PPI table:

- Cluster, dictionary, and journal archives are not supported.
- It is recommended that tables containing large objects (BLOB and CLOB columns) not be archived with selected partitions (using PARTITIONS WHERE) because a number of manual steps are needed to restore the data. Instead of using selected partitions, use a full table archive and restore for tables that contain both PPIs and LOBs.

PARTITIONS WHERE Keyword

Use the PARTITIONS WHERE option to specify the conditional expression, which contains a definition of the rows that you want to archive. To be effective, limit this expression to the columns that determine the partitioning for the table you want to archive.

These restrictions apply to the use of PARTITIONS WHERE:

- The object is an individual table (not a database).
- The source table has a PARTITIONS BY expression defined.
- The archive is an all-AMP archive (not a dictionary, cluster, or journal archive).
- The INDEXES option is not used.
- If the table belongs to a database that is specified in the **ARCHIVE** statement, the table is excluded from the database-level object (with EXCLUDE TABLES) and is individually specified.

- Any name specified in the conditional expression is within the table being specified. (Using table aliases and references to databases, tables, or views that are not specified within the target table result in an error.) It is recommended that the only referenced columns in the PARTITIONS WHERE condition be the partitioning columns or system derived column PARTITION of the table. References to other columns do not contribute to partition elimination, and might accidently qualify more partitions than intended.

Archiving Stored Procedures, Triggers, UDFs, and UDTs

There is a system database, SYSUDTLIB, which contains the definitions of all UDTs and UDMs. When database DBC is archived, the ARC utility automatically archives SYSUDTLIB. DBC first, and then SYSUDTLIB is archived second before any other objects are archived. Therefore, do not archive SYSUDTLIB as a separate object. If you use the EXCLUDE option to exclude DBC on an archive, SYSUDTLIB will be excluded automatically.

The ARC utility allows you to specify the following objects as individual objects in Archive, Restore, or Copy statements.

OBJECT	TD 12.00 or earlier	TD13.00 or later	TD14.10 or later
Tables	Yes	Yes	Yes
GLOPs	No	Yes	Yes
Indexes (Join and Hash)	No	Yes	Yes
Macros	No	Yes	Yes
Stored Procedures	No	Yes	Yes
Triggers (cannot be Copied)	No	Yes	Yes

UDFs	No	Yes	Yes
UDMs	No	Yes	Yes
UDTs	No	Yes	Yes
Views	No	Yes	Yes
Table Function (Operator)	No	No	Yes
Parser Contract Functions	No	No	Yes

Figure 15.7

The EXCLUDE TABLE list may not contain any views, macros, stored procedures, or triggers. Only table names are allowed.

Online Archive

Archive a table or database when update transactions are still concurrently occurring by using the ONLINE option. ONLINE archive allows you to archive without using the GROUP READ LOCK option, which requires after image journaling.

The system creates and maintains a log for each table. It then captures all changes on the table in the log. The log of all changed rows is archived as a part of the archive process and will be restored and applied to undo the changes. These change logs are activated when the consistency point is established on the tables. The consistency point is set by getting table-level read locks on all the tables specified to be in the same consistency point, starting change log on all those tables, and releasing all the locks.

Establishing the consistency points defines the state of the tables to which they will be restored. While waiting for the table read locks required to set the consistency point, new write transactions will wait behind those read lock requests. If it is important to reduce impact to the write transactions, then there are some important considerations for reducing the time to establish a consistency point. New write transactions can be expected to wait for at least as long as the longest running write transaction in the system that accesses one of the tables in the consistency point.

Practice Questions

1. In which phase does ARC insert rows into RCEVENT and RCCONFIG?
    a. Dictionary
    b. Data
    c. Loading
    d. Acquisition

2. What is the default value for the SESSIONS runtime parameter?
    a. 2
    b. 4
    c. 8
    d. 16

3. What is the maximum number of ARCMAIN jobs ARC can handle at one time?
    a. 130
    b. 240
    c. 350
    d. 460
    e. 570

4. Which of the following statements is false?
    a. Other than DBC and SYSUDTLIB, databases are archived in alphabetical order.
    b. Other than DBC and SYSUDTLIB, tables are archived in table id order.
    c. Archives cannot contain both data tables and journal tables.
    d. If an archive of DBC is interrupted, you must restart the entire archive.

5. Which object can now be archived in TD 14.10 that couldn't be archived in earlier releases?
    a. GLOPs
    b. Join Indexes
    c. Table Function (Operator)
    d. Triggers

Chapter Notes

Utilize this space for notes, key points to remember, diagrams, areas of further study, etc.

Chapter 16 – Restoring

Certification Objectives

- ✓ Describe the features and functions of Partition Archive and Restore.
- ✓ Identify the archive and recovery implications of user defined functions, table functions, user defined types, and stored procedures.
- ✓ Identify maintenance implications of triggers.
- ✓ Given a scenario, identify the outcome of partition maintenance.

Before You Begin

You should be familiar with the following terms and concepts.

Terms	Key Concepts
Referential Integrity	How it's defined and managed by the system
Triggers	What they are and where they are stored
UDF	What they are and where they are stored

Understanding Restore Operations

The ARC utility provides several recovery control statements you use during restore-related operations. Each command is described in the following table.

Restore-Related Statement	Function
ANALYZE	Reads an archive tape to display information about its contents.
BUILD	Builds secondary indexes for fallback and non-fallback tables. It also builds fallback rows for fallback tables, and can build journal tables by sorting the change images.
COPY	Restores a copy of an archived file to a specified Teradata Database.
DELETE DATABASE	Deletes data tables, views, and macros from a database. Does not remove journal tables.
DELETE JOURNAL	Removes a journal subtable from the Teradata Database.
RELEASE LOCK	Releases host utility locks from specific databases or tables.
RESTORE	Restores a database or table from an archive file to specified AMPs.

Figure 16.1

A restore operation transfers database information from archive files backed up on portable storage media to all AMPs, clusters of AMPs, or specified AMPs.

You can restore archived data tables to the Teradata Database if the Data Dictionary contains a definition of the object you want to restore. For example, if the object is a database, that database must be defined in the dictionary. If the object is a table, that table must be defined in the dictionary. When restoring at the table level, tables must be defined in the dictionary prior to the restore.

A dictionary table archive contains all table, view, macro and trigger definitions in the database and dictionary entries for stored procedures and user-defined functions. A restore of a dictionary archive restores the definitions of all data tables, views, macros, triggers, and stored procedures. However, it does not restore any data.

RESTORE Statement

The following is the syntax diagram for the RESTORE statement.

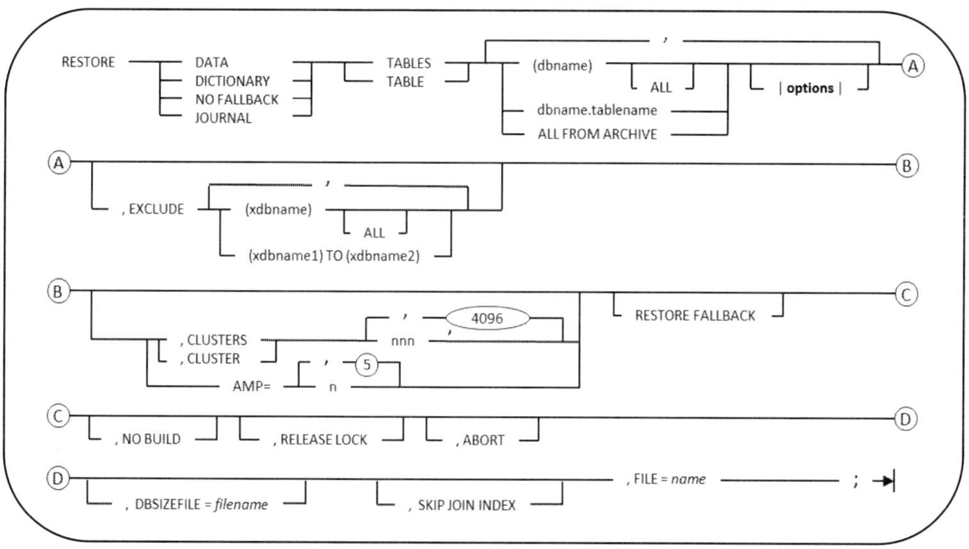

Figure 16.2

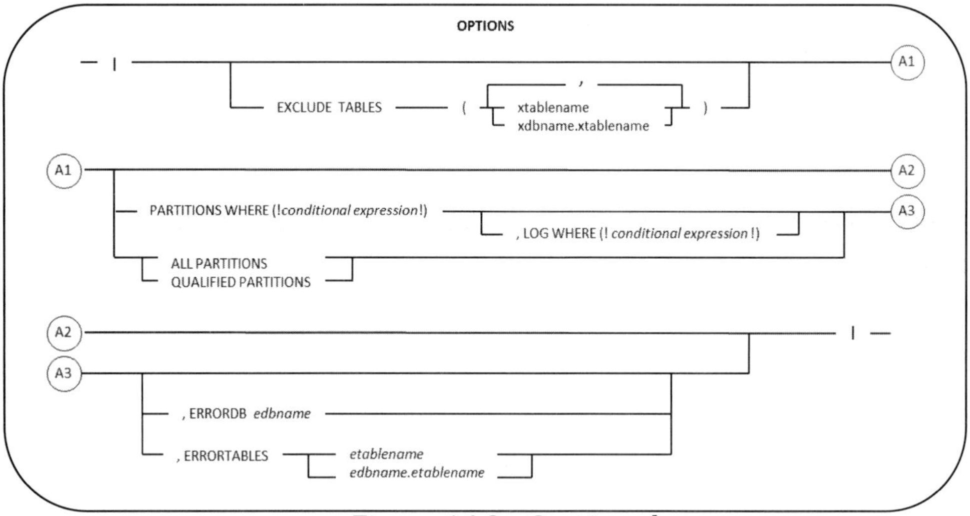

Figure 16.2 - *Continued*

Restoring Selected Partitions of PPI Table

You can restore selected partitions of PPI tables. This allows you to archive and restore only a subset of data in a PPI table.

Restrictions on Restoring Selected Partitions

The following restrictions apply to restoring selected partitions:

- Restoring selected partitions is not allowed to a machine with a hash function that is different from the source machine, but a different configuration is allowed.

To RESTORE or COPY selected partitions, a table must already exist on the target system.

Restoring selected partitions is not allowed to a table that has undergone any of the following major DDL changes:

- Changing primary index columns

- Changing from PPI to NPPI, or vice versa
- Adding or changing referential integrity constraints
- Adding, modifying, or dropping columns.
- Certain changes during RESTORE and COPY operations.

Restoring UDFs, UDTs, Triggers, and Stored Procedures

As mentioned in the previous chapter, database DBC and SYSUDTLIB are linked together. When you restore database DBC, the ARC utility automatically restores database SYSUDTLIB and its UDT definitions. Therefore, you should never restore SYSUDTLIB as a separate object, and if you EXCLUDE database DBC, SYSUDTLIB will be excluded also.

You should only specify either DBC or SYSUDTLIB on a COPY FROM statement. This allows DBC and SYSUDTLIB to be copied to another database. Either DBC or SYSUDTLIB can be specified as separate source objects, but neither of them can be specified as separate target objects.

If you are copying UDFs, UDMs, or external stored procedures from one system to another and any of their definitions include an EXTERNAL NAME clause which specifies a library or package, make certain the library or package exists on the target system before doing the copy, otherwise an error will occur.

Doing a COPY of a full database is the same as a restore operation. However, views, macros, stored procedures, and triggers cannot appear in the EXCLUDE list, and triggers cannot be copied. Triggers must be manually recreated with SQL.

If the views, macros, or stored procedures you are copying have embedded references to objects that do not exist in the target system, they will not work. If you copy or recreate the referenced objects on the target system, then they will work.

When you do a COPY, partial names are fully qualified to the default database name, which may not be the database where the object exists in the target system. To avoid any errors, fully qualify all table names in views, and all table, stored procedure, and view names in macros.

COPY Statement

The following is the syntax diagram for the COPY statement.

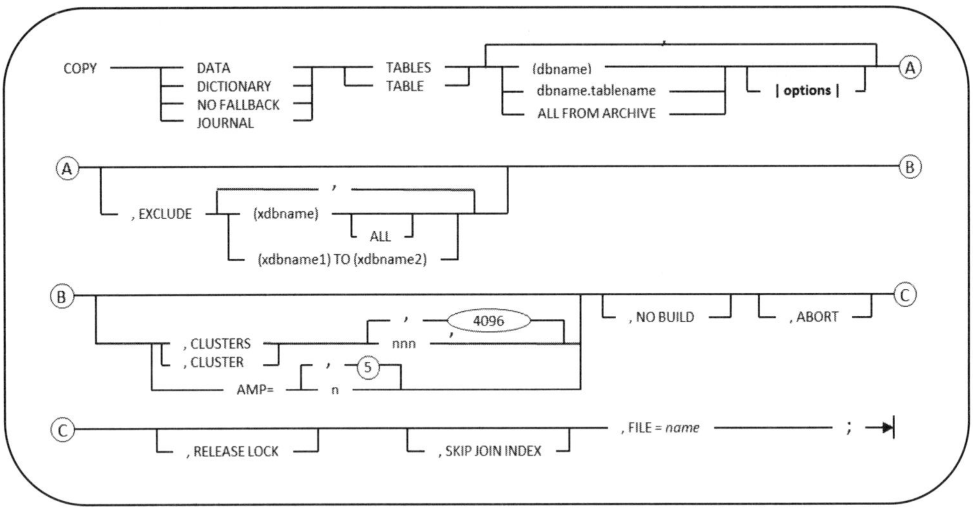

Figure 16.3

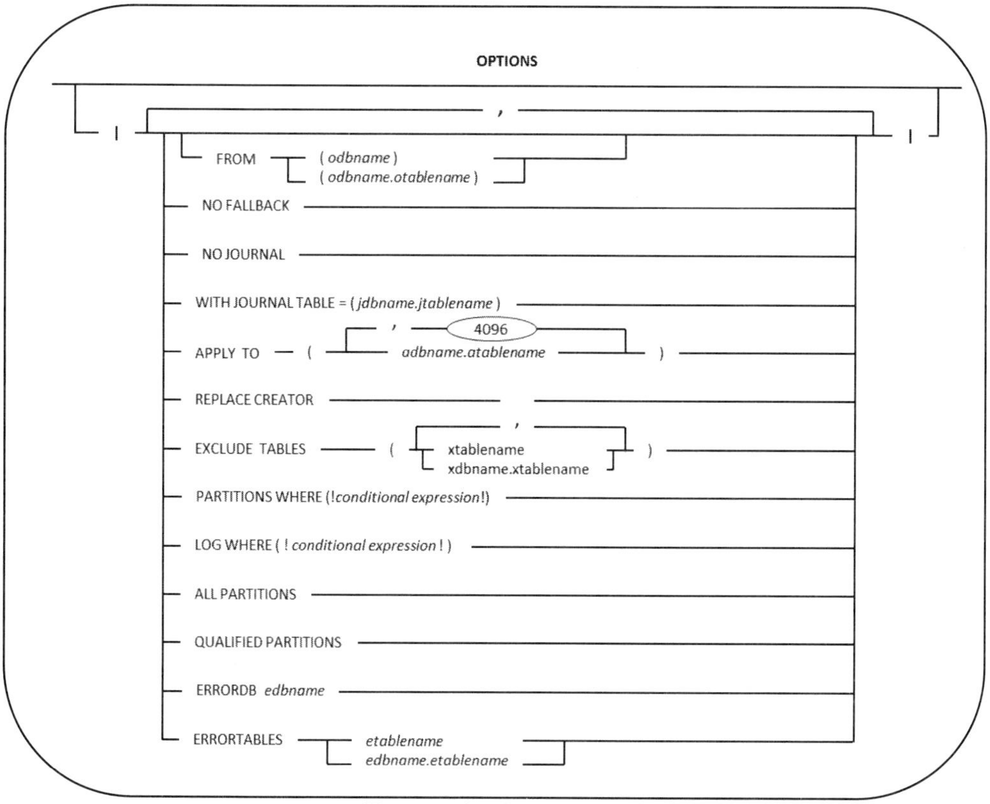

Figure 16.3 - *Continued*

Copying Partitioned Data

Typically, the table you want to copy does not have to be on the target database. However, when you want to copy selected table partitions, the table must exist in the target database. In addition, the target table needs to consist of the entire table definition, and not just the selected partitions.

Copying Objects

Use different Teradata users for each archive job when running concurrent archives against the same objects. This ensures that locks placed by one job are not released by another.

Copying a full database archive is the same as a restore operation. Teradata ARC drops all existing tables, views, macros, stored procedures, triggers, UDFs, UDTs, and dictionary information in the receiving system. The data in the archive is then copied to the receiving database.

Triggers however, cannot be copied with the **COPY** statement but rather manually recreated via SQL.

You cannot copy one or more stored procedures from one database to another using the **COPY** statement. They can only be copied as part of a full database.

If your views, stored procedures, and macros have embedded references to databases and objects that are not in the receiving environment, those views, stored procedures, and macros will not work. To make any such views, stored procedures, or macros work, recreate or copy the references to which they refer into the receiving database.

If your views, stored procedures, and macros have embedded references to databases and objects that *are* in the receiving environment, they will work correctly.

Note: Fully qualify all tables, stored procedures, and view names in a macro and all table names in a view. If you do not, you may receive an error. When you execute a **COPY** statement, partial names are fully qualified to the default database name. In some cases, this may be the name of the old database.

After an all-AMPs copy, copied tables do not have referential constraints. First, referential constraints are not copied into the dictionary definition tables, database DBC.ReferencedTbls and database DBC.ReferencingTbls, for either a referenced (parent) or referencing (child) table copied into a Teradata Database. Moreover, all referential index descriptors are deleted from the archived table header before it is inserted into the copied table.

UDFs & Triggers

A restore of a user database drops any new tables, views, macros, stored procedures, triggers, or UDFs created since the archive of the database.

If you restore a database from a dictionary archive created by specifying individual tables, only the dictionary rows for the specified tables are restored. The following table lists the dictionary rows that are restored by an all-AMPs data restore or a dictionary tables restore of a user database.

Table Rows	Description
Indexes	Definition of all indexed columns in the data tables and views
IndexName	Definition of named indexes in the table
TVM	Definition of all data tables, views, macros, stored procedures, triggers, and UDFs in the database
TVFields	Definition of all columns in the data tables, views, macros, stored procedure parameters, and UDFs.
TriggersTbl	Definition of all triggers in the database

Figure 16.4

Keyword Options with COPY

The following table describes the keyword options of the COPY statement. Triggers cannot be copied.

Syntax Element	Description
DATA TABLES	Copies data tables.
DICTIONARY TABLES	Copies dictionary tables.
JOURNAL TABLES	Copies journal tables.
NO FALLBACK TABLES	Copies non-fallback tables to specific AMPs.
ALL FROM ARCHIVE	Copies all databases/tables in the given archive file.
EXCLUDE	Prevents objects in specified databases from being copied.
ALL	Excludes the named database and all descendants.
FROM	Names the object in the archive different from the target object.
NO FALLBACK	Copies fallback tables into non-fallback tables. If the archived table is already non-fallback, this option has no effect.
REPLACE CREATOR	Replaces the LastAlterUID, creator name, and Creator ID of the tables in the target database with the user ID and the current user name, i.e., the user name specified in the **LOGON** command.
NO JOURNAL	Copies all tables with journaling disabled, whether journaled in the archive or not.
WITH JOURNAL TABLE	Specifies that a copied database has journaling for the specified database and journal table.
APPLY TO	Identifies the tables in the target system where the change images apply.
NO BUILD	• Prevents the Fallback and Secondary

Syntax Element	Description
	Index rows from being created. • If NO BUILD is requested when restoring database DBC, the request is ignored. • If the NO BUILD keywords are used during a **RESTORE** statement, a separate **BUILD** statement must be run for all databases and/or tables that were restored. The tables will not be accessible until a **BUILD** statement is run.
ABORT	Aborts the copy operation if an AMP to which a non-fallback or journal table to restore is offline. This option affects only an all-AMPs copy.
RELEASE LOCK	Releases client utility locks when the copy operation completes.
FILE	Copies a file.
EXCLUDE TABLES	Prevents individual tables in the listed database from being copied.
PARTITIONS WHERE	Specifies the conditional expression for partition-level operations.
LOG WHERE	Specifies the rows that are logged to an error table for manual insertion and deletion.
ALL PARTITIONS	Restores all archived partitions for an archived PPI object.
QUALIFIED PARTITIONS	Copies the same partitions specified in a previous selected-partition copy.
ERRORDB and ERRORTABLES	Specifies the location of the error log for partition-level operations.
SKIP JOIN INDEX	Skip the restore of join and hash indexes.

Figure 16.5

BUILD Statement

Database DBC cannot be restored by clusters, because it does not have non-fallback tables defined. Therefore, ARC will not attempt to build indexes or fallback data on any table in database DBC.

A BUILD operation on a specified table will create unique and non-unique secondary indexes. In addition, this operation will generate the fallback tables if you use the DATA TABLES option.

The BUILD statement is used in the following cases:

- Restoring a specific AMP of non-fallback tables
- Restoring a Cluster archive
- Series of all-AMPs restores where the hardware configuration has changed.

Note: To increase recovery speeds on all AMPs, it is recomemend to use the NO BUILD option in the **RESTORE** statement. This will prevent non-fallback tables from being built after the restore is completed.

During a BUILD, if an AMP is offline, all unique secondary indexes of non-fallback tables will remain invalidated. As a result, queries will run more slowly because the secondary indexes are no longer being utilized for the query.

Note: Insert and update operations will not be able to function.

You must rebuild indexes for non-fallback tables after a restore operation if any of the following situations occur:

- An AMP is offline during a dump or restore
- The restore operation is not an all-AMP restore
- The archive did not include the INDEXES option
- The restore included the NO BUILD option

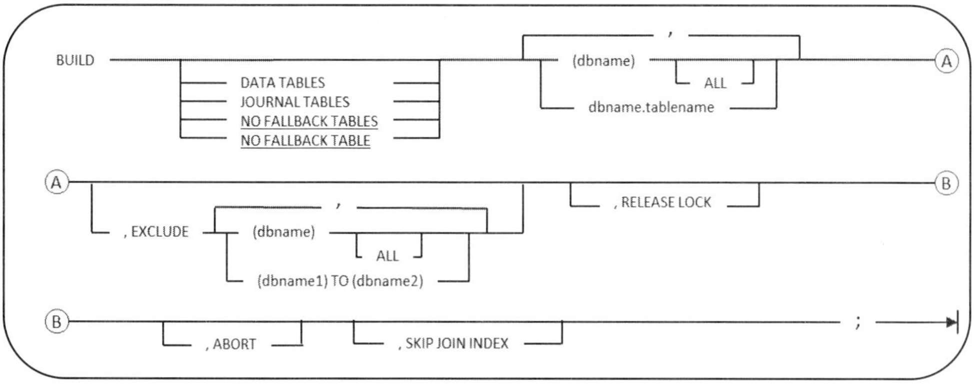

Figure 16.6

RELEASE LOCK Statement

BTEQ, FastExport and TPump use transaction-based locking via the Transient Journal. FastLoad, MultiLoad, and Archive/Recovery (ARC) set a field in the table header which is automatically released by FastLoad and MultiLoad, but not by ARC.

The ARC utility uses HUT Exclusive locks when restoring, copying, rolling back, rolling forward, or building a database. These locks remain active during a Teradata Database or client restart, and must be released manually by the **RELEASE LOCK** statement or by the RELEASE LOCK keywords available on the **ARCHIVE**, **REVALIDATE REFERENCES FOR**, **ROLLBACK**, **ROLLFORWARD**, **RESTORE** and **BUILD** statements. The command syntax is shown in the next figure.

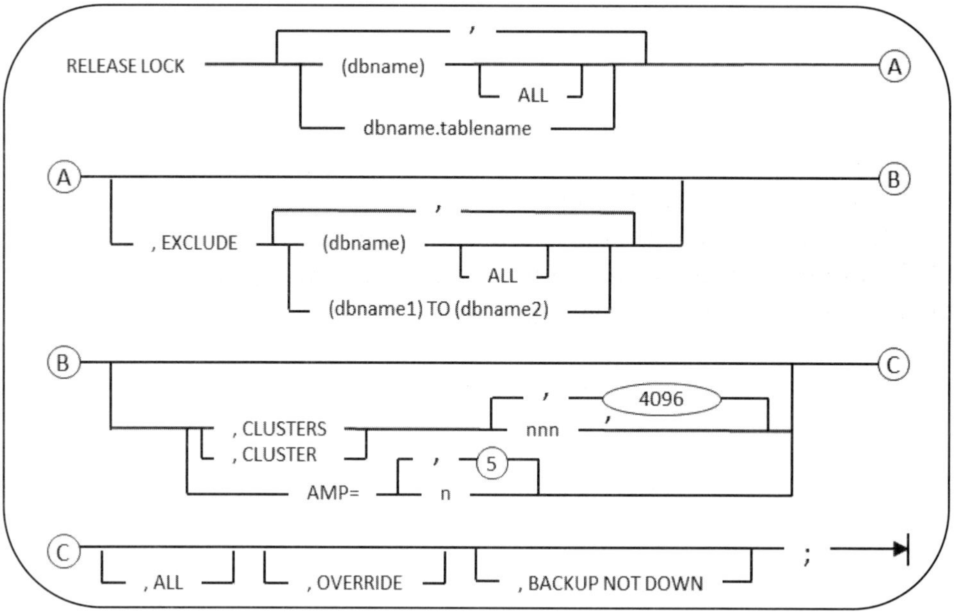

Figure 16.7

ARC issues a message to report that the release operation is complete. It releases HUT locks when the AMPs return to online operation.

Revalidate References

When either a parent or child table is restored, the reference is marked inconsistent in the database dictionary definitions. As a result, the system does not allow UPDATE, INSERT, or DELETE statements on such tables.

The REVALIDATE REFERENCES FOR statement validates the inconsistencies, thereby allowing users to execute UPDATE, INSERT and DELETE statements on the tables. The functions performed by this statement include:

- Inconsistent reference index is validated on the target table

- Creates an error table
- Inserts into the error table, rows that fail the referential constraint specified by the reference index

If inconsistent restraints remain after you execute the statement, you can use the ALTER TABLE DROP INCONSISTENT REFERENCES statement to remove them. To use the REVALIDATE REFERENCES FOR statement, the username you specified in the LOGON statement must have one of the following privileges:

- RESTORE privileges on the table you are re-validating
- Implicit privileges on the database or table

Note: The REVALIDATE REFERENCES statement does not validate soft RI (tables with NO CHECK option.).

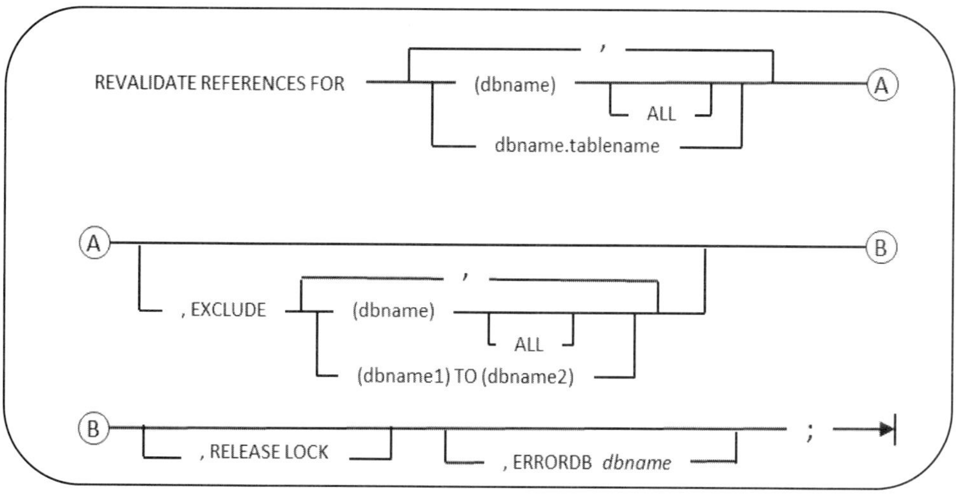

Figure 16.8

Recovery Control Data Dictionary Views

Several system views contain information about ARC utility events. You can use these views for recovery control.

This view	Provides information about
DBC.AssociationV[X]	Objects (databases, users, tables, views, macros, indexes, stored procedures) that you imported from another Teradata Database system or created via the Archive/Recovery COPY statement
DBC.EventsV[X]	Archive/recovery activities, with a row (audit trail) for each archive and recovery event
DBC.Events_ConfigurationV[X]	Archive and recovery activities that did NOT affect all AMPs
DBC.Events_MediaV[X]	Archive and recovery activities that involved removable media

Figure 16.9

Association View

The Association view allows you to retrieve information about an object imported from another Teradata Database.

An existing object created with the ARC COPY command also appears in the Association view. If you later drop a copied object from its new destination, the information is deleted from the Association table and is no longer available.

Events View

The Events view tracks ARC activity. ARC inserts a new row in the Events system table each time another ARC activity begins. The Events view returns a row for each activity tracked.

The following table describes events the system creates depending on the type of object on which the activity was performed.

A row for this event type	Is created for each
Checkpoint Event Row	journal checkpointed.
Delete Event Row	journal deleted.
Dump Event Row	database or table dumped.
Restore Event Row	database or table restored.
Rollback Event Row	database or table rolled back.
Rollforward Event Row	database or table rolled forward.

Figure 16.10

Events_Configuration View

The Events_Configuration view stores rows for each archive activity. If the ARC command specifies all AMPs and there are one or more AMPs offline, a row is inserted in the system table for each offline AMPs. If the statement is for specific AMPs, a row is inserted for each specified and online AMPs.

Events_Media View

The Events_Media view provides information about ARC activities that used removable storage media. This information includes the volume serial numbers assigned to portable devices.

Practice Questions

1. Which of the following can be restored, but not copied?
    a. Stored Procedures
    b. Triggers
    c. UDMs
    d. UDTs

2. Which of the following will not prevent restoring selected portions of a PPI table?
    a. Adding columns
    b. Changing primary index columns
    c. Changing referential integrity constraints
    d. Configuration change

3. When doing a full database COPY, which of the following can appear in the EXCLUDE list?
    a. Macro names
    b. Stored procedures
    c. Table names
    d. Triggers
    e. View names

4. Which of the following statements about an all-AMP restore of a user database is true?
    a. Any new tables, views, or macros created since the archive will be dropped before the restore begins.
    b. Any new stored procedures, triggers, or UDFs created since the archive will be dropped before the restore begins.
    c. Any new objects created since the archive will be left undisturbed, and only the archived objects will be dropped and then restored.
    d. All new objects created since the archive will be dropped before the restore begins.

5. Which of the following about the REVALIDATE REFERENCES FOR statement is false?
    a. It creates an error table.
    b. It validates inconsistent hard RI constraints.
    c. It validates inconsistent soft RI constraints.
    d. It must be run to allow UPDATE, INSERT and DELETE the table.

Chapter Notes

Utilize this space for notes, key points to remember, diagrams, areas of further study, etc.

Appendix

Answers to the Chapter Practice Questions

Chapter 2	Chapter 3	Chapter 4	Chapter 5	Chapter 6
1. a 2. d 3. d 4. b 5. c	1. d 2. c 3. c 4. b 5. d	1. e 2. b 3. d 4. c 5. c	1. e 2. DBC = DBC,DBC,DBC B = DBC,DBC,DBC C= B,DBC,DBC D = B,C,C+DBC E = D,B,B+DBC F = D,E,E+B+DBC 3. a 4. c 5. b	1. c 2. d 3. c 4. b 5. a

Chapter 7	Chapter 8	Chapter 9	Chapter 10	Chapter 11
1. a 2. c 3. e 4. d 5. a	1. b 2. c 3. b 4. a 5. d 6. c	1. c 2. a 3. b 4. c 5. e	1. d 2. b 3. a 4. b 5. a	1. c 2. b 3. d 4. b 5. c 6. b 7. c 8. c
Chapter 12	**Chapter 13**	**Chapter 14**	**Chapter 15**	**Chapter 16**
1. c 2. d 3. a 4. c 5. c 6. b	1. a 2. b 3. c 4. d 5. b 6. c 7. d	1. a 2. d 3. a 4. c 5. b	1. b 2. b 3. c 4. b 5. c	1. b 2. d 3. c 4. d 5. c

Index

S

T

U

V

W

X